SHARP

Road to Abraxas

Part One: 1942-1979

THE BIOGRAPHY OF
MARTIN SHARP AS TOLD TO
LOWELL TARLING

ETT IMPRINT
EXILE BAY

First published by ETT Imprint, Exile Bay 2016

This book is copyright. Apart from any fair dealing for the purposes of private study, research, criticism or review, as permitted under the Copyright Act, no part may be reproduced by any process without written permission. Inquiries should be addressed to the publishers.

ETT IMPRINT
PO Box R1906
Royal Exchange NSW 1225
Australia

Copyright © Lowell Tarling 2016
Artwork cover © Estate of Martin Sharp 2016

ISBN 978-0-925416-58-9 (paper)
ISBN 978-0-925416-59-6 (ebook)

Design by Hanna Gotlieb

Christ is more of an artist than the artists — he works in living spirit and flesh, he makes men instead of statues.

Vincent van Gogh
Letter to Emile Bernard, 27 June 1888

THANKS

The first and greatest thanks to Martin,

whose cooperation and assistance made this book possible.

Secondly, I would like to thank my family: Amber, Joel and Zoë, and especially my wife Robbie who urged me to transcribe my taped interviews, pushed me to write this book, listened to every draft chapter and made innumerable editorial suggestions.

Thanks to Tom Thompson who made this production possible.

Thanks and gratitude to the following people, most of whom agreed to be interviewed on tape and many of whom contributed in other ways too:

Jim Anderson, Mic Conway, Melody Cooper, Peter Draffin, Roger Foley-Fogg, Susan Jensen, Sebastian Jorgensen, Marilyn Karet, Peter Kingston, Jeannie Lewis, Jon Lewis, Tim Lewis, Lex Marinos, Ted Markstein, Philippe Mora, Richard Neville, Michael Organ, Mal Ramage, Adrian Rawlins, Ian Reid, Peter Royles, Alexander (Sandy) Sharp, Roslyn Sharp, Russell Sharp, Garry Shead, Gary Shearston, Clayton Simms, Max Skeen, Tiny Tim, William Yang, Greg Weight.

And to all those who I have not mentioned by name, who spoke with me and emailed me, whose words and ideas I have used, my heartfelt thanks.

TABLE OF CONTENTS

1. The Little Prince 04
2. Art Father 17
3. Arty Wild Boys 30
4. OZ is a New Magazine 46
5. OZ Trial – London Calling 57
6. Fresher Cream 75
7. Art of Pop 93
8. Muybridge, Vincent & Tiny 107
9. Art About Art 121
10. Underground Meets the Underworld 133
11. The Yellow House 149
12. Yesterday's Papers 168
13. Counterculture Goes Mainstream 183
14. Out & About in Paris & London 198
15. Preparing for Tiny 207
16. Kold Komfort 223
17. Street of Dreams 233
18. Revenge of the Clowning Calaveras 246
Notes 260
Index 282

1.

THE LITTLE PRINCE

Finger painting, I remember doing that.
Miss Koulson was very good, my first art teacher.
MARTIN SHARP

Martin Ritchie Sharp was born in Sydney, 21 January 1942, the day of the first Japanese air strike on Rabaul, Papua & New Guinea. His first home was his Ritchie grandparents' place, Wirian, 3 Victoria Road Bellevue Hill.

For the duration of the war, Martin's father, Dr Henry Sharp had been assigned to the Medical Branch of the RAAF with the rank of Flight Lieutenant. At the time of Martin's birth, he was working on the RAAF Recruiting Train, which carried staff to deal with enlistments for the war effort. On hearing the joyous news, Henry hurried home the next day to welcome his newborn son. (1)

Within six months, Henry was shipped overseas where he joined the Spitfire Squadron 453, an Australian air control unit of the RAAF in England. (2) Martin said, 'He loved those years but the worst thing was having to examine the pilots and give them a health clearance. It's like writing a death warrant. The average age was 22 and he knew that 45 per cent of the time he'd never see them again.' (3)

That was Henry's life for the next three and a half years while his wife Joan (Jo) and son Martin were living an extremely comfortable life back home. Their only indication of World War 2 was the night of 31 May when three Japanese midget submarines entered Sydney Harbour and attempted to sink Allied warships. (4) Wirian has distant harbour views from the first floor verandah. Jo took baby Martin upstairs and watched the action like fireworks. She later told him the bombardments shook the house. Too young to comprehend those 'fireworks', Martin has a clearer memory of wartime double-decker buses painted in camouflage colours.

Martin spent his first three years in the company of his mother, grandparents Stuart and Vega Ritchie and their home-helps - cook, maid, gardener-chauffeur and Martin's 19-year old nanny Roma Leonard ('Nursy'). These were the most significant adults in Martin's early life. (5)

The Ritchie surname appears in both Martin's mother and his father's family. They are not connected. His mother's Ritchie line is Scottish, his father's is Irish. The Northern Irish Ritchies established in Bega NSW in the 1850s. Whereas from his mother's Scottish line, Martin's great-grandfather James Ritchie and brother, came to Australia with enough funds to start a tool-making business, making ploughs and farm equipment. The Ritchie Bros succeeded very quickly. In 1900 James Ritchie purchased a superb property called Telford, with absolute water frontage at the Royal National Park, Port Hacking.

After James' passing, his only son Stuart inherited everything and Stuart always improved massively on everything he touched. He transformed Telford into a grand residence and expanded Ritchie Bros into a major manufacturing and engineering firm. Located at Auburn, he built rails and carriages for NSW Rail. BHP was among Stuart's directorships (Commonwealth Steel Newcastle). It provided one-third of the Trans-Australia rail lines across the Nullabor and a quarter of the steel used to erect the Sydney Harbour Bridge.

After his marriage to Vega (Vee) Kopson, a Swedish-Australian, Stuart and Vee settled in 105 The Boulevarde Strathfield where Martin's mother

Joan (b. 1915) was raised and schooled at the local Meridan Girls College. Shortly before the Second World War, Stuart bought Wirian (3 Victoria Road, Bellevue Hill) located next door to Cranbrook School, which Martin and many Sharp relatives attended.

Says Martin, 'I'm not sure what Wirian means. The closest I've got is David Gulpilil - the wonderful actor - said it was the name of the tribe that lived around here. The house was built in 1920 and my grandparents and my mother moved here in 1937. I grew up there as a baby during the Second World War.' (6)

Henry returned from the war in 1945. Jo had married a doctor but a Flight-Lieutenant came home. Martin recalls, 'I remember the day he came back. I was about 3½. He was lying on the floor. He and my mother were loving and cooing while I was wondering, "Who's this guy? He's a bit fat. He's got hairy underarms…" (that sort of thing). Anyway, he was my Dad!

'When my father came back he didn't really connect with me. I think my mother knew him well but I didn't know who he was and in a strange way he never changed much from that person. He was always with adults and found it difficult dealing with children. He didn't like me as a baby. I don't get that feeling – he holds me up in a picture and sniffs my bottom. My mother said, "your father never liked children".

'My mother would've loved more children but she got sick. She got a staphylococcal throat. He came back from the war with something that infected her. So I think the war indirectly poisoned her health.' (7)

But the lounge parties continued – attended by socialites and sometimes celebrities. 'Cocktail parties were it,' says Martin. 'You never had such civilized, lovely people. The jabber of voices, the drinks, someone at the piano playing, it was a lovely thing but you'd never get the idea they'd been to a war and lost half their friends. You can imagine coming from the Battle of Britain to Bellevue Hill and trying to get back into civilian life!' (8)

On his return, Henry served in the RAAF section of Concord Hospital and later as Deputy Principal Medical Officer Eastern Area, NSW. In 1945-1946 he went away again, to serve as Principal Medical Officer in South Australia. His enlistment had committed him to a further 12 months after the end of the war.

Also back from the war was a group of artists who became known as the Merioola group. Merioola was a colonial mansion-cum-boarding house on Edgecliff Road Edgecliff, walking distance from Wirian. It was managed by Melbourne chatelaine Chica Lowe who encouraged artists, dancers, writers and theatre people to take up residence and form an artistic community. Artists included Donald Friend, Margaret Olley, Harry Tatlock Miller, Arthur Fleischmann and Justin O'Brien.

Jo knew Justin from the days when she had enrolled at the Julian Ashton Art School. She rekindled those art contacts while Henry was in South Australia. (9)

Henry came home proper in 1946 and stayed put, having served for the duration of the war plus the requisite 12 months. For the married couple, Grandfather Stuart purchased 25 Cranbrook Lane, Bellevue Hill, who moved in with 4-year old Martin. Henry returned to General Practice and started his academic work in dermatology, studying late in the room next to Martin's bedroom.

Martin recalls their family unit of three, plus maid and a nanny, 'When Dad came back there was a maid called Francis who he'd inherited from his Bega relatives. She was very old. My mother didn't like having her there. She couldn't eat her food. She used to spoon it into all the pewter jugs that were around, which was all right until the mould came out. Francis found the food had been dumped while my mother was getting thinner and thinner!'

Henry played his part in family life, enjoying cocktail parties and family get-togethers where Martin says, 'Henry loved playing piano badly, singing music hall and Gilbert & Sullivan songs'. He bought a beautiful

AWA walnut veneer radiogram to play his 78 records. He also made home movies and bought a sloop, Epacris.

Martin's paternal grandfather, Dr Walter Ramsay Sharp was a leader in his church community, an Alderman on the Vaucluse Council and an outstanding doctor. He died three years before Martin was born, leaving his wife Elizabeth Mary Alexander (known as Bessie) an independent income, three properties (including a Sharp holiday home in Bowral) two beautiful daughters and three handsome sons - all doctors - over whom she had a controlling hand. Martin recalls, 'She was in some ways quite severe'.

From Bessie's five children – Henry, Alan & Katherine (twins), Frank and Elizabeth – came 16 Sharp grandchildren. Bessie made a point of treating all her grandchildren equally. Still, Martin was proud to be the firstborn son of Gay's firstborn son. Conversely, on his Ritchie side Martin had no cousins. He was the only grandchild. This drew him to his Mother's side, especially in his childhood. Martin explains, 'I was the child of Jo my mother and I had to be.

'Although my mother tried very well to make me happy, I didn't grow up in a happy home. My father was very good at some things, we used to go to Port Hacking when things were going well.' (10)

Martin often spent his days going for walks with Jo around the suburb. They would regularly call on his grandparents at Wirian. Jo was always smartly dressed. (11)

Martin's earliest pieces include a letter 'To Mrs Sharp' and a 'Happy Easter' message. He wrote the following story: 'I am a wild bird and this is my story. I was born in a nest, in a tree near a church. My mother a pretty brown bird was soon able to fly. It was a joy to stand on the roof, to turn in the…'.

Another piece was based on his mother's sketch. It read: 'That morning as the ship left port a rainbow was seen in the sky an hour later. And it grew so dark that it soon lost sight of the coast. We had not even passed the cape before the storm struck us. It was so sudden.'

'My mother got me my first paints', said Martin. 'In fact she kept my first drawing. It's in a letter she sent to my father, Martin's First Drawing. He replied, "It's an animal. I don't know what sort though…" (a comment like that). I think all kids like to draw - as soon as you get a pencil and a bit of paper! I was always encouraged by my mother.' (12)

But for his parents' deteriorating relationship, Martin would have enjoyed an idyllic childhood. Instead, the fights, separations and ensuing divorce became a core of unhappiness that Martin would bear all his life.

Forever after he would idealise his parents' courtship: how they met in 1937 on a P&O liner traveling to London when Jo accompanied her parents to the coronation of King George VI. She - the beautiful wealthy heiress and Henry the dashing ship's doctor. Martin would treasure his mother's letters, describing the shipboard romance, the sites of London, and their theme song, 'that certain night', A Nightingale Sang in Berkeley Square. (13)

Sadly, Henry and Jo's marriage 'didn't get going after the war', said Martin. 'They worked very hard at it. I blame it on Hitler rather than anything else. To be a doctor is a very tough job. My mother was very supportive, she did everything she could'. (14)

He clarified, 'I think they were very keen on each other when they were young. Even the early marriage was good enough until Dad went away. I think they were comfortable. They both regret they didn't get married at that time but they waited. Then it all goes into letters. Until I read the letters, I never had any idea of how keen they were on each other. I can't imagine it from what I knew of them. I never saw them "in love" really. (I did actually, but only briefly).

'I think it was pretty tight after the war. They never quite got back those three years. I reckon it was difficult from then on. I can remember them fighting – shouting, shouting, and my mother saying, "Not in front of the child!" but it didn't stop. I can remember that sentence amidst all of this'. (15)

Both parents struggled to make the marriage work and Martin's grandfather was determined that it must. Henry, somewhat awkwardly played the fatherly role - swimming and fishing with Martin, sometimes reciting him poems but usually he was not around or not available. Henry worked all day in his medical practice and closed himself away at night, studying for his Diploma in Dermatological Medicine.

Martin's response was to retreat into himself or spend time with his mother and Ritchie grandparents. He enjoyed his first trip to the cinema with Jo to see Disney's Pinocchio. She had no difficulty being a loving mother and dutiful wife. She embroidered and made collages cut from magazines. Martin copied her. He made collages and drew pictures, many of which were treasured by his grandparents and found amongst their effects some 50 years later. Throughout his life, Martin appropriated images that go back to when he was as young as six years old. Boofhead and Ginger Meggs are childhood references.

Privately, Stuart drew occasional cartoons, so from an early age Martin was well aware of his grandparents' love of cartoonists like Phil May and Livingstone (Hop) Hopkins. (16)

Says Martin, 'There was a real love of cartoons in this family. My grandparents used to cut out Daily Mirror strips of Nancy and they'd make a little book. They loved cartoons. Boofhead was their favorite comic character. (17)

'I even learned to read with comics!' says Martin who, after an interest in Disney, graduated to Superman. When he was nine, DC Comics teamed Superman with Orson Welles in a 'the Martians are coming' edition. This puzzled Martin because 'a real person had entered into the comic strip world'. (18)

'My grandmother was a very good artist in a Pop sort of way. She used to make comic strips up for me – cut the Boofhead comics out of The Sun when it came out, bind them into a comic book. I liked tin soldiers as well. I used to have tin soldiers. I got so cross once, an arm fell off or something. He wouldn't stand up. I got cross and threw him and then his leg and head fell off, I got crosser still.'

Grandmother Vega amused Martin by making figurines out of wishbones. 'I wish I had some of those, they were beautiful,' said Martin. 'She used to make me little toys. Their legs would be the wishbone with little feet. She'd build the body around. They'd all be beautifully dressed and hand-painted, bride and groom, all sorts of funny characters'.

Martin also loved the mascot screwed on the front of his grandfather's 1930 Cadillac car, a squat silver policeman figure with a brown enamel face and a funny smile. Later in life Martin tried to locate it. He did not succeed.

Jo kept a novelty collection in a glass trinket cabinet that was full of little things she had collected or that Henry had sent back in his travels. Among them was a funny little mouse with red pants and big black ears. Martin didn't know who it was but, because of the colour and shape, it really caught his attention. Martin said, 'It was the most interesting in the whole cabinet - which was full of wonderful things. I think perhaps it was the plastic and the colour. That led to my interest in Mickey Mouse. (19)

'I first noticed Mickey Mouse among adult things that don't appeal to children, because your eye's too simple as far as recognising images is concerned. There were many other china bits there but the bit I loved most was this little figure of Mickey Mouse, which was probably off a charm bracelet. It was plastic - red, black and white, very bright. Everything else was crafted and beautifully done. This was real Pop. And I responded to it. I didn't know it was Mickey Mouse at the time. I didn't know Mickey Mouse from anyone. But I responded to that. I was always interested in Mickey Mouse.' (20)

There were songs too. Martin loved Bing Crosby's take on the Christmas story, a 78 record called The Small One sung from the point of view of the donkey. (21)

In 1949 Martin registered at Cranbrook for 'day school'. (22) Sometimes he was chauffeur-driven to school in the Cadillac. And although Martin describes himself as 'shy', day school seemed to be okay.

About that shyness, Martin said, 'I think the extrovert as a child depends on the relationship with the parents. And because it actually wasn't good, I think I was fairly introverted at that stage. It's like there's a piano in the house, but it doesn't get played.'

Painting class was one highlight. Martin's first art teacher was Miss Koulson who he describes as 'very good'. He says, 'There's a dinosaur painting from those days - a pterodactyl. Kids all paint dinosaurs at that age. Finger painting, I remember doing that'. (23)

On his father's desk back home, Martin noticed binoculars capable of seeing a much bigger world, and also a microscope capable of seeing one that was much smaller. Martin would peer into both while his father was away. 'I probably messed up his slides', he added.

'We used to have a verandah room next to my bedroom and in it was a microscope because my father used to study slides. There was also a huge pair of Japanese binoculars Uncle Frank had brought back from New Guinea, the "prize of conquest". So I was looking at the microcosm and the macrocosm'.

Martin was also using the binoculars to spy nude women at their windows. He was horrified when he spotted one. It was not the goddess for which he had hoped.

Said Martin, 'No one gave me any sex education except my mother and her friend. Her friend had a farm and they took us down to watch the horses having it off. I thought, "God, how embarrassing, do they realise we're watching?" And their cocks were that big…! That was my education into the birds & the bees.'

Roma (Nursy) was the first woman Martin saw nude. He said, 'when she was bathing, I could be there. It was completely natural and there was no thought about it because I'd never experienced it before. She wasn't seducing me, she was just natural – educating me. She was like Justin

(Justin O'Brien – later art teacher), one of those figures in my life – a metaphysical family'.

But when Henry made a pass at Nursy, she had to go. Martin found this out later in life but at the time he saw no reason why his favourite should have to leave.

In 1949, the Blake Prize was established as an incentive 'to raise the standard of religious art'. It was named after the artist and poet William Blake. (24) In 1951 Justin O'Brien, a Merioola artist, now Art Teacher at Cranbrook, was the inaugural winner of the Blake Prize for Religious Art, and Jo took Martin to see it. It was the first art exhibition he attended. He would never forget it.

Neither would Martin forget the Vincent Van Gogh reproduction of The Artist on the Road to Tarascon that Jo purchased to decorate Henry's consulting rooms after he attained his Diploma of Dermatological Medicine in 1952. With the help of Jo's parents, Henry set up rooms in Macquarie Street. He later moved to Wyoming (also in Macquarie Street) where his father Ramsay Sharp previously had rooms. Says Martin, 'My grandparents Ritchie were right behind the relationship. They backed him of course, the husband of their only daughter'.

Martin said, 'I remember them having a fight once when I was very small. She'd cornered him a bit in their suite. My father belted me once when I interrupted them. He belted me a few times. Anyway, she had him cornered in that room. And with those binoculars she'd see him rowing some girl out to his boat. He loved sailing. She said, "that bloody boat!" He'd escaped her again! He was a free spirit really.' (25)

Martin also remembers the Hornby Double-O train set given him by Grandmother Vega. He feels it was really bought as a celebration of Stuart's career. The adults played with it more than Martin did. To accommodate the train set, Henry built a shelving unit in Martin's bedroom. Henry loved model trains. He'd bring his friends into Martin's room to show it off. 'Suddenly I found my room taken over almost with this huge train set!' said Martin. 'When my parents were fighting I'd set the trains to have a head-on collision!' (26)

The Sharp family had a holiday house in Shepherd Street Bowral. In the late-40s/early-50s Uncle Frank, Aunt Edith (known as Dinks), Phillip, Erica, Russell and Rozzie lived there for a time. Martin and his mother stayed at the Bowral house with Uncle Frank and his family during an early break in the marriage.

He recalled, 'It was when the bogon moths moved. I can remember vividly because my mother hated moths. She had the lights on, they were battering themselves against her, she was screaming and she was a bit sad. She thought it was an attack. Perhaps I can recognize the sadness there. I remember walking with her and picking blackberries, it was nice. But I only went there once.' (27)

Telford on Port Hacking was the Ritchie retreat. In 2002, Martin wrote about it as if being there was amongst the happiest times in his late childhood. Telford – bought by Martin's great-grandfather in 1900. Improved to a point of magnificence by his grandfather. Visited sometimes every weekend by Martin, his parents and grandparents. Later, with his father less and less.

Martin wrote, 'I am a boy and I'm sitting with my mother Jo on the rocks, to the right of the boatshed at Telford. It is afternoon, my mother is telling me that when I'm older we will come to Port Hacking for holidays. I don't remember the journey there, with my mother and my father Henry, and grandfather Stuart, or the house. But I remember the rock pools, the waves, the afternoon sun and Jo's words. There are so many memories but this is where they start.

'My childhood and young teenage years in those holidays at Telford were shared most especially with Jan and Ian Skinner. I have a good photo of Jan Skinner, their mother Ida and their pup. I don't remember his name now but I do remember him eating all the frogs Jan, Ian and I collected as youthful naturalists.

'The main house at Telford was a beautiful house. It's seen many happy family days from my great-grandfather's time to the courtship and marriage of my grandparents, and my own parents.'

He goes on to describe himself as 'such a shy kid' who was befriended by the Skinner family, caretakers of the premises, living in the smaller residence on the acreage. With the children Jan and Ian, Martin shared games, jokes and cups of tea. Whereas there was a distance and a sadness in the big house, there was a warmth in the Skinner household.

Martin writes, 'There was love in your family and your home, and I became a part of that love. The silence between my parents is not something one understands at the time. Their marriage was beginning to fall apart. One feels it, not knowing what it is that is missing.

'As a child I took all the beauty and graciousness of Telford for granted, like the air one breathes.' (28)

Port Hacking is where Martin learned to love the blue groper fish, an image he later used in his pictures. 'It used to stop my heart when I saw it. It was so majestic – this fish – it was huge. I was always trying to catch it but it was never interested in anything I had to offer. It wouldn't flap away like it was scared, it was a very slow and elegant pace.'

Martin recalls a moment where Jan took his hand as they walked behind her father. Martin was slightly younger than Jan. They were following her Dad who was checking a bushfire. About having his hand held Martin says, 'It must have been the first time anyone had. I was so shy. I didn't hang onto it. She let it go. The whole walk I had my hand so close to hers but she never took it again.'

Ian, Jan and Martin discovered Pop Music together at Port Hacking by playing Bing Crosby, Al Jolson and novelty songs on Jo's 78 record player. Recorded by Kay Kyser and His Band, Three Little Fishies seemed to encapsulate their experience of learning to swim and learning to live, with encouragement from the Mother Fish.

Johnny Ray was popular too, especially with Jo. Other favourites included Guy Mitchell's 1950 hit The Roving Kind and Danny Kaye's punchy rendition of I've Got A Loverly Bunch Of Coconuts.

Much later in life, these memories came flooding back when Tiny Tim drew his repertoire from the same songbook, regularly including songs like I've Got A Loverly Bunch Of Coconuts in his marathons. (29)

Said Martin, 'When I first saw him at the Albert Hall I was sort of primed in that way.' (30)

2.

ART FATHER

My parents took me out of Cranbrook because they didn't like those marks on my leg, hit by rulers, bruises and things like that.

TIM LEWIS

As a consequence of his parents' deteriorating relationship, Martin switched from dayboy to boarder at Cranbrook School. 'I think things were getting tight and tense at home, so it'd be better if I were out of the scene,' said Martin. (1)

There was a marital storm brewing and, if Martin was shy before, now he simply closed down. He recalls, 'I could feel the tension in the air: Dad, in the kitchen nook where we'd have breakfast. His head would be in the Sydney Morning Herald. As soon as he sat down he'd be eating behind the paper. It was as severe as that – silence. Stony silence. The marriage truly fell apart and I saw it years before the divorce'. (2)

Being aware of his family connection to the school in a general way, Martin was puzzled about specifics. He obviously knew his father Henry attended 1919-1927 as the second student to enroll. Honour Rolls were a constant reminder that Henry distinguished himself both academically and in sport. And Walter Ramsay Sharp – Martin's grandfather - was on the provisional committee that set up the school. With a sense of discovery Martin exclaimed, 'I'm in Cranbrook School for my father because his father was one of the founders!' (3)

Martin could not understand how his grandfather could be one of the actual founders without his name being listed? Staring at the Honour Roll, Martin could see the name Walter Ramsay Sh… almost scuffed off 'because it was the bottom one on the list'. Martin didn't comprehend the 'Ramsay' bit and he couldn't read 'Sharp'. He said, 'I wasn't sure if it was my grandfather because Ramsay Sharp wasn't a name that was used or even mentioned'. (4)

Walking distance from his parents' place and next door to his grandparents at Wirian, Martin became a boarder at the school. He was in for a rude shock. Australian high schools were cruel places in the 1950s. You couldn't get away from the brutality anywhere, not even at Cranbrook. Corporal punishment was not banned in New South Wales state schools until 1987 and not until 1995 in private schools. (5) Indeed it was encouraged in the 1950s. Everyone was familiar with the maxim, Spare the rod, spoil the child.

Attending the school from the age of eleven and a half to 17, Martin was caned 'plenty of times'. He said, 'I found it pretty tough. My housemaster told me that caning was good for a boy. They weren't allowed to kill you. That was about where they had to draw the line. I didn't even know where the bathroom was. I was too shy to ask anyone. So I wet my bed. The first night there. Can you imagine!' (6)

Juniors were subjected to ongoing victimisation, in and outside the classrooms and in the dorms. Martin got a couple of into scraps ('I wasn't that good a hitter'). He felt that fighting was 'institutionalised'. Boxing was in the sport curriculum ('bashing up your friends'). And, he added, 'there was a lot of bullying in the school hierarchy system. They're so cruel.' (7)

For most Australian schools of the time, the school hierarchy system meant all new boys, juniors and especially 'first formers' would be subjected to humiliating initiation rites. For the rest of the year they served as punching bags, and sometimes servants, to senior students. Next year everything would change, second formers were mostly left alone as a new bunch of first formers were subjected to the bullying – or what some call 'fagging'. On the other side of the Harbour Bridge, Martin's future friend, bespectacled Richard (Richie) Walsh was enduring similar experiences at Barker College. The rugby bullies dangled Richie from locker room clothes hooks and he was repeatedly caned. Said Martin, 'Richie had a rough time of school, because he was small. (8)

Martin was sexually assaulted in junior high. He bitterly recalled, 'The guy molested me when I was a first year junior'. Then, '…we worked out as a network that all the junior boys had been persecuted. So we got together and turned the tables on him, went to the teachers and said, "This guy's been molesting us…". They may have spoken to him or chastised him but he was made prefect as soon as he got to the fifth. He was given official power!'

Five decades later, Martin was still angry. He blurt out these events on public radio, unconcerned that he may damage the school's reputation or that he might reveal too much of himself. He said, 'The ABC rang me up and said, "Have you got any memories of schooldays?" and I said, "As a matter of fact I have…I remember this guy used to bully us and molest us when I was at school…".' The interviewer cut in quickly and changed direction.

'They terrorised people!' Martin continued. 'You got used to having a rough time there, as par for the course. That's the system of those schools, training you to do the same in business when you get out. Thank God Justin (ie. Justin O'Brien) was there, I believe that was a miracle. There were some good teachers there, some terrific people'. (9)

In 1970, Martin lampooned the school motto in his Yellow House Catalog, featuring the Cranbrook School badge and reversing the school motto from 'To Be Rather Than To Seem To Be' to 'To Seem Rather Than Be'. He also quoted the William Blake poem, The Schoolboy.

But to go to school in a summer morn
O! it drives all joy away;

Under the cruel eye outworn,
The little ones spend the day
In sighing and dismay. (10)

Until he discovered the Art Room, Martin appeared to have no outstanding talent nor was he noticeably 'bad' at anything. He read a bit - not much, watched no television, enjoyed geography lessons, was useful at field sports and a reasonable swimmer. He was neither a champion rower like some cousins nor a champion footballer like his Dad. If Martin could be bothered with any ambition it might have been 'singer in a Rock band' - which wasn't in his consciousness at all until his senior years. (11)

Art was a compulsory subject that everyone studied at Cranbrook. It was also an extra-curriculum activity that students might pursue after school hours, like debating, dramatic society, cricket, football, swimming, rowing and a Scout group, only less structured. At first, Martin didn't know where the art room was located. 'No one ever told me and I never asked,' he said. He eventually found it and, instead of cosying up to Justin O'Brien, the art teacher – his mother's friend and winner of the 1951 Blake Prize that Martin had attended – initially Martin would not be coaxed in and just watched from outside. (12)

When Martin was in his second high school year, one of his future friends, Peter Kingston (Kingo) enrolled in form one. One imagines the two juniors in short pants passing each other in the corridors. Martin and Kingo shared the same art teacher and both used the art room as a sanctuary. Justin was a gay man. His art room provided safety from the sexual bullying instigated by heterosexual toughs. (13)

Justin had an informal approach to teaching, usually one-to-one, never didactic. Martin is grateful that Justin saw the importance of providing good paints and good brushes. 'Poster paints' Justin called them - water paints in jars. 'It was a dynamic art painting scene', said Martin, 'very different to the other classes. I didn't even think of it as a class. (14)

'Justin was wonderful. He was a human being to us. He wasn't the only teacher who was a human being I'm sure. But he taught by being a considerate and thoughtful person. Justin doesn't consider himself a practicing Christian but he was very religious as a younger man. He became gay late in life, when he was 36–37. He would have been chaste up til then. Virtually a priest I suppose. Then that side of him came out.

'He never gave me any trouble – never, ever, not once. So there is a lot between us because his morals are very good. I'd say Justin is definitely a Christian but he's out of the church because they won't accept him.'

In junior school Martin tried to make sense of the religious instruction. He said, 'I can remember absolutely distinctly - just gone to boarding school - and we're doing prayers - a sheet of paper, all beautifully printed. The first prayer said, O Lord, Our Father, forgive where we have erred and strayed, like lost sheep we have done those things which we ought not to have done and left undone those things we ought to have done, there is no help in us. I'm kneeling, reading this stuff. I'm just a kid and I don't know what they're talking about because I don't think I've done anything wrong!

'Now I can say, "Yes, I've done things wrong". Now I can say "I've erred…",' said Martin as a 52 year-old. 'I'm glad I learned the prayer but it seemed a very primitive way of instructing and wrong to inflict on children. It's the sin and guilt of adults. Kids are like they're still in the Garden of Eden, still connected to God.' (15)

Meanwhile Stuart Ritchie started thinking of his successor to the Ritchie Bros engineering operation. He had only two direct heirs, daughter Jo and grandson Martin. In those days it was unthinkable that a woman should hold the position of CEO, so Jo was out of the question. That question didn't even arise. Jo had no interest in running a huge engineering firm.

And - apart from being curious about the art room and getting himself into the second-15 football team – teenage Martin showed little interest in any career. Still, Stuart reflected on his grandson, in his mid-teens. One day he asked Martin to accompany him to look over the Newcastle plant. It was a non-event. Martin said, 'My grandfather took me up - only once - to see if I was interested. I wasn't fascinated by it. I was just horrified by the noise! He never said he'd train me to take it over nor did he expect me to.' (16)

In some ways, it was his father's side that was more career-conscious. Under the governance of grandmother Sharp, like their father Ramsay Sharp, their sons had become well-accepted group of charming doctors - Drs Henry, Alan and Frank Sharp – My Three Sons. Uncle Alan's work in vascular surgery was earning him huge accolades.

While some may have expected Martin - the son of a doctor's son - to be a medico, he felt no family pressure. Martin said, 'they didn't encourage me to become a doctor. They wanted me to become one but they never said, it's a beautiful thing making people well – or something like that - so there wasn't a lot of communication. There was no engagement about interesting me in medicine. I was not an intellectual so I was to them a bit dyslexic I think.' (17)

Without fail, the Sharp family celebrated every Christmas at Grandma Sharp's Vaucluse home and later at her Astor residence. Twelve cousins and their parents. On such occasions Martin mostly hung out with cousin David Massy-Greene (whose career as a pilot would earn him two world records in the late-80s). Martin (b. 1942) and David (b. 1943) were the 'older cousins'.

The main crop was Jane, Sandy, Phillip, Roger, Erica, Katie, Kate and Russell – followed by the 'littlies' - Andrew and Roslyn (Rozzie) both born in 1953. Four other cousins, Lizzy, Margie, Meme and Sally Millear lived in western Victoria and did not attend.

Martin describes the Sharps as 'very ho-ho-ho adults, very theatrical, laughing loudly, telling jokes.' He described Grandma Sharp's Family Christmas get-togethers as a 'strong family ritual, which demonstrated a strong family'.

While Grandma Sharp's daughters had enduring marriages - notwithstanding their wit, charm and success - her three sons were travelling a path that would some day break up each of their marriages. The children sometimes swapped scraps of information about their respective parents' antics. And Martin? He became plain surly when Grandma Sharp insisted that he and David should do Santa-duty and Martin should wear the whole damn costume.

The problem now with family get-togethers was that Jo and Henry's marriage was just a veneer. A decade of Henry's infidelities was an open secret. Said Martin, 'I believe he couldn't be true to her. She was always true to him, until a situation evolved where they accepted he had a mistress who was his secretary but he had many before. He even made a pass at my nanny!'

On weekends spent at home with his parents, Martin watched the marriage breaking down. Then Dorothy Muller, Henry's secretary, started calling around. To Jo's irritation, she and Henry worked tête-à-tête on the Woollahra Action Committee.

Some time later, Martin recalled a tradesman called Keith Hollingsworth spending more time than necessary talking to his mother. Martin describes him as a Beatnik Carpenter. (18)

Martin's parents separated in his mid-high school years.

'I was probably 15 or 16 when they separated,' said Martin. 'I remember my father saying, I've had enough, I'm getting out, that's what he said to me'. (19) Until he could find his own place, Henry moved into the Astor Hotel with his mother. He walked to work and spent his weekends sailing his sloop around Sydney Harbour, looking for a property appropriate to his new circumstances.

Martin's relationship with Henry was strained, probably because it was so strong with Jo. He received no sex education from his father. Said Martin, 'I didn't know how you get married. I thought you all got dressed up. No one said to me, you fall in love with this girl and get married to her. My father said to me, "if you get into trouble, let me know". Trouble he called it!' Stuart Ritchie did not fill in as Martin's absent father. 'He was a grandfather, not a father. He didn't give himself in that way.'

Martin found something of a replacement father in Justin, whose art room had evolved from a safety zone to a place of genuine interest. 'I wouldn't say Justin became a father figure,' said Martin, 'but he became an Art Father or something like that.'

Spending more and more time around Justin, Martin began painting a whole series of 'characters' evocative of real-imaginary characters - where did they come from? 'Maybe Justin,' said Martin. 'Maybe they came out of his unconscious or something?

'I would have covered just about every type imaginable. Roman emperors, racecourse people, gangsters, boxers, miners, conquistadors, the dentist, a beautiful picture of a tired boy holding up a Siamese cat - the only one I ever did of a kid.'

Martin would reproduce two of these pictures in his Yellow House Catalog - a piano player and a long-faced man holding a bird captioned, 'The saddest painting the lonely boy ever painted'. (20)

Another inspiration came from Sydney's Royal Easter Show. Artist, Arthur Barton was the acknowledged master of the Digger Cartoonist tradition. For 35 years Barton was affectionately known as the 'Rembrandt of Luna Park'. (21) He certainly captured Martin's attention.

Martin described Barton's impact, 'I loved the Easter Show. It was a mixture of everything. It was life itself. I loved those great rows of cattle, the big ring, thundering hooves of the trotting races. The Show was a passionate place. Jimmy Sharman - drum beating - and the boxers. All these fantastic archetypes - half-man/half-woman, the Pygmy Princess…so that was absolutely interesting.

'The Easter Show was where I saw some great poster artists at work – Arthur Barton was one of them, the painter from Luna Park. He had an assistant. They used to stand on a big scaffold at the Easter Show. A great wad of huge sheets of paper and two guys in white overalls and hats were up there, and they'd paint! I learned about lettering from watching them.

'They'd do these shapes, block it off into seven different squares, do a bit of a drawing, fill in few corners of the square and suddenly you'd have a Tarzan's Grip ad up there! It was like magic the way they'd paint so fast, or create these things, but there was suspense – they'd bring them up – they were very good. I always liked that sort of thing. You can see it in my character The Toff - that I painted when I was at school – the neon signs and the sense of Pop.' (22)

Enthused by the discovery of art, Martin entered a school drawing competition, which he won. Says Martin, 'The prize was so much $credit of art materials at the shop. It was strange - they didn't think I needed the prize, so they didn't give me the prize!' (23)

Being exhibited was even better than winning a drawing comp. Justin exhibited the best student pictures around the school corridors. But the pick were exhibited in the stairwell, positioned where every teacher and boy saw them as they walked up or down the stairs.

One day, Martin started painting an English Bobby. Martin explains, 'Somehow it turned into the toughest teacher in the school called Mr Bell – Cheery Bell, his nickname was. I did this painting of Cheery Bell with all the kids sitting at their desks. If you didn't bring your books you'd have to polish the bookshelves and I painted myself – or a boy equivalent to me – polishing the shelves in the background. No one had ever painted teachers before – real people.'

Justin hung Martin's cheeky portrait eye-height, halfway up the stairs. A crowd gathered 'jam-packed around the picture'. It caused quite a stir. 'I knew I was onto something,' said Martin, 'that's where one learned about the significance of exhibiting. First goal that one!' Far from being insulted, Cheery Bell felt flattered enough to want it. Negotiated through Justin, Cheery Bell got the picture and Martin got something else.

Cheery Bell was the English teacher who introduced the Bernard O'Dowd poem Australia to Martin's class. It remained with Martin for life. In 1988, Martin framed his OZ? Tapestry (commissioned for the State Library of New South Wales) with words from this poem, 'Last sea-thing dredged by sailor Time from Space…'. Martin said, 'He'd play the authoritarian to the boys, but he wasn't a shit, he was a very good teacher.' (24)

American singer, Johnny Ray's 1954 tour of Australia was the first live concert Martin attended. Johnny Ray – known as the Nabob of Sob - was his mother's 'heartthrob' at the time and Martin accompanied her to the show. Jo dressed as a Bobbysoxer and even wore an American sailor's cap to look the part. She simply loved Pop concerts, many held at the Sydney Stadium in Rushcutter's Bay, which (under promoter Lee Gordon) showcased acts like Ella Fitzgerald, Artie Shaw, Buddy Rich, Andrews Sisters, Louis Armstrong, Nat King Cole, Harry Belafonte…the list goes on and on through to the late-1960s.

Next, came Rock and Roll music, the rise of the teenager and a period that some social commentators have identified as a 'Youthquake'. From Coca-Cola, Levi jeans and 45 rpm singles, it came from several cultural fronts at the same time.

The film The Wild One starred Marlon Brando cast as the leader of a motorbike pack and Rebel Without a Cause starred James Dean in a constant state of teenage angst. Suddenly every male teenager wanted to dress like a grease monkey, which held no appeal for Martin, It was the music that attracted him. Not leather jackets and American World War 2 Army surplus clothing. 'At the time, I didn't see all those films we were supposed to have seen,' he explained.

Martin said, 'My early teens and Rock and Roll coincided. I was in Wirian upstairs. I was sick, I had a cold, I was listening to the radio. My grandmother must have been looking after me and I heard this weird sound come out of the radio. It was Elvis - Heartbreak Hotel. I remember the sensation in the house. Boy, did he make a huge impact, Elvis the Pelvis. Photos of him going wild. Incredible records. I had some of his - Rip It Up, Don't Be Cruel and Old Shep. See You Later Alligator - Bill Haley – fantastic graphics on this. I loved Rock Around The Clock. And Johnny O'Keefe became big. He was exciting. He had a great hit with Wild One.'

Martin's interest in British Rock started in 1958 with the release of He's Got The Whole World In His Hands by Laurie London, a 13-year old black kid from East London. 'I really love him singing, "He's got the whole world in his hunds". He sings hunds! Only rare things like Laurie London and Rock Island Line by Lonnie Donegan broke into the Australian pop charts. (Maybe Cliff Richard but I never had any interest in him.) Five years later the Beatles erupt out of Liverpool, break the domination of America on the popular music scene.' (25)

In his late-teens, Martin frequently accompanied his mother to concerts and shows. One was Water Ballet, created by American competitive swimmer and actor, Esther Williams. Held at the White City Tennis Courts in Rushcutters Bay, the organisers flooded one of the courts to enable this aquamusical featuring synchronised swimming and acrobatic divers. Meanwhile, at the Sydney Stadium, a short walking distance away, promoter Lee Gordon mounted his first Rock and Roll Show, featuring five big-name American acts.

Said Martin, 'I was watching Water Ballet. There were clowns, acrobatic swimmers and Esther Williams was the star of the show. It was "okay". And then I heard this incredible screaming and noise coming from the Sydney Stadium about 100 yards away. It was Bill Haley and the Comets. I wished I was there - not watching clowns diving off high-boards!'(26)

As he became more senior, Martin's school life had become "okay" too. The Cranbrook building boom was underway throughout the 1950s. The Cranbrook Memorial Hall was constructed during Martin's junior years and the purchase of Leura in Victoria Road from the Knox family provided additional accommodation for 60 boys in his senior years. The expansion brought the total number of students to 450, placing Cranbrook on the same level as other Associated Schools (private schools) in size. (27)

In his final year, the question for Martin was – where next? Clearly he had no interest in following in either grandfathers' footsteps. Martin didn't think he was good at anything but art. (28)

'At school I was an individual artist who was creating stuff. That was my most consistent period. I was a proper painter at school – (not that I knew at the time). But looking back on it I could see that I was. I was a painter and didn't even know it - then the rip hits the delta, you drop your load and you wonder? I went all over the place after that, but on purpose.' (29)

Vincent then came back into Martin's life. As an art prize, Justin awarded Martin Lust for Life, the fictionalized biography of Vincent van Gogh. The book was made into a film of the same name, starring Kirk Douglas as Vincent and Anthony Quinn as Gaughin. Released in 1956, it was a visual sensation. The book and the film, Martin loved both.

Martin said, 'I was very struck by Vincent's pictures as a child. I liked his style, it communicated to me. A film was made about his life called Lust for Life. I got that book as a prize in high school from Justin O'Brien and also another special prize from Justin, which was some paintings of his. I did a copy of one of Vincent's pictures - a still life which Justin gave me to copy.' (30)

Did Vincent make any actual impact on Martin's painting style? 'I think at school he did', said Martin. 'I also think I learned a bit from El Greco about how to shade a face.' (31)

Before leaving Cranbrook, Justin painted Martin's portrait as part of a series of young boys. Justin depicted Martin as a melancholy youth who seemed as world-weary as possible without losing one's innocence. During the sittings, Martin insisted on playing Rock and Roll music, an area where Justin's tastes didn't run. (32)

Martin repeated his final year at Cranbrook, 'an indignity intensified by his failure to be appointed prefect'. Like Martin, Richie Walsh was compelled to repeat his final year (Barker College) and 'was also deemed not to be prefect material.' (33)

Martin finished high school and Justin left for Europe within 12 months. He was replaced at Cranbrook by Peter (Charlie) Brown, who became friends with Martin and Jo. Charlie Brown would play a significant role in the formation of the Yellow House.

By the time he got around to leaving school, Martin had dropped the concentration camp rhetoric. 'I was quite happy in it by the time I left', he said. (35)

Where to next? Architecture was one possibility. Or maybe Justin was right - maybe Martin should go straight to Art School?

3.

ARTY WILD BOYS

Martin had a different attitude.
Money was no object. You can see how he grew up.
GARRY SHEAD

In 1960, Australia was governed by a conservative status quo. This was true of all levels of society – school, clubs, local councils, State governments, everything. The Prime Minister and Leader of the Liberal Party, Sir Robert Menzies, did his damnedest to out-Brit the Brits. He stood for stability, more of the same and remained untroubled by the Opposition Leader Arthur Calwell, who wore a shabby suit and never expected to win government. The Liberal Party had somehow convinced the whole country that all right-thinking Australians should vote Menzies. It went on for 17 years. Menzies came out with things like, 'I detest some of the wretches that get into universities. They are a collection of ratbags and larrikins!'

By the early-60s, the small farmlets that ringed Sydney were being bulldozed into dormitory suburbs - 3-bedroom homes that idealised what writer Afferbeck Lauder satirised as 'Gloria Soames: a spurban house of more than 14 squares, containing fridge, telly, wart wall carpets, pay-show and a kiddies' rumps room'. (1) Dull, that's what it was. The rise of the Australian middle class handed the PM a constituency of don't-rock-the-boat voters. You were weird if your parents didn't drive a Holden or a Ford Falcon. It's like the whole country was doing it in the missionary position with the lights off. 'Norman Normals' is how Martin would soon cartoon the male of this species – sometimes 'Alfs'. (2)

Nevertheless, there was a small subversive element and Australians enjoyed satire if they knew where to look. Comedian Barry Humphries fingered the spot as far back as 1958 with the release of his Wild Life in Suburbia EP record, featuring characters Mrs Edna Everage and Sandy Stone. It was successful enough to launch his stellar career. (3) Another well-accepted piece of satire was the novel (later the 1966 film) They're a Weird Mob, by John O'Grady - taking the pseudonym and point of view of Italian migrant 'Nino Culotta'. (4)

Australians espoused all things British and adopted all things American, right down to its comics, which came via Mad magazine - the funniest thing in the newsagency.

Clearly there were lots of jokes yet to be mined at the expense of the Norman Normals - True Blue Aussies who (in 1960 Australia) reckoned you wouldn't wanna be a Commie, Spag, Reffo, Kike, Poof, Pom, Wog, Ruski, Derro, teetotaler, 'JW', Abo or a woman. In 1960, there was much to protest about. The national referendum granting the vote to Indigenous Australians was seven years away and feminism was a decade away.

Teenagers had disposable income but that didn't give them a voice. 'Get a job', 'get a mortgage', 'respect your elders' - it was all that stuff in their ears. The post-War Baby Boom added four million to the population between 1946-1961. Teenagers sure had the numbers. Four million emerging voters whose input into society was being stonewalled. Right down to the acceptable length of a teenager's hair, everything had been figured out by their parents.

Everything was figured out. Even – or especially - the arts. Australian poetry was tightly controlled by two publications Poetry and Australian Poetry. If you couldn't impress them, you couldn't get in. There were few independent art galleries. In Sydney, the Art Gallery of New South Wales called 95% of the shots.

But what about Rock n Roll, that catalyst of social unrest? Not in this country. Pop Music television appearances were limited to Channel 9's Bandstand, hosted by the good-natured - 'square' - Brian Henderson. Male performers wore suits. Female performers dressed like debutantes. All media came from Sir Frank Packer, the ABC or some other power-group that excluded young people. Don't even mention independent ham radio stations. They were for geeks.

It was difficult to get a voice even via a simple thing like printing. The general public could only print two ways. (1) Silk-screening (for posters) and (2) duplicating machines, known as 'Gestetners', was how poets, propagandists and voluntary associations (churches, clubs, etc) self-published. (However, innovations to offset printing were well underway at the time.)

One thing that the media did right was to identify teenagers as a separate demographic. The discovery coincided with the rise of the advertising sector, which suddenly became sexy in the 50s when Madison Avenue NY discovered brand image. People with a non-specific creative talent often ended up in the advertising sector.

That's where social commentator Phillip Adams got his start, as well as entrepreneur John Singleton, photographer Greg Weight, artist Brett Whiteley and 'know all' (as Jenny Kee dubs him in her autobiography) Richard Neville. (5) About his brief time in advertising, Richard wrote, 'Adland taught me the basics of printing, layout and come-hither headlines'. (6)

In 1960, Martin followed Justin's advice and enrolled in the National Art School (East Sydney Tech). He remained in contact with his former art teacher, dropping in to see him from time to time until Justin left for Europe. Says Martin, 'Art school - that's where I met Jenny Kee and lots of great people – Peter Powditch, Geoff Doring and Peter 'Charlie' Brown. A good crowd of people, art students are'. (7)

Martin's life suddenly got a whole lot more exciting. He started dating Anou Kiisler, a student at Sydney Girls High School. He discovered Vadim's, a hangout for the Sydney Art intelligentsia. He also discovered Gauloises cigarettes, Double Bay clothes shops and interesting cars that he flagrantly mistreated. His friend, Garry Shead describes Art School Mart as 'extraordinarily witty - there would always be a little phrase. You'd be working it out – he was just so smart'. (8)

At this stage, Martin was really an artist by default. He said, 'I went to East Sydney Tech but I'd really stopped being a painter after school. I did a few pictures, not many. Maybe 3-4.' (9)

Art was one of several options, with the idea of studying architecture not totally buried. About his career path as 'artist' Martin said, 'I would have liked to have been other things as well. There was nothing else that I was any good at. I'd like to have been a singer. I admire people who can sing. That would have been something that was talked about. A couple of friends of mine were thinking of forming something when I was a teenager - something to take on Bandstand. Richard Neville was always dancing in the audience. He should have been performing!' (10)

Being a surfer was another crazy option. Sydney's Northern Beaches replaced Telford as Martin's weekend retreat. He enjoyed hanging out at Whale Beach and Newport. 'I would have loved to have become a surfer', he reminisced, 'I think they're magnificent. To watch them, courage and health – dancing on the edge of eternities - Infinity - just riding that wave. I might have sat on a board once or twice, but surfing evaded me. I probably wouldn't be sitting here if I'd been a surfer. I'd have gone in a whole new direction. I didn't get a surfboard - but I painted one once.' (11)

The Sydney Stadium at Rushcutters Bay was still a fascination. Martin described it as, 'the best venue I've been to. It was our Albert Hall, in a way. It should have been preserved!

'It was built for a prizefight with Jack Johnson and Tommy Burns. (Johnson was the Muhammad Ali of the 1910s.) A simple building. They eventually put a corrugated iron roof over it, the biggest in Australia. Concrete in two corners and then this big octagonal, corrugated iron flying saucer. The atmosphere was superb. The great neon sign with two boxers out the front. Gladiators.

'The stage revolved, so everyone could get a good look. It was very challenging to the performers – they had their backs to half the audience all the time. It was a strange way of doing it but it worked. Also their silhouettes cast these huge shadows against the back walls, people screaming and dancing – amazing! Police-shields to bring stars onto the stage, it was a sensationally exciting place.

'Lee Gordon put on a lot of shows there. Judy Garland sang there. I saw Johnny Cash there. (1959) It was exciting! I saw Peter, Paul & Mary there, what a fantastic show! Mary tossing her wild hair, oh boy, was she the belle of the ball! I've seen great shows there – Harry Belafonte, Louis Armstrong. I had a great Pop education I guess.

'It would seem to me that they would bring the whole Top 20 out in one show. I like Bobby Rydell (in a way)…Gene Pitney, Del Shannon – and Elvis of course was dominating from afar. You've got a second crop of Elvis would-bes - Frankie Avalon. Johnny Restivo was good, he had the Hippy Hippy Shake. Brenda Lee/Chubby Checker. Brenda Lee was the star of the bill but Chubby Checker stormed the show with The Twist. Everyone did the Twist. It still gets me moving!' (12)

Martin was also curious about the back room of the Royal George Hotel where a group of libertarian drinkers met. Known as the Sydney Push, the idea was the bastard child of Professor John Anderson, who occupied the Challis Chair of Philosophy at the University of Sydney 1927-1958. In his prime, Anderson questioned everything – aesthetics, literature, politics - and he outraged Sydney's clergy and conventionally minded citizens. (13) Rejection of conventional morality and authoritarianism was the common bond of the Sydney Push. They used phrases like 'non-utopian anarchism' and 'permanent protest' to describe their activities and theories. It was the kind of place where anyone silly enough to put up a proposition would get flattened.

At its core, the Sydney Push was dominated by a group of men like Darcy Waters, Roelof Smilde, cartoonist George Molnar and poet Harry Hooton. However, slap bang in the middle and often vehemently taking the floor, undaunted by her gender, was the outspoken and outrageous Germaine Greer. On the outer circle were people destined for greater things like Clive James, Paddy McGuinness, Mungo Macallum, Bob Gould and Margaret Elliott (Fink). (14)

Sometimes painter/art critic Robert Hughes would attend. Martin knew him from Vadim's. Sometimes Peter 'Charlie' Brown was there too. Curious, Martin would join the outer circle, smoke his Gauloises and sip pernod. Left-leaning anarchism wasn't exactly Martin's scene. He was more interested in the people. Had he been bothered with politics, Martin would have probably tilted to the right, like his family.

Not that his family offered reassurance. Henry had located a harbour property at Neutral Bay where he was building his future home for himself and Dorothy. And Wirian, once a haven, was a battlefield – with Jo and her father constantly fighting. As if the impending divorce wasn't bad enough, Jo had fallen in love with Keith Hollingsworth, which was completely déclassé. He was a tradesman for chrissakes! This was Lady Chatterley's Lover revisited!

Said Martin, 'Keith was about 10-15 years younger than my mother. Keith was not a posh person. He was a lower class person, an artisan. Because of her affair with Keith, my grandfather was distraught. Grandfather Ritchie said to her, "unless you break off your relationship with him…!" Whether that came from my grandfather or society's orders, I don't know. I don't think he would have done that because he adored my mother, she was his only child.

'She could have had anyone in Sydney if she wanted to play the game but she wasn't a person who played the game. They tried to court her, the divorced ones, the ones who thought she might be a loose woman, but she fell in love with this guy. She conceived with him!' (15)

Grandfather Stuart worked less and less until he retired. Says Martin, 'Then they sold up the Ritchie Bros engineering works. They demolished it for developers'.

Martin didn't want to be a managing director. He wasn't even sure that he wanted to be an artist. In 1960, the big names in Australian art were Sidney Nolan, Russell Drysdale, Albert Tucker and Arthur Boyd. Said Garry Shead, 'They were treated like gods. They were way out there. We didn't see them (I didn't anyway). You didn't criticize them. They were BIG painters.' (16)

Australian Modernism had been a battleground since the early 40s. Nobel prize winner, author Patrick White was the freshest thing on the menu, having won his second Miles Franklin Award. His 1957 novel Voss, with its Sidney Nolan cover, was studied in high schools. The Fair Dinkum School of Australian culture didn't like that. They believed the Bush Balladeers were the nation's best writers and the Heidelberg School were Australia's real artists.

Notwithstanding Melbourne's post-War bohemia (1937-1947), the Angry Penguins (1940s), the Heide group (1934-), the Ern Malley poetry scandal (1943), William Dobell's Archibald Prize controversy (1944) and success of Australian Modernism in London (1961 - Nolan, Boyd, Tucker amongst them), Australian art was as conservative as the rest of society the early 1960s.

No one wants to remember Addled Art, Sir Lionel Lindsay's 1946 book, which was essentially a rant. Lindsay writes, 'I am convinced that Modern Art (self styled) will die the death. I found that a three-colour photograph had been pasted on! The morality of this hoax, the mendacity without spendour, need not be discussed; beside it Picasso's pasting on of Le Journal is but a nursery pleasantry'. (17)

Lindsay was friends with Sir Robert Menzies - who as Prime Minister never shied from commenting on aspects of 'proper' Australian culture.

Then out of nowhere, London's Tate Gallery purchased a picture by former East Sydney Tech student, 22-year old Brett Whiteley. Titled

Untitled Red Painting he was the youngest artist in 90 years to be bought by the Tate. (18) Martin and Garry couldn't help notice Brett's international success - a young Aussie from Sydney's Lower North Shore! He lived up the road from Martin's Uncle Frank's family, in Longueville! If Brett Whiteley could, maybe other young Aussies could too!

Martin's lecturer John Olsen, was another success, in a modern vein. His one-person exhibition at the Terry Clune Gallery in October 1960 crowned him, according to writer Geoffrey Dutton, 'the most dynamic figure in the Sydney art world until 1963 when he went to Portugal…'. (19)

Despite these surges of interest, Martin's first year at art school had not proved the success for which his family had hoped. He had turned dilettantism into an art form. He was – I suppose – a 'face' - the student more interested in coffee shop conversations than attending lectures, the snappy dresser who splattered paint on clothes no one else could afford to buy. Said Martin, 'I liked dressing and finding interesting clothes. When you're a teenager you really do. It's such a language. I had a pink and black thin tie – very shiny.' (20) But no, Martin's first year at art school had not proved the cornerstone on which his parents hoped he might build a career.

In 1961, Martin quit art school and attended Sydney University to study Architecture, a nod to his drawing ability. In the same year, Richard Neville quit advertising and enrolled for an Arts course at the University of New South Wales and Richie Walsh switched from studying Arts-Law to Medicine at Sydney Uni.

Martin moved into St Paul's College, an all male residential college on campus. Like the Cranbrook School, there was a weighty Sharp heritage at Sydney Uni. Martin's grandfather, Dr Ramsay Sharp, left a bequest named after his parents (Martin's great-grandparents) the William Henry and Eliza-Alice Sharp Prize in operative surgery. Grandmother Bessie's brother, Dr Harold Ritchie, and Martin's father and uncles all graduated from medicine from Sydney Uni. This was Martin's new stamping ground, although his architectural course was not the focus of his attention, he was attracted by the drama society.

Needless to say, Martin's father had been there before him. Henry was co-originator of the Sydney University Revue in 1929. He performed on stage and wrote at least two plays – Mississippi Melody and Suppressed Desires. And now – in 1961 - Martin was creating posters for the Sydney University Revue. His art school reputation made him a natural choice. Martin's attendance coincided with the Golden Age of Sydney Uni drama: Clive James, John Gaden, Lyn Collingwood all took the stage at Sydney University in 1961.

Martin reels them off, 'There was some fantastic humour when I was there. Germaine Greer was the star of university, an absolutely riveting star of the stage. Great writers - Bob Ellis and people like this. I saw Bob Ellis acting in The Birthday Party as Petey – (by Pinter). Fantastic performance. Arthur Dignam - absolutely a star! John Bell putting on amazing plays. It was a very exciting period to be in touch with that crowd'.

Student Balls was another outlet for Martin's posters. Martin returned to art school after two university terms. He explained, 'I was meant to be doing architecture but I was hanging out with some artist friends from art school. I was living a double life really'. (21)

Art School is where Martin met Garry Shead, an art student with a mischievous turn of the pen. Schooled at Shore Grammar, Garry went to the North Sydney campus of the National Art School four days per week, the other day Garry would cross the bridge and attend the East Sydney campus. He met Martin through one of his teachers, David Strachan, who said, 'There's somebody you should meet...' and what a fortuitous meeting that turned out to be. 'I saw so much of him when we were at art school', said Garry, 'we became very good friends'. (22)

Garry hailed from the same North Shore locality as Richie Walsh and remembers noticing Richie way before he met him. Says Garry, 'I used to see him going to school (Barker) in his huge great boater, this little guy with a big suitcase. I didn't know who he was at that time. Only later on I realized it was him'.

Garry was full of ideas, one of which was Australia's first truly underground movie. In 1961, Garry started filming what became Ding A Ding Day at East Sydney Tech. It took five years to complete. Martin appeared in some early footage, on-and-off all the way through. Garry also attended Film Society screenings of the French New Wave cinema. This put him in contact with Albie Thoms and a whole new crowd.

Said Martin, 'Garry was doing poetic sort of stuff. He's always had a very romantic vision, a fantastic artist and a great filmmaker. He was the wave before the New Wave - the really New Wave! He had the nerve to get up and do it. He made very interesting films with nothing, just friends and nerve.' (23)

'Garry will be acknowledged as a great pioneer, being one of the first people who was onto it. A real innovator, very beautiful films. I had the good fortune to be in a couple of them, one - surprisingly - on the merry-go-round at Luna Park'. (24)

Garry was also cutting it as a cartoonist in the commercial world. August 1961 saw him filling in for Les Tanner as guest cartoonist in The Bulletin, followed by contributions to Sydney Morning Herald and the Sydney University paper Honi Soit. Martin followed suit. He recalls, 'I was sending cartoons to the Bulletin and they were getting published in the size of a postage stamp. Garry was getting these fantastic full pages! He was hot as a cartoonist - boy! Les Tanner was a wonderful cartoon editor of The Bulletin, he was a great friend of both of us'. (25)

In 1962 two exhibitions by a group known as the Subterranean Imitation Realists (also Annandale Imitation Realists) created quite a splash in the Sydney-Melbourne art world. It was the first group-Art salvo from the emerging generation. Cop this.

The works by Ross Crothall, Colin Lanceley and Mike Brown seemed to come from nowhere. Much of it was junkyard assemblage, with a nod to primitive art, Dada, the objet trouvé and urban larrikinism. Boyd,

Nolan and Tucker weren't even on their spectrum. This was an attack on Abstract Expressionism. The Subterranean Imitation Realists were pre-Pop. They anticipated Pop.

While drinking endless cups of coffee at Vadim's where - in the days of strict licensing laws - actor Kate Fitzpatrick served booze in coffee cups, Colin Lanceley recalls, 'We often played a game we called Aesthetic Chess which was played on table tops and involved placing and moving miscellaneous objects from our pockets to create visual tensions and patterns. We loved art and literature and we loved primitive art especially. We intensely disliked the kind of fifth-rate Abstract Expressionism which prevailed in Sydney at the time.' (26)

Martin and Garry knew - or knew of – this group as the previous batch of John Olsen's students from East Sydney Tech. In February 1962 the Subterranean Imitation Realists mounted their first exhibition at the Melbourne Museum of Modern Art and Design. Their second and final exhibition in May 1962 was held at the Rudy Komon Gallery, Sydney.

Martin describes the group, 'Colin Lanceley is a really fine artist who had a group who influenced me a lot. The Subterranean Imitation Realists used to do fantastic pictures, like Luna Park, Mug Lairs Picnic, all made of bottle tops. They painted a whole gallery out and hung their pictures in it, so their freedom was a terrific excitement to me. (27)

'The Subterranean Imitation Realists were a real inspiration because they'd taken over an art gallery and painted over it inside and outside, made a big mess of the place - painted a big car. They were three guys like a visual pop group. Talk about Pop Artists! They were an influence on me – more than Peter Blake or any of these overseas people.' (28)

What was known as Commem Day (University Commemoration Day) was a big thing in Sydney in the early 1960s. Parades through the city, floats, pranks. It was a day when everyone was tolerant of uni students' antics, like 'kidnapping' a celebrity – maybe a deejay, like Bandstand's Brian Henderson – and holding him/her to ransom (the money went to some cause). Another famous prank was when some students told a group of road workers that a bunch of uni students dressed as police were about to regale them. They then told the cops that a bunch of uni students were digging up the road as a prank. The students stood back and watched/enjoyed/photographed the confrontation.

Special editions of the university papers Tharunka and Honi Soit were sold by students up-and-down inner-city streets. Every railway station was manned. These were spoof papers – like a facsimile edition of the Sydney Morning Herald bearing the headline 'Sydney Harbour Bridge is falling down!' They usually featured a racey photograph of a female student baring slightly more flesh than readers were used to seeing in print. So once every year, clerks, shop assistants, schoolkids, factory workers - anyone near a train station, got treated to the students' take on things. The whole thing was a bit of a giggle. There was a good-natured acceptance of these uni pranks by the city at large.

In 1962, Richard Neville was made editor of the University of New South Wales' student publication Tharunka. At Sydney Uni, Richie Walsh and Peter Grose were the newly-sacked editors of Honi Soit. They were sacked for being too edgy and about to be reinstated.

Sydney Uni had a student publication, New South Wales Uni had one too, the Art School didn't. One night Garry had a dream that would lead to two courts cases and a heap of legal and artistic arguments for the next three years. Instead of cartooning for the Bulletin – why not do it for ourselves?

Said Garry, 'I woke up in the middle of the night with this idea for a newspaper – "sowing your wild oats" – and something arty to connect with it. I told Martin, "let's do a magazine for the Arts" and we got it together'. (29) Said Martin, 'I don't think Garry realizes how he inspired me in the early days – The Arty Wild Oat, which led to OZ magazine. Such a wonderful, gentle and humorous person!'(30)

The Arty Wild Oat was put together under the general editorship of Garry, assisted by Martin along with secretary Sue Wood, art editor John Firth-Smith, advertising Ernest Rushton, circulation Ian van Wieringen and production Robert J. Mayne. Its first issue was April 1962. (Copies may be viewed online.) (31)

Albie Thoms remembers it well, he writes, 'The Arty Wild Oat: its first issue featured an interview with Bob Hughes, who courted trouble by attacking the purchasing policy of the AGNSW, a trustee of which was the head of their school.

'Honi Soit now was edited by Richie Walsh and Peter Grose, with Mungo MacCallum as its theatre critic, Richard Brennan as film reviewer, and Penny McNicoll, the daughter of the editor of the Daily Telegraph, as news editor. She soon took up with Bob Ellis, who was writing long and usually long-winded features for the paper, including a somewhat envious one about Bruce Beresford's forthcoming film. For its cartoonists, the paper had the Architecture student, Geoff Atherden, later a leading television comedy writer, as well as occasional contributions from Martin Sharp'. (32)

So there were crossovers.

Tharunka editor, Richard Neville was curious. Martin remembers noticing him before meeting him. Martin says, 'I first met him when he was working for Tharunka. He came in to get some artwork for the advertising agency at a house in Neutral Bay. He came around to pick up a drawing and I thought he was rather strange - very straightly dressed yet he was a character. He clashed a bit with the bohemian house that he'd come into. I remember noticing him. We didn't communicate - I just noticed. But later on, of course, we became the greatest friends'. (33)

Richard Neville organized to meet Martin and Garry formally at the University of New South Wales Roundhouse in the third week of April 1962. It was a business meeting of sorts. Garry introduced himself, holding a copy of Arty Wild Oat and Martin lurked shyly in the shadows muttering, 'Art is pretentious'.

Over countless cappuccinos, Garry suggested collaboration between Arty Wild Oat and Tharunka and then Martin drove Richard home. On arrival, Martin asked Richard to pass him a tin opener. He jumped out of the car, sawed off the roof of his Triumph sedan, turned it into a convertible and – writes Richard, 'With a wave he was gone, taking a part of my heart with him'.

Next day they went spear fishing together. (34)

The second issue of Arty Wild Oat came out in July. Garry said, 'we did two issues. There was an interview with Norman Lindsay in the second one. I wrote to him and asked him to write something for our newspaper and he said, "Oh I'd love to - young people – I'll give my point of view on things…". That was the front main story of course. We did actually go and see him. Martin organized that. It wasn't that interesting. Norman Lindsay came out - then went inside to his little officey part of the house. I happened to follow him and he was actually doing his hair! We talked to him for about 20 minutes. He didn't invite us in.' (35)

Martin said, 'Garry Shead got Arty Wild Oat together and I worked on it with Ian van Wieringen, John Firth-Smith and a few others. Colin Lanceley wrote an article for it. We had an interview with Norman Lindsay. It was only a fold-over 4-sheeter - but it went quite well. It was like a student paper but it hadn't started from the Student's Representative Council (SRC), it started from some cartoonists.'

That was the point, Garry didn't ask anybody's permission to start The Arty Wild Oat, it was started by cartoonists. Although it came from the students, no student politics were involved and the editors couldn't be voted down. As it was not an official or semi-official organ of East Sydney Tech, its 7499 print-run seemed to invite an off-campus readership.

Said Garry, 'We did the Arty Wild Oat and we had students selling it. We distributed it to the art school, the University of New South Wales and the University of Sydney. That was where Richard Neville and Richard Walsh got the idea for doing OZ. We could create a newspaper from just throwing in our own money to make it, so that led to OZ. We had a journalist friend from school who organized the printing.' (36)

As well as Richard Neville, the art student 4-page flyer led to Martin and Garry meeting Richie Walsh. Martin said, 'This put us in contact with the editors of the universities Richard Neville and Richard Walsh, and their plan was to bring out a student newspaper - but on the streets.

'Commem Day spoof papers used to come out every year and they were sold to the public. This was an idea to do the same thing once a month, but amalgamate outside the actual university magazines and bring out our own magazine. Richard Neville and Richard Walsh were the experienced publishers. I was just there for the art and a bit of design'. (37)

And then Garry got suddenly taken out of the picture. In the 60s schools could discipline students for vagaries such as 'attitude', 'insubordination' or similar ill-defined transgressions. In the June issue of the Bulletin, Garry wrote an article with this opening paragraph, after which he was not readmitted to East Sydney Tech:

Teaching Artists How The Power Game Works. 'The benevolent attitude of the civil service toward its employees amounts to the stagnation that often accompanies senility. If some of the teachers who have been with the department 20 years or more were dismissed they would stand very little chance of keeping their heads above water. Therefore there is a moral obligation to keep them on to which there seems no immediate remedy…'. (38)

Said Garry, 'I was only at art school for two years 1961-62. I was a bit of an obnoxious kind of upstart, cocky. I wrote a piece for the Bulletin that was fairly critical of the art school teaching. Douglas Dundas was the head teacher there and he told me to come to the office and said, "Shead, I don't think you should bother coming back to art school next year".' (38)

Booted out of Art School – well, 'not readmitted' - Garry spent a long time out of work, wondering who on earth might want his talents? 'I wasn't allowed to go back so I had to get a job. For six months I was without a job. I didn't know where to start. I was in the laundry of my parents' place in Pymble at that time, writing, fiddling around and suddenly the mother of a friend of mine rang to say "there's a job at ABC Gore Hill, you should try for it as a scenic artist". So I went along and got the job'. Garry got a job as a set painter. He left home immediately. (39)

The ABC was an ideal environment for Garry, who need editing facilities to finish his film. It took until 1965 for him to complete it. (Ding a Ding Day has had several screenings over the years, including the Yellow House in 1970 and the Yellow House Retrospective at the Art Gallery of New South Wales in 1990.)

But before quitting art school and working at the ABC, there was telling moment when Garry showed Martin his latest cartoon for the Bulletin. It had three elements, the character, the gag and on the pavement the word Eternity.

Martin handed it back without comment.

Eternity.

'He took a good hard look at it', said Garry. (40)

'The first time I saw Eternity. I must have been about seven or eight, maybe a bit older,' said Martin. 'I was definitely on my own and I don't know when I was allowed out on my own. I was walking back from the Rose Bay Pier in Cranbrook Road. I saw it written on the pavement, on the left hand side of the road coming back around the second corner, and I wondered what it meant. I'd never seen anything written on the pavement before'. (41)

4.
OZ IS A NEW MAGAZINE

*After its lame beginning,
OZ became stronger with each issue.*
ALBIE THOMS

In 1957, publisher Lawrence Ferlinghetti and manager of the San Francisco City Lights bookstore, Shigeyoshi (Shig) Murao, were charged with disseminating obscene literature in the form of the Allen Ginsberg poem Howl. The poem contains references to illicit drugs and both heterosexual and homosexual sexual practices. In October of the same year, US Judge Clayton Horn ruled the poem not obscene. (1) This case was an early goal in a long-running generational war about censorship.

The team who would subsequently create OZ were in their early teens and may not have noticed the case at the time. They would later see the Howl trial as setting some sort of precedent for their own experience.

As an eighteen-year old, Martin definitely heard about the next literary scandal, the 1960 Lady Chatterley's Lover trial brought against Penguin Books under the British Obscene Publications Act. It was big news in certain circles, like the Sydney Push and amongst the next generation of writers. That the publishers escaped conviction by arguing it was a work of 'literary merit' created a legal precedent. (2)

Meanwhile, the Arty Wild Oat pushed a few boundaries, attracted lots of attention but after just two issues its small team was running out of puff. The publication needed much more content. It also needed to make the jump from art-stream to mainstream. Yet Arty Wild Oat certainly caught a mood, a target-readership and an attitude. The genie was out of the bottle. The two Richards knew it.

Editors, Richard Neville and Richie Walsh teamed up. Before Garry left art school and worked for the ABC, they organised a meeting with him and Martin, drank plenty of coffee and reached an agreement. Instead of issuing three separate publications - Tharunka, Honi Soit and Arty Wild Oat – they agreed to join forces and create one - with broader content and more pages. It would be political, sassy and funny.

The agreement led to a formal meeting held at Richard Neville's place. Not quite a Board Meeting, it was a type of party which welcomed friends as potential contributors. About 15 turned up. Richie brought cadet journalist Peter Grose and Richard gave a speech, while Martin and Garry formed a sub-group with Tharunka artists, Peter Kingston and Mick Glasheen and giggled at everything being said. (3)

Said Martin, 'Richard Neville called everyone over, had a party and everyone was excited by the idea of combining the papers and releasing a regular combined-talents university student paper on the streets. A rough memory of the times - Alex Popov…Michael Glasheen was cartooning, Peter Kingston for Tharunka, Richard Neville running full-page comics on the front. Writers: Gina Eviston, Robyn Cooper, Anou my girlfriend and Ann Kaiser a girlfriend of Richard's. That night OZ was born.

'Richard Walsh suggested the name, which I thought was silly at the time. I had my own idea - ASP for Australia's Satirical Paper. But OZ was perfect, of course. It's got a lot of angles to it: OZtralia, the Wizard of OZ. It's a paradoxical name – humorous, good-natured. It was just right actually. And so, there it was - OZ.' (4)

Meanwhile the coffee drinking sessions continued at Vadim's. Martin introduced Richard to Robert Hughes who was playing to a table of admirers as usual. Martin also introduced him to Sydney Uni arts student Louise Ferrier and Richard was dumbstruck. Richard wrote, 'Her beauty shriveled my savoir faire, her composure drove me nuts'. He babbled something about starting a magazine, tried to hold her interest until a bloke came to retrieve her. It was Peter Grose.

One night in late March, Martin and Richard drove all over the city plastering up posters that read, 'OZ is a new magazine'. Issue No 1 was released on April Fools Day 1963. It was launched on £50 working capital, 30 subscribers and no fulltime staff. A 12-month subscription cost £1 and the cover price was 1/6. Six thousand copies were distributed from an office in the Rocks area of Sydney found by Gina Eviston's father. It sold out by lunchtime, Richard ordered a reprint and described it as the happiest day of his life. (5)

The team comprised: editors - Richard Neville and Richie Walsh. Art Director - Martin Sharp. Artists - Garry Shead, Mick Glasheen and Peter Kingston. Staff - Anou Kiissler and Aggie Read. Melbourne editor - Paul Lawson. (6)

Summing up the spirit of OZ, social commentator Craig McGregor wrote, 'They know, to the faintest whiff of snobbery in a charity dinner, all about hypocrisy, pretense, cruelty, intolerance and authoritarianism of so much of Australian life. Like most young people they can't stand phonies and the smug self-satisfaction of many adults. They know absolutely what they are against, and it is a measure of their talent that their opposition finds bitter and memorable expression. But they are not sure what they are for.' (7)

There were 16 pages per month, mixing text and illustration. Necessity being the mother of invention, Martin was required to faithfully produce drawings on a regular basis each month. Not just cartoons, but also ads for Binkie's Burgers, Suzie Wong's Restaurant, Clune Galleries and the Gas Lash, an after hours speakeasy where his friends hung out.

Former Gas Lash manager, Ted Markstein described the place that so regularly bought the entire OZ back page for a Martin-drawn ad, 'A guy called Ron Murphy had a place called Binkie's, a late-night burger place on Elizabeth Street. The Gas Lash was next door. I ran it. It was a folk-singer joint. You couldn't get liquor in Sydney after 6.00 at night, so we ran it as a speakeasy and all society used to come down there.' (8)

Said Martin, 'It wasn't until I started drawing cartoons (which I've always been keen on anyway) for OZ magazine, that I was put into that position where I was working fast and spontaneously - a bit of collage, a bit of this, a bit of that and a bit of fast handwriting. John Olsen was one of my teachers. His spiky handwritten paintings were an influence, the vitality of his style.' (9)

Olsen broke away from East Sydney Tech and opened his own art school, The Rocks Art School. Cynthia Byrne (later married to Robert Klippel), Peter Powditch and Martin were part of Olsen's small class of six students. They left their East Sydney Tech courses and followed him there. In Cynthia's words, 'as if he were the Pied Piper'. It only lasted six months. (10)

Satire was busting out all over, Barry Humphries' monologues, the Mavis Bramston Show on TV. Canberra Times had a satirical column and the Phillip Street Theatre ran satirical revues. Even the Kings Cross Whisper claimed to be a satirical paper - all pushing boundaries in their own cheeky way.

Albie Thoms was certainly pushing boundaries at the Sydney University Dramatic Society with his Revue of the Absurd. Like everyone, he too was curious about OZ. Albie summed it up the first issue. 'My first response was that it seemed a bit roughshod and juvenile, with a crude collage on its cover depicting a man in a chastity belt, while an article inside lampooned sexual abstinence. Smugly, I found it all too unsophisticated and lacking in bite, and believed it vastly inferior to my own revue.' (11)

Censorship and free speech were issues of the time. Things were getting silly. American censorship required married couples in films to dress in neck-to-knee pyjamas and sleep in separate single beds. Nipples were airbrushed from magazine photos. Nudie magazines weren't nudie at all but usually dollybirds in underwear. Stocking tops were risqué. The Australian censors combed through each month's issue of US men's magazine Playboy seeking something that would enable it to be banned.

OZ 1 was exciting for readers and the editorial team. OZ probably felt invincible and enjoyed poking fun at right-wing establishment figures like radio commentator Eric Baume, modernist architect Harry Seidler, Queen Elizabeth II, Robert Menzies PM and Sydney's Social Top 20. Three more issues continued in this jocular vein before the law caught up with them.

The police contended that OZ 1 contained an article about chastity belts, which was deemed offensive, as well as an interview with an abortionist (an illegal practice at the time). Richie's father was so deeply shocked by the charges that he suffered a heart attack thought serious enough for the Walsh family solicitor to have the case adjourned until September.

In panic, the printers would not proceed with OZ 4. Now the OZ team had two problems - the printer and the law. Then Richie phoned Richard with a left-field idea - the Anglican Press. Of all things! Said Richard, 'Isn't it owned by the church?' Richie replied that its proprietor, Francis James, was a champion of free speech and a maverick.

Richard, Richie, Martin and Anou met Francis James on his premises. They came to an agreement and set a date for the press to roll. As they took their leave, the slightly world-weary proprietor shot out, 'You lot might think of yourselves as angry young men. Piffle! Young Walsh here will take to the establishment like a duck to water!' Richie didn't like that at all.

In an attempt to avoid a conviction, the OZ boys backed down. On a September Monday in 1963, at the Central Court of Petty Sessions, Richie's solicitor entered a plea of guilty on behalf of Richard, Richie and Peter Grose. The big shock came when Peter's solicitor told the court that his client was no more than a consultant, had completely disassociated himself from his two associates and on reflection, found OZ to be utterly worthless. The magistrate fined them £20 apiece and supporters of OZ hissed Peter as he walked out. (12) Peter Grose has since gone on to become a highly respected publisher.

Albie wasn't pleased with any of them for pleading guilty. He too had been picked up by the Police on a charge of obscenity relating to his Sydney Uni Revue of the Absurd. The charge related to the use of the word 'shite' and 'arseholes' in one of the songs in the Alfred Jarry play The Song of the Disembraining.

Albie writes, 'I was set back by the news that the editors of OZ had pleaded guilty to their obscenity charge, and wondered what bearing it might have on my own case, due to be heard the following month. When I next saw him, I castigated Richie Walsh for caving in, but he explained that he had been misled by his lawyer, who had recommended this course, believing that their convictions would not be recorded because they were first offenders.'

The lawyer reasoned that a conviction would not help Richie's future medical career nor Peter Grose's journalistic hopes. It would also mean Richard Neville probably could not travel to America. Richie explained to Albie that there was everything to be gained by avoiding conviction - which proved mistaken as they were convicted anyway.

At least Martin found it amusing. Writes Albie, 'The affair was gleefully mocked by Martin Sharp in Tharunka with a cartoon that showed Richard at first relishing the idea of a trial and the publicity it would bring, before putting on a suit to plead guilty'. (13)

In a subsequent issue, Richie saw to it that OZ took Albie's side in a piece titled 'Obscene or Absurd?' OZ particularly enjoyed the moment when the policeman said to Albie, 'Get me Alfred Jarry!' to which Albie replied, 'If you'd read your program you'd see he died in 1908!' The reprint, from the Sydney Push's Libertarian Broadsheet, also pointed out that it is 'probably a triumph for the freedom to be vulgar and in bad taste without being obscene'. (14)

This article led to Richie introducing Albie to the OZ crowd. Everyone seems to remember Richard Neville from their first meeting. Albie writes, 'He was a ball of energy, with sparkling eyes and an awkward way of standing, with his head held at an angle while he engaged you with a distinctive, toothy smile that Martin Sharp later made symbolic of OZ. Richard was most enthusiastic about my censorship victory, expressing genuine interest in my future plans, and invited me to contribute to his magazine, though I then had more pressing concerns.' (15)

OZ suited Martin. In his quiet way, he was an angry young man. He found himself in OZ. It gave him an artistic identity. Martin said, 'I went to art school and lost my style completely. It took OZ to pick it up again.' (16)

The OZ team had a thing about the parochial Aussie male. They called him 'Alf'. He was their equivalent of Barry Humphries' Sandy Stone character. Sometimes also known in OZ as 'Normal Normal', Alf is the typical owner of a 3-bedroom brick veneer house with a Holden to polish in the driveway. He's looking forward to a date with the wife at the RSL and a beer with the boys while watching Saturday football. 'Terrible drug that marijuana' complained a beer sodden Alf in Martin's OZ cartoon. (17)

This guy was almost everybody's father!

Like the two Richards, Martin was angry about the humiliations of his school life. Said Martin, 'Most satirists sat back pretty quietly at school and had a pretty rough time of it. That's certainly my case and certainly Richie Walsh's. Richard Neville is a bit more extrovert but he was still the brunt of a lot of pranks at school – so that was an interesting motive in OZ. It's the sort of rage that comes out quietly later.' (18)

For their heavy condemnation of his mother, Martin was also angry with his father's side of the family. Notwithstanding Henry's many infidelities, nor that Jo only took a lover after the marriage breakup, she was made to wear the blame for the impending divorce. Aunts Barbara and Edith (Dinks) were the only ones who gave her any family support. No doubt having married Drs Sharp themselves gave them certain insights.

Of the Sharp family, Martin said, 'The males did not talk to my mum. When it broke, which is a bit earlier than when they were divorced, it was pre Decree Nisi - no blame. "We won't put your name all over the papers if you don't make a fuss", which is what they were doing to my mother. It was terrible. And they were so bloody self-righteous about it. It was all bullshit!

'I guess my mother must have been considered a fallen woman. Society dropped her, not only the Sharps, except the wives of the Sharps who loved her, they used to come and see her – Dinks, Aunt Barb – but the Sharp family under the command of the hand that rocks the cradle...!' Martin was quoting the idiom 'the hand that rocks the cradle rules the world' which is how he regarded Grandmother Sharp's grip on her three influential sons. (19)

Martin had attitude, not uncommon among undergraduates in their early-20s. Martin was hanging with a crowd of young upstarts who were getting themselves a bit of a name around town as a precocious group of (probably) poseurs refusing to go along with the status quo. Art school friend Jenny Kee describes Martin and artist Peter Powditch as 'leaders of the pack' at art school. (20)

In this pre-Beatle era, surf culture was the thing in Sydney. Says Martin, 'The surfing-thing hit very big and some very exciting music came out of it. The whole sound was a terrific. I used to go to Surf City at Kings Cross – the Stomp was a great thing.' (21)

What Martin probably didn't know was that this was possibly his first brush with the Kings Cross underworld. Surf City was a former cinema owned by Lee Gordon and Abe Saffron that they converted into a disco called the Birdcage. After Lee Gordon left Australia it was leased to John Harrigan, or the Harrigan family, presumably by Abe Saffron himself. In fact Abe Saffron was involved in all the Sydney shows Martin talked about - Harry Belafonte, Chubby Checker, Bobby Rydell – the lot. (22)

Surf City featured surf music, Sydney's latest craze. Young men 'peroxided' their hair blond and, along with their surfie girlfriends, they pounded their feet on the dance floor, with their hands held behind their backs. Thoonk-thoonk. Following the bass lines. Thoonk-thoonk. That was known as the Surfer's Stomp.

The music might be 14-year old Patricia Amphlett (Little Pattie) singing her hit song Blonde-Headed Stompie Wompie Real Gone Surfer Guy. Or perhaps a new band called the Aztecs who started out at Surf City playing surf instrumentals. Around this time a singer called Billy Thorpe joined them and they completely changed that routine, becoming more like those Liverpool Mod bands that Australians were hearing about, like the Beatles whose first Australian release, Love Me Do was setting them apart from Gerry and the Pacemakers, Brian Poole and the Tremeloes and those other Pommie bands.

There were lots of Surfies around Surf City. They probably didn't even own a board! Meanwhile, Surfers – the real deal – were to be found at riding the waves, especially on the northern beaches. Sometimes Martin would leave his Paddington apartment/studio and spend Saturday afternoons with Richard, pretending to drink beer at the Newport Arms hotel (the 'Arms').

Though seldom venturing the surf themselves, Martin and Richard sometimes sat on the beach, watching the wave-riders. Martin got ideas for sketches from watching what beach people did. One Saturday afternoon he saw the full drama, wheelies, a punch up and a 'well-aimed chunder'. Richard recalls being with Martin when it happened, after which Martin raced to the OZ office where he wrote/drew the controversial cartoon, The Word Flashed Around the Arms, written in the first-person voice of the Ocker gatecrasher. (23)

On those northern beaches, Martin got to know surf-filmmaker Paul Witzig – a Sydney Uni guy - who Californian Bruce Brown hired to shoot Australian footage for his upcoming movie The Endless Summer. Witzig later worked as Brown's Down-Under liaison, screening Brown's films in New South Wales and Queensland.

Now with a track record as the poster artist of preference for student balls and art school events, Martin was asked to create a surf-themed poster for The Endless Summer, which he did. Not the famous pink, yellow and orange poster with the surfer carrying the board on his head. Another one. 'It wasn't very original', said Martin. (24)

Barry Humphries knew – or had met – Martin. Around this time he penned a poem, which he dedicated to him. The Old Pacific Sea is an odd one to associate with Martin, though it may have been inspired by Martin's The Word Flashed Around the Arms chunder-cartoon. It's the 'chunder in the old Pacific sea' song that Barry Crocker would sing in the 1972 film The Adventures of Barry McKenzie - by which time, whatever connection it may have had to Martin was surely lost. (25)

Their court case behind them and a surge of youthful energy before them, Martin, Richard and Richie at last agreed that OZ was on the right track. Richard was glowing in his mother's glory, having formally graduated as a Bachelor of Arts. Richie was doing well, studying medicine. Martin never stopped drawing. The circulation of OZ had doubled.

Albie writes, 'After its lame beginning, OZ had become stronger with each issue, featuring a Bob Hughes' caricature of God on the cover of the second, the send-up of the Bogle-Chandler murders on the third, and a satire on the Profumo Affair for number four. Each issue was crammed with small items ridiculing politicians, priests, and the pretensions of Sydney society, while Bob also lampooned the CND, Bob Ellis swiped at US politics, and Bruce Beresford offered criticism of contemporary cinema. They were supported by scratchy illustrations from the magazine's art director, Martin Sharp, together with cartoons by Garry Shead, Peter (Kingo) Kingston, and Mick Glasheen. Best of all were Martin's full-page monologues, combining small drawings with lots of written text, reversing the usual comic convention that limited words to slim panels and speech balloons.' (26)

The OZ team held a meeting after which they felt confident that they had ironed out whatever problems they had. Their readers were most forgiving. They seemed to understand that OZ was nobody's fulltime job and some of the team, Richie for example, actually studied while at university. Readers also sensed they were on the edge of something in a city where teenagers were growing longer hair and asserting their youth in all art forms. Agitprop theatre, underground film, Pop poetry and especially Pop music. Hairdressers were turning into celebrities. Fashion designers too. Clothes shops and record shops were where the teen dollar was being spent. Art galleries were suddenly interesting.

While parents were still arguing about the demerits of Abstract Expressionism, the art students were way beyond that. New York Pop artists Andy Warhol and Roy Lichtenstein were over-defining the images that the Abstract movement had lost. They painting down-to-earth subjects like comic books, money and tins of Campbell soup, taken straight from the commercial world. Said Martin, 'Pop Art was like a flavour. It was around. I was a bit younger than most of the Pop artists. I wouldn't say I was influenced, it was a flavour that was around'. (27)

Yes, things were going well for OZ, which they all agreed in their April meeting. Before the month was out, Martin, Richie and Richard each got a summons to appear at the Court of Petty Sessions for publishing an obscene magazine, OZ 6 – the one with the urinal cover.

'This time it's serious,' said Richard to his father. (28)

5.

OZ TRIAL LONDON CALLING

OZ was vulgar, abrasive, sometimes funny, sometimes embarrassing, but good for Sydney. It was certainly doing no harm to anyone when in 1964 the full ferocity of the old-style repressive laws of censorship and criminal libel were unleashed on it.

GEOFFREY DUTTON

To date, apart from brief forays by Barry Humphries into London's comedy circles, this Australian generation had yet to make its overseas impact. If they would not go to England, England first came to them.

In the time between entrepreneur Ken Brodziak's handshake agreement with manager Brian Epstein and the Beatles' arrival in Australia in June, the band transformed into an international phenomenon. Overnight, the £3000 Brodziak-Epstein deal seemed a pittance.

In March, Can't Buy Me Love, the band's sixth single was released and went straight to No 1. John's first book In His Own Write also came out that month and sold 50,000 copies on its first day. Also in March the John, Paul, George and Ringo started filming A Hard Day's Night.

Madame Tussaud's famous waxworks put their effigies on show. Everyone changed their hairstyles. Everyone changed their tastes. Even the Queen arked up. But Epstein would never renege on his bond. Shortly before the OZ trial – June 1964 - the Beatles were booked to play concerts in Adelaide, Melbourne and Sydney. (1)

With an eye on the Rolling Stones, Martin didn't think the Beatles actually called the shots. Rather, they spearheaded a movement with many players. He initially poked fun at them in OZ. Said Martin, 'I like to think I had long hair before the Beatles! Their hair was short! I think they cut it to become the Beatles!'

Until the Beatles tour, Martin was still looking to Australian bands for inspiration. Moving right along from former-hero Johnny O'Keefe, a Sydney-based band called the Missing Links was OZ magazine's pet rockers.

After name-checking 50s singers Laurie London and Tommy Steele, Martin explained, 'Not much had been coming out of London. It had been pretty silent at this stage. Suddenly England became interesting. The Beatles and the whole Liverpool Sound. Brian Poole the Tremeloes were great, Do you love me, now that I can dance…! The excitement of that scene! The Beatles had that fantastic Liverpool humour which really kicked in with similar Australian humour.'

So Martin had a change of heart - he liked them. No, loved them! He got completely caught up in the phenomenon and it had much to do with Greg Weight's ex-girlfriend, Jenny Kee, a proper livewire.

When the Beatles hit town, Jenny was in her second year at East Sydney Tech. Jenny and Martin knew each other from art school and also from Vadim's where Jenny recalls the OZ boys tête-á-tête, regularly scheming something up. She and her friend Vickii Maher had accompanied Martin and Richard to Luna Park shortly before the Beatles were due to arrive. They told the boys they were targeting the band and Martin thought he should tag along. Martin bought tickets for himself and his Mum to see the Beatles play the Sydney Stadium and he took Anou to see them arrive at their hotel, where Jenny and Vickii were sure to be.

The Beatles staying at the Sheraton Hotel, 40 Macleay Street Kings Cross, was the worst kept secret in town. Thousands of fans showed up. Thousands. Said Martin, 'I was a bit of a Stage Door Johnny in a way. I admired performers. I was always interested in meeting performers.' (2) He tried to smuggle Anou inside in a laundry basket, to no avail. It was impossible to get close. Yet Jenny and Vickii somehow cut through the pack.

Jenny and Vickii hung around the lifts, got to the 8th floor where they were greeted by a wall of bodyguards so they went back down. Then back up. Again they faced the wall of bodyguards, but this time Beatles' press secretary Derek Taylor was there too. Taylor beckoned them in and seconds later Jenny and Vickii were in John and Paul's suite. Later in the evening Jenny scored John Lennon. She wrote, 'He had his way with me and it was hot: a genuine emotional charge for us both'. (3)

Martin surmised some sort of agreement was reached that if Jenny came to London, John would take care of her – see that she got a job maybe? Something like that. Said Martin, 'There was this call for Jenny to get over there'. (4) Richard wrote, 'By morning she (Jenny) had decided to save up for a passage on a cruise ship to Carnaby Street.' (5)

What none of them yet knew was that Bob Whitaker, who was about to become a close friend, had received the same call. So impressed was Beatles manager Brian Epstein by Bob's photo-montage portraits of himself taken in Melbourne (two days before Sydney), that he appointed Whitaker as court photographer to the Beatles for the next two years. Bob's oeuvre is recorded in his book The Unseen Beatles. (6)

Said Martin, 'When they toured here Bob Whitaker did some portraits of Epstein and Epstein said they were fantastic. Rather imperial photos. And he got the job of being Epstein's personal photographer to the Beatles and went to London. So he was a contact.' (7)

Martin was about to find all this out when he and Anou accompanied Colin Lanceley to Melbourne to help hang his exhibition at South Yarra Gallery. Lanceley's first group show was organised by owners of the Heide Gallery, John and Sunday Reed, patron of so many artists. By 1964 the Subterranean Imitation Realists had split up and this was 25-year old Lanceley's second solo exhibition. (8)

Lanceley knew the Reeds and the Reeds knew everyone in the Melbourne arts circle, including Georges and Mirka Mora - who also knew everyone in the Melbourne arts. The Mora family spent many weekends at the Reed's gallery-home and at their beach house in Aspendale. Regular drop-in guests included artists Charles and Barbara Blackman, Fred Williams, John and Mary Perceval, Albert Tucker, Barrett Reid, Arthur Boyd, Sidney Nolan, Joy Hester, Asher Bilu.

In 1954 Georges (Gunter Morawski) founded the Mirka Café in Elizabeth Street, Melbourne, which exhibited Joy Hester's first major solo exhibition. Georges' wife Mirka was also a painter. And the eldest of their three sons, 15-year old Philippe, was already making short films. Artists dropped in, artists dropped out. Martin's visit to the Mora home may have been the first time he saw an all-family art environment at work and play. He was always interested in art/live-in environments.

The day Martin and Anou called on the Mora family, Martin's former art teacher, John Olsen, was present. Olsen and Georges got engrossed in conversation, leaving Martin and Anou to somehow talk Mirka into being photographed wearing a truly ghastly mask for the cover of August OZ. That is - the OZ in preparation - the one to hit the newsstands after/during the July court case. (9)

Photographer Robert (Bob) Whitaker was there too. That's how Martin met him. Mirka writes, 'Robert was wearing lovely tight shorts and I couldn't help seeing an air ticket popping out of his pocket as I was lusting over his tight, round bottom. Divine. He was so happy, he was going to London to photograph the Beatles, and Brian Epstein had given him the air ticket.' (10)

Said Martin, 'Bob Whitaker's mother is Australian. His father is English. I met him through the Mora family. I went down to Melbourne with Colin Lanceley to help him mount an exhibition. I met the Moras then and also got to know Philippe – a friendship developed.' (11)

Twenty-three year old Bob Whitaker was running his own photographic studio at the time. 'I soon became bored with fashion,' wrote Bob. One day, promoter/journalist/poet Adrian Rawlins phoned to announce that he'd got himself commissioned by Jewish News to interview Brian Epstein and he needed a photographer. Sure, said Whitaker.

The pair showed up at the Guest Lounge of Melbourne's Southern Cross Hotel. Epstein arrived 'immaculately dressed: well-pressed trousers, gingham shirt, smart shoes, silk socks an expensive watch and a gold bracelet'. Whitaker 'cautiously at first' took some shots then Epstein relaxed. At the end of the interview Eppy asked if he could see the pictures when developed.

In the developing room, Whitaker tricked them into photomontages, enshrouding Epstein's face with peacock feathers in one shot. Bob struggled through another mad crowd, handed an envelope to Epstein who promised to call when he'd had a good look. Eppy loved the shots. Which is how Epstein came to invite Whitaker to the UK as his Artistic Adviser. (12) Although he had only briefly met John, Paul, George and Ringo in Melbourne, in London Whitaker got to know them real well.

Shortly before the OZ trial, Australian's first national newspaper was launched in Canberra, Rupert Murdoch's The Australian. Working on the paper were a number of Honi Soi youngbloods, including David Solomon, Mungo MacCallum, Peter Grose and Martin, who supplemented the work of Bruce Petty by providing occasional cartoons.

In those days, Martin was doing a lot of b/w pen and ink work. He says, 'When I was about 22 I got a job when Petty went on holidays. For two weeks I worked in Canberra. They offered me a full-time job but I didn't want to live in Canberra. It was a good opportunity in way but it wasn't the way I wanted to go. One cartoon a week, I could handle.' (13)

At this time Martin was ensconced in a studio behind the Windsor Castle Hotel in Paddington Lane. He had a pet guinea pig, which unfortunately ate rat poison and died. He said, 'I'd left home and moved into a little studio in Paddington which I loved but then OZ broke and my mother said, 'you'd better come home'. (14)

The OZ trial, cast its long shadow on Martin's family life. While his grandfather Stuart seemed a little bit proud of Martin, his Sharp grandmother probably blamed Jo for her delinquent grandson. About her response to the trial Martin said, 'It was embarrassing. It must have been.'

Jo probably wanted Martin's company, that's why she invited him back. Apart from domestic help, she lived alone while Martin's father Henry was often gloriously sailing Sydney Harbour with his wife-to-be Dorothy, while his mother coped all blame. Even Stuart Ritchie turned his back on his daughter, appalled at the events that had led to the impending divorce. Martin overheard all this.

The Sharp side of the family was worse. Forsaking Jo's actual name, Grandmother Sharp had taken to referring to Martin's mother as 'Jezebel'. Remembering the music from his childhood Martin voiced the demonic sentiments, 'They were calling her Jezebel in their family discussions! That's what they described her as! Frankie Laine had a big hit called Jezebel - if ever the Devil was born, without a pair of horns, it was you Jezebel…! But she said to me, "I never regret marrying your father because otherwise I wouldn't have had YOU". And she always had a lot of young friends.' (15)

Jo started writing for OZ. The Social Top Twenty, 'An authentic survey of Sydney's most popular socialites, compiled by an independent OZ reporter…'. (16) That was Jo.

Said Martin, 'My mother was writing for OZ, we had the Social Top 20 in there. Richard Neville - they all really liked my mother. I envied her, because she had such charm. They'd go to her as soon as they arrived. So I was a bit jealous of my mother. She pinched my friends by the handful!

'And she ran that house as a hospitality place. She brought me up. Dad tried but he was too straight or something like that. She loved dancing, she was a bright young thing of the day, "laughing at danger…", said Martin, referencing the Noel Coward song Poor Little Rich Girl. 'But she really tried to be a perfect wife and perfect mother in every way she could.' (17)

Next, the Supreme Court of New South Wales. 'I was in trouble with OZ magazine,' Martin continued, 'my Ritchie grandparents were totally supportive because their dream was for me to be a cartoonist.' Martin was also proud of his father's support and he bragged to all his friends that Henry bought him an immaculate suit that he never wore to court. (18)

And so OZ went to trial and the publication became famous for being allegedly obscene, which was never its intent. OZ was not there to 'deprave and corrupt'. It was there to annoy. They saw themselves as satirists not pornographers! Said Martin, 'Youth always revolts against the leadership of age, I'm sure about that. I suppose we were satirists. I think that's the best description.' (19)

Richie Walsh agreed, 'In its heyday Australian OZ was probably more famous as an allegedly obscene publication than as the satirical magazine we aspired to be'. Walsh heads a long line of social commentators who can't see what the fuss was about. He wrote, 'Today that particular issue could be passed around among kids in a pre-school without causing alarm; but what was truly amazing was that the NSW Vice Squad, which took responsibility for pressing these charges, had found enough time to get affronted by our puny efforts: they devoted most of their daylight hours to organizing prostitution and illegal gaming houses for their mutual benefit!' (20)

Martin and the two Richards – the First Triumvirate - were charged under the Obscene and Indecent Publications Act. It was a criminal charge. If found guilty they could be sent to jail.

The prosecution argued that the cover illustration of Richard and two others fake-urinating into the Tom Bass sculpture-fountain on the front of the P&O building in Sydney was also morally dangerous. No disrespect to Tom Bass the artist was intended, it was a Richard Neville prank: a joke. That's all. (21)

Historian, Geoffrey Dutton, summed up the situation. He writes, 'OZ was vulgar, abrasive, sometimes very funny, sometimes embarrassing, but good for Sydney. It was certainly doing no harm to anyone when in 1964 the full ferocity of the old-style repressive laws of censorship and criminal libel was unleashed on it.' (22)

Social commentator Craig McGregor describes the anachronistic setting of the trial: 'No 1 court of the Court of Criminal Appeal, where the case was heard, continues the penal colony theme of the entire building: a grim, drab room of dark wood and masochistic benches, a huge stained-wood carving of the Royal Arms (Dieu et Mon Droit) at one end and high monastery pews at the other, the judges' bench set in the shadow of a massive overhanging canopy, and lowering over everything the portraits of red-robed past Chief Justices: John Nodes Dickinson, 1860-61, Sir Philip Whistler Street, 1925-134, Sir William Portus Cullen, 1910-1925…'. (23)

Nicely dressed, the three defendants and publisher Francis James took their places as the Crown opened with an argument about Martin's strip, 'The Word Flashed Around the Arms'. They sparred over colloquialisms like 'king birds', 'fairies' or somesuch.

Notwithstanding that the 1956 Howl trial and the 1960 Lady Chatterley's Lover trial had amply dealt with the word fuck in print, the prosecution pretended to be terribly shocked by Martin's 'Get Folked' caption. Martin's cartoon-satire on the folk singing revival was accused of being dangerous to public morality. John Olsen took the stand and said, 'It's just a colloquial term your Worship, no big deal'.

The trial generated so much attention that circulation of the next issue of OZ blew out to 40,000. Martin's OZ sketch of the trial was a judge dressed as a clown, the speech bubble captioned with a Judge Locke-ism, 'Young people, this is a court of law, not a circus'. (24) Judge Gerald Locke did not take kindly to being lampooned.

Right here, Martin and the two Richards earned their stripes as heroes of whatever youth culture was doing. The justice system turned them into folk heroes. In the face of a likely prison sentence, they were not backing off. It's a glimpse of the sheer confidence of a generation that was about to invade London in the form of Robert Hughes, Germaine Greer, Clive James and another 20 or so significant Aussies.

On 23 September 1964 Stipendiary Magistrate Mr GA Locke sentenced the two Richards to six months jail with hard labour and Martin to four. The company, OZ Publications Ink Ltd was fined £100 and printer Francis James was fined £50. In her sad diary, Jo penned, 'Mart had up for obscene article. Headlines in all the papers. You find out who all your friends are. You have very few.' (25)

Said Martin, 'We got sentenced by a very tough Catholic magistrate, who we did stir a bit as OZ was coming out. We published a few cartoons about him, which provoked him. I drew them. We were feeding the case back into the magazine as it was happening. The whole argument against OZ seemed absurd to us.'

Despite bringing a 'certain degree of fame', a glamorous trial and thrusting OZ forward in the battle against censorship, it sure took its toll. It seemed inconceivable that the sons of Colonel Neville, Dr Sharp, and a north shore Anglican stalwart would be incarcerated by the justice system. But the lads were 'taken down', handcuffed, fingerprinted, fed fish heads and given a taste of what a six months' sentence might feel like. Just overnight. Until Martin's father fronted the bail money.

The two Richards and Martin were released on bail, pending an appeal. Said Martin, 'My father was very good, he came to court every day and bailed me, Richard Walsh and Richard Neville out. He always said Richard Walsh never sent the bail money back. Richie Walsh doesn't remember that.' (26)

Writes Geoffrey Dutton, 'As soon as the OZ prosecution was announced, a defence appeal was launched by RF Brissenden, Clem Christesen of Meanjin, Max Harris and Rosemary Wighton of Australian Book Review, Professor Peter Herbst, Professor H Munro (of the Freedom to Read Association), Stephen Murray-Smith of Overland and James McAuley of Quadrant. Thus almost every editor of an intellectual journal in the country was supporting OZ, including Tom Fitzgerald who gave evidence as an expert witness at the trial. The defence was that there was literary and artistic merit, and that the publication was justified in that it would not deprave or corrupt. The expert witnesses included Dr Harry Heseltine, Professor May, Elwyn Lynn, Mungo MacCallum, John Olsen, the well-known headmistress of Abbotsleigh, Betty Archdale and Gordon Hawkins.' (27)

OZ had an excellent legal team. Organized by Richard's solicitor, Martin lists, 'Paul Landa, Neville Wran, Lionel Murphy, John Kerr… all Labor apart from Edward St John – who I thought was one of the best legal minds. I think they were looking for a civil liberties case. They were looking to test the defence that was used successfully by Penguin for Lady Chatterley's Lover in England, which was "artistic merit". I think it possibly opened the door that lead a lot of stuff that hasn't got any artistic merit at all.

'We were defended on the grounds of artistic merit. We won on appeal. A lot of great witnesses appeared for us, it was a bit of a cause.' But Martin wanted to get in the dock and speak for himself, which he says they were not 'allowed' to do. Looking back, he said, 'I thought that was pretty strange - and that's when you realise maybe something else is going on…!' (28)

Martin, Richard and Richie were front-page news – a dirty little rag, whatever. Said Martin, 'I'd been very quiet before OZ. OZ was the thing. I think it brought a certain degree of fame at a young age from an unusual angle. The court cases and the severity - particularly of the initial sentence - polarized the community.' (29)

Free, after what would not be his last taste of prison, Richard schlepped over to New Caledonia for a break. When he returned Richard wrote a feature about Sydney's illegal abortion clinics, widely believed to have been granted legal immunity by lucrative police protection rackets. Also, around this time, Australia sent a battalion to fight in the Vietnam War, giving OZ a strong political angle.

Martin went back to Melbourne for an art opening and also to help Mirka paint leaves and roses on the doors and windows of a restaurant she and Georges had recently purchased. (30)

While Martin was gone, Richard – who was in love with Louise – kept company with Anou. He writes, 'Two or three times a week, I rushed from my copywriter's desk to a five o'clock movie. Then it was a brisk walk to the OZ office to type out my Herald review. A lonely routine. When Anou tagged along, I was delighted. She was bright, flirtatious, original. Anou created her own outfits, sewing and trimming the gingham as I typed banalities. When Sharp went to Melbourne for an opening, all those hours in the back stalls took a toll on our self-control. The sex was hot, the guilt immense. My best mate's bird – how could I?' (31) Martin returned and for a while nothing was said.

Meanwhile, working for the ABC, Garry had the facilities to complete his seemingly never-ending project, Ding-A-Ding Day. The film includes historical footage covering the birth of OZ magazine. Said Garry, 'It took me years. When I got to the ABC I got access to editing equipment, which I learned and I finished the film in 1965. When Martin saw Ding A Ding Day - in the film there's a shot of Richard grabbing Anou and kissing her in the OZ office - and I think that shocked him.' (32)

Martin confronted Richard. Richard fessed up.

In his book, Hippie Hippie Shake Richard says, 'I confessed to my friend, who was rather piqued…for about two days. Then all was forgiven.' (33) Not quite. Friends recall Martin still fulminating about this incident 40 years later! Garry shrugged off the incident, 'That was the times – free love. People treated it very lightheartedly then.' (34)

After all he'd been through, maybe now was time for Martin to paint, which he had not really done since high school.

At this time, Greg Weight worked in an advertising agency. As an 18-year old, Greg was fascinated by the Sydney Push and sought them out after work. Folkies like Jeannie Lewis, Gary Shearston and Black Allen

Murawalla sang in the back room while the virtues of Philosophical Anarchism were being vigorously discussed out the front.

One night, at a Push session, Greg ran into the art teacher who replaced Justin at Cranbrook. Greg said, 'I was talking to Charlie Brown, bemoaning my fate of being trapped in the art department of an advertising agency and how I was more interested in the art world. Pop Art had emerged. It was an area that I was keen on and Charlie said, "Maybe you'd be the right person to meet Martin Sharp?"

'I was enthralled by that possibility because I'd been an ardent follower of OZ magazine. Charlie gave me his number. I rang up Martin and asked whether he needed any help. He agreed he needed as much help as he could possibly get because he was painting an exhibition. I became his studio assistant.

'I worked with him for about six months before he went to London. We got on really well. I sometimes did the over-painting, stuck silver leaf on paintings, painted frames, putting paper maché on a sculpture he was working on. It wasn't about creating museum art, it was about creating ideas. So the materials weren't Belgian linen and Matisse oil paints, it was whatever paint Martin felt inclined to use that had the right colour - straight out of the tube or straight out of the tin. There was a freedom in the making of things and the doing - so I really did learn a lot about just letting myself go creatively there.' (35)

Martin and Greg painted Martin's first exhibition, Art for Mart's Sake, to be held at Clune Galleries in March of the following year. In those days, Martin never thought to have Greg co-sign the pictures, as he did later when Tim Lewis played a similar role. Oil and lacquer, on paper mounted on board - pictures like Love Machine and Seventeen Minutes to Four are typical of the style. (36) The works resembled what Monty Python's Terry Gilliam would come up with five years later.

Said Martin, 'All those images were based on collages. I cut up old catalogues of dental equipment and made these collages out of them. I then had them blown up photographically and painted over them. That was 1965.' (37)

January 1965 marked the arrival of another pop sensation from England - the Rolling Stones.

Martin and Richard had gotten themselves invited to a party at Elizabeth Bay, held for the Stones. To Richard's surprise, Jenny Kee arrived at the party with Mick Jagger on one arm and Keith Richard on the other. 'Howdja do it?' spluttered Richard. (38)

Jenny writes it in her book, A Big Life. 'Janthia (Walsh) and I set out for the Chevron, where the Stones were staying. Although there were thousands of fans everywhere, plus police, plus bodyguards, the works, just as there had been for the Beatles, I must admit it didn't excite me nearly as much. We got ourselves invited to a publicity bash thrown on the roof of the hotel. I wore an exotic red floral silk kimono. Without any effort we were singled out by the Stones' manager, Andrew Loog Oldham, and asked to his room, where Janthia bathed herself in perfumes. She was paired off with Mick Jagger. I with Keith Richards, who was intense, silent and morose. I felt sorry for him. He didn't seem to be coping too well with his fame.' (39)

At the party, Richard chatted to Mick Jagger as much as he could and Martin connected too. However, before anyone could get too deep, Jenny and Janthia whisked their boys off to the Gas Lash – the speakeasy near Central Station that had added to its legend by recently being raided by the Vice Squad. Martin's convivial response to all this excitement was a cartoon in OZ, featuring a bare-breasted woman wearing sunglasses saying, 'I was rolled by the Stones'. Some say he drew Jenny, others reckon Janthia. (40)

To date, the Australian folk singing scene had been quite cultic. For Lefties only, it surfaced in the back rooms of pubs and often made heroes of unionists. The Basic Wage Dream by Don Henderson is a classic example. But there was something about Gary Shearston that set him apart from his older folkie peers - maybe his looks, his youth or his spirit. Gary was the only Folkie to appear on Brian Henderson's Bandstand, that's for sure.

Sydney radio stations began playing a track from his newest album Australian Broadside. The single Sydney Town was a Top 10 hit. The words included:

Have you heard about OZ magazine
Convicted on a charge of being obscene
Seems you're not allowed to satirise
If you tell the truth they call it lies. (41)

In April, Louise Ferrier sailed to London, which got Richard twitchy. He moved into investigative journalism and published The OZ Guide to Sydney's Underworld – with Martin's Dick Tracey cover. It listed a Top 20 of Sydney major criminals. The list deliberately left the No 1 spot blank but at No 2 Richard listed the name 'Len' who he, somewhat unwisely, described as a 'fizz-gig' (police informant).

Soon after the list was published, the fearsome Lenny McPherson called on Richard's house in Paddington. McPherson's primary concern was whether the OZ editors were part of a rival gang. They weren't. Just silly uni students. McPherson restrained himself from decking Richard for calling him a fizz.

The OZ Top 20 crim-list reportedly played a part in the death of Sydney felon Jacky Steele, who was shot in Woollahra in November 1965. Steele, who had been trying to take over protection rackets controlled by McPherson, had taunted McPherson that he was not No 1. OZ published extracts from the minutes of a confidential meeting of Sydney detectives held on 1 December 1965, leaked to the magazine by an underworld source. (42)

Less concerned about the underworld, Martin continued poking fun at establishment figures. Sydney's artistically-minded set were affronted that the NSW Minister for Public Works, Sir Davis Hughes, was high-jacking architect Jorn Utzon's original Opera House design. Hughes brought about Utzon's resignation and had the Opera House completed with designs that were inconsistent with the architect's original vision.

Martin drew a nasty-faced Hughes for OZ. He lampooned the Minister as the sinister face of Luna Park, his first drawing of a place that would constantly appear in subsequent prints, posters and paintings. (43)

Jo and Henry divorced in 1965.

Said Martin, 'My grandfather and my mother were fighting after the divorce. It caused a rift with them. My mother broke off the relationship (with Keith) and my grandfather didn't believe her. That caused a complete trauma. So he turned his back on his daughter. (44)

'It was a cataclysmic divorce. I stayed with my mother. She suffered terribly from the divorce – I know! And she was ripped off - I know! She had few loves in her life, she only had two. She fell in love with her doctor.' (45)

There was a lot of cross-pollination in Sydney's art-bohemia of the time. Musicians, actors, visual artists and writers worked in constant collaboration. Artists made films and filmmakers painted pictures. Along with David Perry, Aggy Read and John Clark, Albie Thoms set up an experimental collective, Ubu Films in Sydney. Albie loved Garry Shead's films. He wrote, 'I was amazed at the way Garry worked without a script, using his intuition and a feeling for location to determine what would take place.'

Garry invited Albie to help him with Broken Hearted, which he intended shooting in a day. It featured Martin playing the male lead, airily smoking Gauloises while his love interest was Judy Carroll, then John Firth-Smith's girlfriend and soon after, his wife. (46)

Another film group was run by Mick Glasheen, Johnny Allen and Peter Kingston. Mick Glasheen was one of the contributors to the UNSW revue where Roger Foley was running light shows. Roger and Albie developed a cooperative relationship because they needed each other's equipment. Said Roger, 'When Ubu were doing their lights shows they'd borrow their lights and film projectors from me and I'd borrow the films from them'. (47)

One of Roger's ideas was to use Martin's OZ magazine monologue cartoons in a UNSW university revue he had devised called First No Pinky, which is how he got to meet Martin. It was the Norman Normal sketch.

One enduring facet of the show is Martin's 'smile on a stick'. It was almost the logo for the show, appearing on the poster and also on the promotional brochure. That smile was the cover of OZ 25.

Next time Martin got involved with Roger (after his London years) Roger had evolved into lightmeister Ellis D Fogg.

Albie wrote, 'Some of our cast and crew were involved in that year's University revue, First No Pinky. Produced by Keith Johnson and Colin Anderson, it had sets by Martin Sharp, who also provided scripts based on his OZ contributions. One of Martin's evoked the ecstasy of the mystery-man writing Eternity on city pavements.' (48)

Shortly before leaving for London, in March, Martin held his first exhibition. Greg - the 'assistant' - was present. He said, 'It was at the old Clune Gallery (the gallery that became the Yellow House) and Martin was primed to do something because he was the darling enfant terrible in the Sydney set. His intention was to go to the UK and do something there but he wanted to leave with a bit of a celebration. That was the exhibition I worked on. Martin was absolutely engulfed by admirers and Anou clinging to his arm.

'It had nothing to do with me at the opening, but it was a lesson. You've got to be the artist, not bloody help the artist!' (49)

Said Martin, 'My first exhibition, I'll tell you about that – to Roma. I held my first exhibition for her unconsciously.' (50)

'I stopped working for OZ for a while and just needed to paint. I was doing very different work. It was quite Pop. I painted that exhibition at my mother's house.

'That's when I got into Dylan, Mr Tambourine Man, I loved that song. While the Beatles were singing about love, girls and that sort of stuff – fantastic stuff - they weren't as interesting lyrically. Dylan was amazing.

He was very impressive but one left the week before he had his concert here. I'd have loved to have seen that show at the Sydney Stadium!' (51)

'When I look at all the pictures I did just before I left for London I hadn't had a clue about dope or acid. I might have had a smoke by then but that didn't have a major influence. I was certainly doing psychedelic pictures, with titles from Dylan songs and things like that. But they weren't consciously psychedelic. Look at any time associated with smoking hashish and marijuana and you'll find that influence comes into art - like the Paris of the 1890s, the Surrealists, Baudelaire and all those people who smoked dope…'. (52)

Jo, of course, was immensely proud of her son. Henry was more standoffish. At the Sharp family gatherings that Martin now dreaded, Uncle Alan – the esteemed pioneer heart surgeon – took Martin aside and condescendingly explained the rudiments of art. And Henry affected a mixture of embarrassment and pride. Said Martin, 'I'm not saying my father didn't realise I was an artist. He'd come to my exhibitions but he'd come with two of his mates that I'd never met. They'd tell me, 'your father loves you' but it didn't feel like it to me!' (53)

Martin and Richard left for London in February 1966. Richie returned to his studies and continued to publish a reduced edition of Sydney OZ until 1969. He included regular contributions by Richard and Martin from London.

Shortly afterwards, Garry held his first solo exhibition at the Watters Gallery in Sydney. Called North Shore, titles like 'Wahroonga Lady in her Naked Lunch' were much more provocative than the actual pictures. Nevertheless, the police raided the gallery, Garry made the papers and surprisingly his pictures were not taken down.

And Greg got a job as photographic assistant to Alan Nye, one of the busiest fashion photographers in Sydney. Nye had his own studio in Yurong Street in East Sydney, constantly buzzing with beautiful models. It was the perfect place for a 19-year old to be.

Stuart Richie died in 1966 when Martin was in London. Said Martin, 'My grandmother said, "your grandfather died a brokenhearted man". I've got my grandfather's Will, he cut my mother off – just like that! Except, he left her an annuity. The excuse was to protect the Will from my father.' (54)

6.

FRESHER CREAM

*Martin held a farewell exhibition at the Clune Gallery:
cartoons, collages, popsicle-bright paintings.
Everything sold, even a portrait of me bopping
in a corduroy suit, the eternal groover.*

RICHARD NEVILLE

Barry Humphries was in London. Germaine Greer was in London. Louise Ferrier was in London. Robert Hughes was in London. Robert Whitaker was in London. Colin Lanceley was in London. Jenny Kee was in London. And more significantly for our two travelers – Martin and Richard - who needed somewhere sling their Army disposal rucksacks upon arrival, Richard's eldest sister Jill had established herself in central London.

In February 1966, Martin left Australia with quite a bang, as he'd hoped. The Clune Gallery exhibition was packed with admirers. It had been a bit of a risk, because although his OZ followers were used to Martin as a b/w cartoonist, he had not yet fully presented himself as a painter of pictures. Martin's Greg Weight-assisted collage-paintings gave every indication that a great career had been launched. Pictures from this series found their way into major galleries in time.

Based on his OZ artoons (or Sharp-toons), the NSW Uni review was running a different kind of Martin Sharp show - First No Pinky, produced/directed by Roger Foley. Martin attended its February launch shortly before leaving for London. Also in Sydney, Garry's film, Ding A Ding Day was shown at last, marking Martin's screen debut. But although Martin drew its OZ magazine ads, he did not catch the opening of Jim Sharman's production, On Stage OZ.

And a North Sydney publishing company, Scripts Pty Ltd, contracted Martin's first book for publication, Cartoons, A Selection from OZ, The Australian, The Sydney Morning Herald, Honi Soit, Tharunka, Etc. A 'best of' publication, this silver-coloured book featured Martin's Get Folked 'toon without controversy. (1)

Meanwhile, writer and Sydney Uni dropout literature student, Peter Draffin had written a novel Pop that had also been accepted by Scripts. (2) Said Peter, 'I'd seen a lot of Martin's drawings in OZ magazine and I knew he'd be a good person to illustrate my book, so I approached him and he liked it.' (3)

OZ and Pop were Martin's main drawing projects while tramping the hippie trail through Asia with Richard. Said Martin, 'I was drawing it on the trip and sending it back. Using Op Art a lot, Bridget Riley, wave pictures…'. (4)

Draffin recalled, '…that's what Martin did in cafés and stuff.' (5)

While Richard and Martin hiked the hippie trail, Richie kept OZ going in Australia. In the mail, he received a three-month burst from Martin, then a lessening contribution.

The cover for the March issue featured Martin's Boofhead, also inside - I Was Rolled by the Stones, The Australian Londoner/The London Australian (full page), plus an ad for On Stage OZ.

April: a full page strip called Two Innocents Abroad, the Adventures of Martin and Richard in cartoon format.

June: Two Innocents Abroad Pt 2 and another full-pager called Darling! depicting a grotesque Dame Edna Everage before Martin's trademark exclamation mark. (6)

With a no-pressure deadline, Martin had also been approached by publisher Ure Smith to illustrate Craig McGregor's People, Politics and Pop, a collection of McGregor's Sydney Morning Herald, Quadrant and Meanjin articles - a social history of these lively times. (7) Other than jokes about gauche tourists, few of Martin's on-the-road OZ-toons reflected his actual geographical location. (8)

In Peter Draffin's Pop, Martin sketches as if he is enjoying himself. The drawings follow the storyline, with pictures of the band, the party, filming and words like Pop and Wow that looked like black and white pre-psychedelic art.

In contrast, Martin's collage-illustrations for Craig McGregor's People, Politics and Pop, are autobiographical and sometimes angry. Private School deals with his impressions of Cranbrook, Three Gaoled Filthy Paper mocks the OZ trial, Martin even seems angry on behalf of Garry Shead's police bust - with bitter depictions of suburban love goddesses.

Completed in London, some of the images in McGregor's book are a type of 'trial run' for Martin and Bob Whitaker's Beatles Calendar and Martin's famous Dylan poster. (9)

In his book Hippie Hippie Shake, Richard gave his account of traveling Asia with Martin. It was a lovesick trip. Richard pined for Louise and Martin for Anou. In April OZ 27 Martin documents 'the adventures of the OZ overseas correspondents at the crossroads of the world – Singapore'. (10)

Martin and Richard traveled through Singapore, the Malay Peninsula, Bangkok, Cambodia, Laos, Burma, Calcutta and the Himalayas. Although the food didn't agree with him, Martin was deeply impressed by some places. He said, 'Richard Neville and myself went to Katmandu. It was certainly the loveliest place I'd visited in ages – the peacefulness of the people, water buffaloes, villages…the things that happened there – terrible wars were raged in such a lovely place.' (11)

It had now been a few months since Martin and Richard had seen the inside of a barber's shop. They were frequently pestered by locals wanting to know if they were the Rolling Stones? It's not difficult to imagine Richard sometimes saying yes. Martin and Richard experienced temples, saddhus, opium dens, cock fights and food that made Martin throw up.

Somewhere in Nepal they asked each other, as if for the first time, what each planned to do in London?

'I'll just wait for you,' Martin shrugged.

Richard admitted that he hadn't a clue what to do, to which Martin insightfully said, 'Do what you're good at - start a magazine'. (12)

Martin confirms, 'Richard didn't know what he'd do with himself in London, so I suggested he bring out OZ'. (13)

After climbing a Nepalese mountain in July, Richard returned to find Martin gone, leaving a note that read, 'See you in Swinging London'. Recovering from his friend's unforeseen exit, Richard wrote, 'A bit of a blow, yes, but I almost felt a sense of relief'. (14) Said Martin, 'Richard stayed in Nepal. I was a bit sick. I went on ahead of him.' (15)

Richard's eldest sister Jill Neville was amongst the early-60s wave of young Aussies to come to London. Between hanging out with the Sydney Push in the late-50s and working as a typist in Sydney's Daily Mirror, Jill saved the £80 'under 21' steamer fare to London. She arrived in 1960 and scored a job as an audio-typist at the BBC.

By 1966, Jill was living in Holland Park with her 6-year old daughter Judy, the child from a disastrous two-year marriage. Jill was witty, sassy and outspoken. She wore a fedora hat, had green fingernails and smoked through a Sally Bowles cigarette holder. Her visitors were the smart publishing and advertising set, plus newspaper and TV journalists. When Martin rapped on her door, she was tapping out her second novel. Her first, Fall Girl had recently hit the bookshops to great reviews. (16) Jill was indeed expecting Martin, though probably not in July and probably not without her brother.

Said Martin, 'Getting to London, one met a whole lot of other people who were rather similar to oneself – sensibility perhaps – maybe a lot to do with art school I suppose. Art students, terrific friendliness, no class barrier. This sense of a contained youth culture was completely different to adult culture. It had its own language, its own world, its own dreams. Very idealistic I think - as is natural with young people – the possibility of a peaceful world'. (17)

Richard arrived nearly two months later, in September, around the time Clune Galleries was holding an exhibition of OZ artwork in Sydney: Martin Sharp, Garry Shead, Peter Kingston, John Allen, Mike Glasheen, Mike Brown, Peter Fisher. It was another of Sydney's 'where is Martin Sharp?' moments. More or less broke, Richard banged on Jill's front door at night and read a note from Martin pinned to it, 'too late, it's swung'. Bang bang bang brought a yawning Martin to the door. Jill too. Richard found her kitchen stacked with Martin's pen and ink works. Richard was raring to reignite with Louise.

Knowing this, Martin played him a track from Dylan's new Blonde on Blonde double LP. The song was Visions of Johanna, which found 'Louise and her lover so entwined…'. Maybe Martin enjoyed seeing Richard squirming as the song progressed. (18) Martin would do this throughout his life: attribute a specific meaning to songs that the songwriter could never have foreseen.

Next morning, borrowing Jill's Mini-Minor, Martin drove Richard to find Louise. They set out for Biba's Boutique, a jungle of Art Nouveau where Jenny Kee worked. She might know where to track Louise. Jenny had reinvented herself as an up-to-the-minute dollybird Mod while Richard presented as a dusty hippie. Jenny wrote, 'He (Richard) came into the store on his first morning in London, fresh from an overland odyssey through Kathmandu and Kabul…a couple of paces behind him was Martin Sharp'. (19) All-round greeting, then yes, Jenny knew where Richard might find Louise. There was an affectionate moment in the backseat of the Mini when he did.

Once settled into London, money became more an issue for Richard than for Martin. In an attempt to get things moving, Jill took both of them to an advertising firm - her employers - with a view of finding them work. Maybe, their portfolio of b/w hand-drawn ads for Sydney's Gas Lash, Clune Galleries and Binkie Burgers wasn't up to their tastes. Either way, Richard still needed that $folding stuff, kinda desperately.

Martin, on the other hand, was living on a semi-independent income that enabled him to occasionally splash out. The UFO, the newest club in town, was where Martin got a close look at cutting edge underground bands. He said, 'The band that really impressed me most at that time was Pink Floyd. Seeing them at the UFO Club was a great scene. Syd Barrett was with them at that stage. I saw him perform light shows'. (20)

Syd Barrett - the guy who played slide guitar with a plastic school ruler! Pink Floyd – the band that played performance events rather than concerts! Martin was having a great time, while Richard wrote, 'mostly I was preoccupied, on the lookout for parties, pocket money and ways of making a splash'.

So Richard did what Richard does best. He simply talked. He got himself noticed pretty well immediately. When the Evening Standard phoned looking for 'that notorious satirist from Sydney' Richard talked himself up. He talked about the important revolutionary role OZ played in sweeping 50s-style Australia aside. He had an answer for everyone. When asked by the media what he was planning to do in London, Richard replied, 'Start OZ of course, the town needs a bomb under it!' The newspaper ran a pin-up shot of Louise (the OZ 'secretary') and described Richard as 'coolly ambitious'. Now that he'd boldly announced on a BBC live-to-air radio show that he was going to start OZ - Richard either had to do it or lose face. (21)

Leaving Jill's place, Martin scored temporary digs with Robert Hughes. Hughes had left Australia in 1964, living for a time in Italy before settling in London where he was doing very well indeed. At the time Martin stayed with him, Hughes was writing for The Daily Telegraph, The Spectator, The Times, The Observer and more. Soon, he would even write for OZ.

Hughes led to Martin re-connecting with Bob Whitaker. Martin moved in with him, but they were hastily on the hunt for better quarters.

Said Martin, 'Bob Whitaker was living out at Greenwich, which was a lovely area in the suburbs, but it was not quite what I was hoping for!'

The Kings Road Chelsea impressed Martin and Whitaker agreed. It was Whitaker, not Martin who found their first premises on the strip, opposite Picasso's coffee shop and handy to London's first 'psychedelic' boutique Granny Takes a Trip. The Kings Road was certainly the place to be - café society, Mod clothes, Psychedelia, colourful shop displays and a world of ideas walking past on the footpath. Designer Mary Quant was said to have shaped her pubic hair into a heart. She ran another famous Kings Road shop called Bazaar.

Martin recalled, 'Bob and I went to Kings Road one day and I thought, "This is fantastic!" Bob agreed - so he found a great place in Joubert Studios Kings Road. A little lady lived next door that we saw very rarely. That was Judy Garland, in the same little alley we were in. She was pretty wrecked. (22)

'It was a difficult-shaped place to live in, because you really only had front door, bathroom, kitchen, lovely glazed corridor and a huge studio – wood panels. I think it had been a display workshop for Joubert (ie. Amédée Joubert & Son) who was a great outfitter. There were samples of his work still lying around. It was a fantastic place for one person but it didn't quite work for two. Bob had the best room. He slept in the big studio, which was a cul-de-sac. I slept in a tent in the kitchen area. He'd found the studio, so it was fair enough. But it didn't give me a lot of privacy!' (23)

Chelsea is where Martin would spend his next three years. He admits it was conspicuously fashionable, though at the time he thought of it more as an artist's suburb. He said, 'Chelsea was always quite an artistic area – there are quite a lot of studios there and the Chelsea Arts Club. Oscar Wilde used to live there, Turner...!' (24)

Ah, Whitaker.

Coming from Melbourne in 1964, Whitaker located in London as part of the official Beatles crew. Whitaker photographed Beatlemania at its American peak. He was their official photographer at the concert at New York's Shea Stadium, attended by 55,000 fans, a world record attendance at the time. In May, while Martin and Richard were backpacking through Asia, Whitaker photographed the Beatles for the Revolver album, after which he toured with them in Germany and Japan.

Whitaker did the cover shot for the notorious Beatles' Yesterday and Today album. Known as the 'Butcher' cover, it features the four looking not so fab, in white smocks amongst decapitated dolls and raw meat. Sick of the usual publicity shots, John Lennon liked it and Paul defended it. Nevertheless in America and Canada, Whitaker's cover was condemned as being in extremely poor taste. It was withdrawn after some 60,000 were pressed. Licking his wounds from that setback, Whitaker showed Martin the Beatles' sanitised Revolver LP with his Butcher Cover replaced by a Klaus Voormann b/w sketch and a Bob Whitaker photo on the back.

About this time, Whitaker's tenure as Beatles photographer was being wrapped up. The band gave its last public performance in San Francisco on 29 August 1966 after which they would have no more need for an official photographer. Whitaker was down to taking happy snaps of George and Patti painting their house in psychedelic colours. In his book, The Unseen Beatles, he admits that both his career as a photographer and Martin's hopes as a Beatles cartoonist got only limited success.

It reads: 'With time on their hands they (Martin and Bob) worked several joint projects. They re-cycled some of Bob's Beatle photographs as poster ideas and humorous cartoons, though none of them were published. Their most ambitious and compelling scheme was for a Beatles calendar. It was never completed. Recalls Bob, "...because we gave up after spilling a bottle of Indian ink over one of the pictures"'. Twenty-five years later Bob published them in The Unseen Beatles. The calendar is b/w fun - Beatles cut-outs, captioned by Martin. (25)

Said Martin, 'I did a Calendar with Bob Whitaker's photographs and OZ lettering. I was full of confidence. Nothing came of it'. Martin dismisses meeting the Beatles as inconsequential. He said, 'I was just another guy they had to cope with'.

The indifferent reception to the Beatles Calendar was a setback. Martin came up with a better idea - he worked on a series of complex poster-images that people might stare at for ages after an acid trip. Psychedelic is how they were described.

Martin rejects that he may have initiated psychedelic poster art. He said, 'Oh no! I'm sure they were coming out in America. I think psychedelic posters came from San Francisco, Moscoso, Mouse, Bill Graham's Fillmore! They got all that Op Art vibration. So no, I didn't start it!' (26)

Psychedelic art grew out of Haight-Asbury's counter-cultural community. Leading proponents were San Francisco poster artists, Rick Griffin, Victor Moscoso and Stanley Mouse. Entrepreneur, Bill Graham used psychedelic artwork on the promotional posters for his concerts. The style was inspired by a blend of Art Nouveau, Victoriana, Dada and Pop Art. Sometimes the hippie artwork resembled what Aubrey Beardsley might have done with lurid colours. But it wasn't all about America. British artist Bridget Riley became hugely influential with Op Art that created optical illusions.

The first poster with which Martin greeted his England audience was the highly successful red and gold Mr Tambourine Man silk-screened 'Bob Dylan'. With the help of scissors, glue and his fabulous Finnish assistant Eija Vehka Aho, Martin created the image in Whitaker's studio using metallic foil, Indian ink and reflective paper. Martin confirmed, 'Yes, that was the first one'. (27)

Its impact grew slowly but grow it did. By the close of 1967 Martin's trippy Dylan poster was pinned up in teenage bedrooms, student dorms and hippie toilets from London to San Francisco and Sydney. Mr Tambourine Man has since been bootlegged, ripped off and even used as a cover of the Bob Dylan 1966 bootleg album. It was also the cover of OZ 7. Forty years later the Bob Dylan image was sold on merchandise (mouse mat, glasses case) by the Art Gallery of New South Wales for their 2014-15

Pop Into Popism exhibition in which Mr Tambourine Man was one of the gallery's six promo banners, waving in the Sydney breezes alongside Pop Art legends, Andy Warhol, David Hockney, Roy Lichtenstein, Keith Haring and Peter Blake.

Martin's next poster was the metallic Donovan, Sunshine Superman. Like the Dylan poster, it too was tremendously popular, with more Martin Sharp posters surely on the way. (28)

Martin explains his approach, 'The lettering are letters in one way, but they're shapes in another – the thing is to try and make the thing work as a visual whole - to convey information. I like the cheapness and the mass of posters, like Pop records.' (29)

Martin produced at least three other metallic-style posters in this 1966-67 period. He also did the OZ is a New Magazine cover for London OZ 1. About Martin's instant poster success, Richard adds, 'OZ associate, Peter Ledeboer, was so taken by my friend's visual flair that he set up a new company, Big O Posters, geared to produce and promote every piece of artwork created by Sharp'. (30) In 2015, it still reproduced Martin's art.

Richard and Louise cobbled together London OZ 1 at Jill's place. Jill was probably desperate for her brother to move out, as OZ was beginning to take over her premises, attracting a smattering of volunteers and callers, including former contributors to Sydney OZ. (31)

Said Martin, 'Richard is an excellent publisher, an excellent coordinator of people. Terrific psychology. Wonderful humour. He always smells a rat and turns it into something wonderful before it turns into a bigger rat!' (32)

London OZ 1 was launched 24 January (Jenny Kee's 20th birthday). Despite terrible reviews, it sold out, followed by OZ 2, which limped a bit. Another underground publication, IT (International Times) was launched only a few months before OZ so - although competitiveness wasn't cool in the hippie era - OZ had a direct competitor.

At this stage, OZ was a rebel without a big cause. The pro-marijuana cause soon came in February after Sgt Norman Pilcher and his Drug

Squad busted Mick Jagger and Keith Richards at Keith's country home, Redlands. That the police had a prepared warrant and an on-the-spot News of the World journalist showed all the signs of a set-up.

In June, Mick Jagger would be charged with possessing four pep pills and Keith Richards for allowing his premises to be used for the smoking of marijuana. Mick was sentenced to three months' imprisonment and Keith was given a year's sentence. Both were immediately imprisoned, but released on bail the next day pending appeal. In the four months leading to trial, the Legalise Pot campaigners cranked up their protests, with OZ magazine getting onboard and Martin creating his Legalise Cannabis poster. In the interim, Rolling Stones guitarist Brian Jones got busted too, again by Sgt Pilcher.

Building on the success of Martin's sell-out metallic Dylan poster, Big O printed and circulated Legalise Cannabis too, promoting what would be in July, a Legalise Pot Rally held in London's Hyde Park.

With OZ off and running, plus a market for his posters, Martin had two regular outlets for his art - except that this time around the OZ-cycle, improvements to offset printing techniques offered him colour. Brilliant colour. It had been a while since Martin had worked in full colour. Although they looked psychedelic, Martin's Dylan, Donovan and Legalise Pot posters were actually 2-colour printed on reflective paper.

The drab 1966 English winter saw Martin homesick for the Australian summer. With Pop at the printer, Draff left Sydney, intending to get to London sooner or later. In the interim, he encamped in a town called Formenterra, on the Balaeric island of Ibiza. Jenny Kee and friends had recently enjoyed Ibiza and returned to London prattling on about the sea the way Sydney-siders do and Londoners don't.

Lovesick and missing Anou, it was time for Martin to take a break from London's depressing weather. Time to visit the sun and Draff. Martin had never known – or didn't think he did – an author of 116 pages of continuous prose.

Said Martin, 'London was bleak. Certainly I was missing Australia. I was missing the beaches and thinking of summer and summer love – those sort of things. I didn't actually meet anyone under those circumstances, I was always thinking of Anou (who was my girlfriend). Peter Draffin was living on Formentera, Ibiza, the Balearic Isles, which are off the coast of Spain. There's a mysterious island just off the coast of Ibiza, which is meant to have been where the sirens sung to Ulysses.'

Martin penned the words: You thought the leaden winter would bring you down forever…(London)…so you rode upon a steamer…

Martin explained, 'I remember going to Formentera on a ferry - not a steamer - it was a small boat. They served cognac. The contrast of the sparkling water - the sun and the sea - to London in the winter, and how a summer love couldn't stand the hardness of the winter. And so you've got to make a choice – staying maybe in London or Australia? The difference between Bondi and the Serpentine!

'With tales of brave Ulysses, how his naked ears were tortured by the sirens sweetly singing… I probably have got more lyrics to that song than what I wrote originally. I wrote it to the tune of Suzanne – "Suzanne takes you down to her place by the river…" to me that was a very influential album by Judy Collins.

'Writing Tales of Brave Ulysses was a thrill to me. Very free and surreal imagery, like Whiter Shade of Pale and that great period of songwriting in the modern era. I was just getting a rhythm and the images came. I wrote some of it at Ibiza and some back in London. Or I may have written it all in Ibiza, (I'm not sure where I wrote it really.) The line the tiny purple fishes run laughing through your fingers - that was more Formentera than Ibiza, trying to catch those little fish. (33)

'I didn't know how to write rock lyrics because rock lyrics have their own special sound techniques. It's really a story-telling song about desire, summer and mythology.' (34)

Writing lyrics was not all Martin did while staying with Draff. Martin also drew up a 24-page book titled, Twice Upon a Time. Martin's may have intended it as his follow-up to Martin Sharp's Cartoons. He was more of a book/magazine illustrator at this stage, than a poster-artist.

Martin's introduction to this little book seems to offer itself to a broad impersonal readership, 'This book is written drawn, climb inside dear reader it is for no one else but you.'

Twice Upon a Time grapples with the cosmos. It is Intelligent Life in the Universe by Carl Sagan meets Vincent Van Gogh's Letters. From Carl Sagan, Martin quotes, 'The saucer myths represent a neat compromise between the need to believe in a traditional paternal God and the contemporary pressures to accept the pronouncements of science'.

And from Vincent, on the second-last page: 'How I wish you could see everything I see nowadays, there is so much beauty…' (turn page) '…before me. I can do nothing but pursue it'. Martin closes with a pen and ink sketch of Vincent on the road to Tarascon. (35)

Martin didn't approach a publisher with Twice Upon a Time but he thought enough of Tales of Brave Ulysses to share it with Suzie Cuthbert (later, Sue Weight). One evening, Suzie and friend Charlotte Martin called to see Whitaker. They were models. Charlotte from France, Suzie from Melbourne, (which is how she knew Whitaker). In the course of the evening, Martin showed Suzie his Tales of Brave Ulysses lyrics/poem. She thought they were great. (36)

Located in Margaret Street London, the Speakeasy Club was a late-night meeting place for record industry executives, artist agency execs and Rock stars who wanted to mix with other Rock stars. Jenny Kee worked at the bar. The Speakeasy is where Jenny caught up with John Lennon after their Sydney tryst. 'I don't suppose you remember me?' she shyly asked John, whose memory may have been sharper had he not been accompanied at the time by his wife Cynthia.

One night Jenny was serving drinks when Eric Clapton walked in with Charlotte on his arm. (37) Martin was certainly taken by Cream, having presented Richard with their first album Fresh Cream for his December birthday. Knowing this, Jenny phoned Martin to proclaim, 'You've got to come down here!'

Martin describes the scene, 'So I went to this club and there was this girl I knew called Charlotte Martin, a French model - very beautiful and quite tough - a very proud young thing - quite brusque with me. I saw her in the Speakeasy sitting with a couple of guys and I didn't know anyone else there, so I went and joined them. It was a Rock Muso's Club. I found out they were musicians and I said, "Oh, I just wrote a song!" One of the guys said, "I just wrote a tune". I said, "Here are the lyrics!" I wrote them down on a piece of paper, gave them to him, and in two weeks Eric turned up with a 45 record. He put that wonderful music to it. The lyrics would have got nowhere without him.' (38)

Martin has repeatedly told that story to interviewers. But Suzie Cuthbert was at that table too and Suzie seldom gets a mention. Suzie's former husband Greg Weight paints a fuller picture, 'Sue claims to have been partially responsible in encouraging Martin to give Eric Clapton - who she was friends with – Tales of Brave Ulysses - the lyrics. Now she is not one to tell lies. Suzie clearly says she was with Eric at a table at the Speakeasy. She'd read what Martin had written, and she encouraged him to give it to Eric.' (39)

Never a 'pop' star, Eric Clapton saw himself as a musician. He'd walked out of a successful band, the Yardbirds, because in his mind, they'd sold out with their pop song For Your Love, which peaked at No 3 on the UK charts.

Clapton next joined Britain's most credible blues outfit of the time, John Mayall's Blues Breakers. After recording the famous Blues Breakers album (often called the 'Beano' album because of the comic that Eric is reading on the cover shot), Eric left them to create what is acclaimed as the first 'supergroup', Cream. The band featured the best drummer - Ginger Baker, the best bassist - Jack Bruce and with Eric Clapton is God graffiti on a much-photographed wall in London – there were no doubts about Eric's credibility.

Cream was actually Ginger's idea. He asked Eric to join him. Eric agreed, providing Jack was on bass. Ginger and Jack argued incessantly ever since that pairing, which was uncomfortable in every way except musically.

The band's debut album, Fresh Cream peaked at No 6 on the UK charts and No 39 in America. It was a mixture of blues covers and compositions by Jack and Ginger. Lyrics were not this trio's long suit. Jack was roping in performance-poet/friend Pete Brown to infuse words into his brilliant riffs, leading to songs like Sunshine of Your Love and Strange Brew.

At this stage, Eric regarded songwriting as some kind of miraculous process. At a stretch, Eric reckoned he was good for about one composition per year and when Martin handed him the written-on serviette, this must have been the one!

In his autobiography Eric recounts, 'As it happened I had in my mind at that moment an idea inspired by a favourite song of mine by the Lovin' Spoonful called Summer in the City so I asked him to show me the words. He wrote them down on a napkin and gave them to me.' (40)

Commenting on the process, Martin said, 'Eric altered the words a little, just to fit them in, but he kept the whole idea of the song'. (41) 'To me it was like an entry into the world of popular song, joining the songwriters and meeting with the musicians on a level of working together.' (42)

What would become the Disraeli Gears LP was recorded at Atlantic Studios in New York, 11-15 May 1967. Atlantic Studio's kingpin, Ahmet Ertegun thought Cream had been signed to the label as a blues unit fronted by Clapton. Wasn't Cream all about Eric Clapton? Eric said no, Jack should sing most of the songs. That Eric claimed to be 'just the guitarist' didn't help. (43)

Ertegun didn't understand Eric's reticence. Neither did he follow the progressive – psychedelic - turn these Cream Blues were taking. But Ertegun had enough nous to hand the problem to someone who did get it, producer Felix Pappalardi. Pappalardi cut the group loose to do their thing. Sunshine of Your Love – okay. Strange Brew – yes. Eric refusing to sing Tales of Brave Ulysses – no problem. Jack improvised the vocals in one take over Eric's wah-wah. (44)

Wah-Wah?

Hearing the wah on Tales was a first for most people. 'What's that?' everyone asked, wondering about Eric's extraordinary guitar sound, mimicking both the human voice and ocean ripples.

The wah-wah effect had actually been around since the 1920s, used by trumpet and trombone players, but the first guitar wah pedal was created by Brad Plunkett at Warwick Electronics US in November 1966 and somehow Eric got one the day before laying down the song. (45)

Pete Townshend of the Who certainly felt Tales had upped the songwriting lyric stakes. In his autobiography he wrote, 'Jimi Hendrix was testing some of his first lyrical ideas at his shows. Eric's friend, the painter and designer Martin Sharp, was helping him write songs, and Martin's lyrics were very ambitious and poetic. Caught between two great emerging songwriting talents, I felt challenged to evolve.' (46)

Cream got Hippie-tinged while touring America. They grew their hair and started dressing in colourful paisley neck-shirts, scarves and jackets. Strange Brew/Tales of Brave Ulysses was rush-released as a 45 rpm single before the month was out.

Having received advanced copies, Eric decided to drop in on his co-writer to give him one. Not anticipating a Rock song, Martin was admiringly surprised. Eric too was another kind of surprised. While he had been in New York recording Disraeli Gears, Martin had moved into an attractive property known as The Pheasantry. Originally built around 1670 for Charles II's lover, showgirl Nell Gwynn, this pad had heaps more ambience than where Eric was living in some kind of apartment.

Sometimes described as an eccentric poseur with artistic connections, sometimes, a fast-talker with regal connections (ie. Lord Boothby). Or even a small-time crim with both cheeks carved into the 'Big Smile' by the hard men of the underworld, the Kray Twins. David Litvinoff (Litva) was really a procurer. The Procurer is the title of Lucien Freud's 1954 portrait of Litva.

Describing Litva, many people grope into the barrel of horrible words and select the worst one. Yet Martin and Eric describe him in glowing terms. Mick Jagger's Jumping Jack Flash was supposedly written about the guy.

Litvinoff could get anything – boys, heroin – whatever. His half-brother Emanuel Litvinoff is a well-respected Penguin novelist. (47) His other half-brother, Barnet Litvinoff, a respected historian. David was nothing like them. His gift was an ability to instantly sum up what anyone might want. When Litva met Martin, Martin was cooped up at Whitaker's place and he desperately wanted space. One day David Litvinoff and friend simply arrived at Whitaker's, right out of the blue. Walked in.

Said Martin, 'One day a couple of guys came through and there was this fast-talking older guy. They just walked in as if they owned the place and started rapping away - and that was David Litvinoff and some friend, Michael Rainey perhaps. Anyway I became friends with him and he said there was a studio going next door, a place called the Pheasantry - £14 a week, so I grabbed it. (48)

'The Pheasantry is where pheasants were raised for the Royal Table. It was a nice building, a bit of a grand entrance and a courtyard. It has a painting of Nell Gwynn on the outside. Also a minstrel's gallery but you had to have midget minstrels. It was a wonderful space. It was next door to a previous studio I shared with Robert Whitaker. There were three bedrooms, bathroom, kitchen, big studio room - that's pretty much it. It had a great atmosphere.' (49)

So when Eric dropped in to see Martin, he dropped into Nell Gwynn's Pheasantry - 152 King's Road Chelsea. At the time Eric was living at Regent's Park in what Martin describes as 'a rather straight sort of flat'. Apart from a sense of friendship that each sensed, Eric saw a fantastic bohemian studio and Martin saw an anchor tenant who would cover his share of the rent without fail, which had not (to date) been achieved by Martin's overnighters and drop-in friends. (50)

So Martin approached Eric with an idea, 'The Pheasantry was £14 a week to rent, I said, Would you like to…? He agreed to join us and moved in. That lead to doing the record covers, the discussions about Tiny and the friendship over the years.' (51)

Peter Draffin was passing through London and staying at the Pheasantry at the time. 'When Eric Clapton arrived I was moved out!' he laughs, adding by way of explanation, 'I was a complete nutter there!' (52)

OZ was finding its feet by July 1967 thanks to the strenuous assistance of Louise and friends. Sometime around OZ 3, Richard and Louise left Jill's place and moved into Notting Hill Gate - the 'thinking person's London' - where they paid half the rent that Martin paid at the Pheasantry.

Richard often called around. Martin recalls the jibes, 'Notting Hill Gate was a different sort of scene altogether, more intellectual, more committed. So, Richard was like: a bit superficial, Chelsea…! But I did find quite a bit of depth in it and a lot of great people'. (53) '

In August, Cream played their first headline venue in America at the Fillmore West in San Francisco. They stretched songs like Spoonful and I'm So Glad into drawn out musical jams, which suited their hippie trippy audience perfectly.

Things were now working out well for Martin - OZ, Big O posters, Cream. Wrote Richard, 'From his Chelsea studio, Sharp was beginning to personify the debonair King's Road glitterati. With his arty sense of style, late hours, prodigious talent and a timely inheritance from an aunt, the upper echelons of the pop/fashion elite drew him to their bosoms'. (54)

'I just wandered into it really', said Martin, 'it was only through cultural suction and time. Bob Whitaker helped a bit.' (55)

Prior to 1967, interaction between art and Pop music had been sporadic. Before the year was out it was de rigeur.

7.
ART OF POP

Martin was a very gentle man, with an insatiable appetite for life and new experiences.
ERIC CLAPTON

Pop Art really hit its straps in the early-60s. But in 1967, Art of Pop was nudging Pop Art to stage left.

The Beatles' sensational Sgt Pepper's Lonely Hearts Club Band album cover was one big reason. Created by British Pop artist Peter Blake - instead of by some Marketing Department - after Sgt Pepper's every frontline band strove for a 'concept' cover. Cream was already ahead of the pack. Disraeli Gears was well into production before anyone – not even Eric - knew anything about Sgt Peppers' cover art.

The commercial push for Art of Pop product came from the flowering of San Francisco's Hippie community and its cultural demands (ie. posters, t-shirts, comix and concept record covers). This would blossom mid-year into the Summer of Love. Martin's artwork anticipated it. Said Martin 'It was great to get to London and find a whole lot of people that were like oneself and they were extraordinarily welcoming, which was the mode of thought of the day - everyone was welcome. London was an immensely hospitable city.' (1)

Eric wrote in his 2007 autobiography, 'I had moved from Regent's Park to the King's Road Chelsea, to share a studio with Martin Sharp, with whom I had become good friends. Martin was a very gentle man, with an insatiable appetite for life and new experiences. At the same time he was very considerate and sensitive to others. An admirer of Max Ernst, who inspired a lot of his work, he was and still is a great painter.'

Martin was in the process of creating his Max – the Birdman – Ernst poster. Later he painted the image on canvas. It featured in the Mick Jagger/James Fox film Performance.

Eric picked up a brush too, painting his room in bright red and gilt, 'a reflection of the times'. (2) They became firm friends. 'Eric was my real connection with the whole scene,' said Martin, speaking about the world of Rock Music. 'I never knew how good he was really...' (3)

Eric became a regular customer of the King's Road fashion boutique, Granny Takes a Trip. He'd had a complete image makeover since his days as a straight-haired long-sideburned Bluesbreaker. He and his peers had moved with the times. Long hair had become a statement of personal freedom and a slap in the face to the old conservatives. Ginger's mad hair stuck out in all directions. Young people everywhere dressed in rainbow colours and grew moustaches, beards and long hair. Eric grew a mo. So did Martin, as painted in his Self Portrait of the time.

Apart from Eric's long absences from the Pheasantry, due to Cream's punishing touring schedule, Martin found living with a Rock star no different from living with anybody else. There was no bevy of teenage beauties hanging out the front and no one came in through the bathroom window. Eric walked King's Road unhindered. 'It was fairly easy-going really,' was Martin's comment about Eric's public fame. 'But King's Road was becoming incredibly fashionable – I guess it had always been so – there was this amalgam - people from every area of life. I think the tripping and the smoking helped. It was where I did my best work of the time.' (4)

As a flatmate, Martin describes Eric as, '...very quiet. He used to play a lot of acoustic guitar.' (5)

Meanwhile OZ magazine was finding its place in the market. 1967 was a boom year for underground publications, many of them running articles and pictures that deliberately provoked their parents' generation. Richard got right into that. London OZ was nothing like Sydney OZ, which Richie Walsh kept going (and which was never connected to the drug culture). The Art of Confrontation is where London OZ was increasing positioning itself.

It was Germaine who came up with the article 'In Bed With the English' in which she maintained that English men were no good in bed - a proposition she was willing to put to the test. (6) That was just one of a string of arresting articles that got OZ lots of attention.

Martin was a consistent contributor. Disengaged from the controversies surrounding Guide to Taking LSD, ads for sex products and deliberately provocative content, Martin said, 'I was just there for the art'. (7)

Everyone was busy at the Pheasantry. 'Obviously you can't be at a love-in if you're working hard,' said Martin. (8) 'I did the Donovan poster in the Pheasantry. I also did some OZ cartoons and things like that - quite a bit of OZ work. Bob (Whitaker) was helping with OZ as well.' (9)

Building on the success of Donovan - Sunshine Superman, Martin continued producing metallic posters for Big O, like, Max – the Birdman – Ernst, Sex! and Live Give Love – the latter credited to 'Martin Sharp and Michelangelo'. Printed with yellow ink on paper, Martin's Mr Tambourine Man was the cover of OZ 7 and was later sold independently as an OZ cover poster on newsprint.

Around this time Felix Dennis came to Richard and Louise's attention as a bit more than young OZ street seller. He could also sell ads, he was opinionated and he could write.

Felix wasn't Australian. He was the son of a part-time jazz pianist who ran a tobacconist's shop. Much later in life, when Felix had become one of the richest men in Britain, he credited OZ with teaching him entrepreneurial skills. (10) At this stage though, he was making a career-shift from hawking OZ along King's Road to hustling ads over the phone.

Released in May 1967 to great anticipation, the album Are You Experienced by the Jimi Hendrix Experience upped the Guitar Hero stakes for Eric. Hendrix was a black American guitarist who looked like no one else in London and sounded like no one else on stage. His fluidity on the instrument was astonishing. Coupled with his natural virtuosity, he was a left-handed guitarist who played an upside-down right-handed Fender Stratocaster guitar. It was impossible to copy his licks. Are You Experienced was only prevented from being No 1 by the Beatles' Sgt Pepper's album. Of Hendrix's arrival, Martin commented, 'There was this new gun in town. I guess there was a bit of pressure on Eric'. (11)

Martin found Hendrix absolutely compelling. In his Pheasantry studio he celebrated the musician with a Hendrix poster, sold by Big O in 1967 and reprinted in 1968. Based on a Linda Eastman photograph, Martin portrays Hendrix as a right-handed guitarist, a mistake that he corrected. Both versions have been equally well circulated over the years.

The mistake came about because Martin was working on Perspex, which is how the image came to be reversed. It also came about because Martin, who never played guitar, never really thought about the difference until it was pointed out.

Eric asked Martin to come up with a cover for Cream's Disraeli Gears. Collage had worked well for Martin in the past and Martin worked well with Bob Whitaker. So he asked Whitaker to take some shots of the band.

Cream had a series of gigs booked for Scotland. Whitaker decided to use the occasion for Martin's photo shoot. On the drive up, Eric, Ginger, Bob, Jack, and Jack's wife Janet, simply enjoyed themselves. Pointing everything out like a tour guide, Jack was especially proud of his Scottish heritage. They took two cars and pulled over at every opportunity to take in the majestic scenery.

Climbing the highest mountain in Britain, Ben Nevis (1344 metres), was Jack's idea. The plan was to shoot the cover shot from the top but, as the LSD took hold, other things happened instead. The band has seldom appeared so relaxed in each other's company. Then Cream got back to being Cream and toured Scotland, Whitaker returned to the Pheasantry and handed the prints to Martin. Martin got his scissors out and merged Whitaker's clipped-up photos into the collage that became the cover of Disraeli Gears. (12)

Quoting Whitaker's The Unseen Beatles, 'Bob supplied the portraits of the group for the day-glo montage. Bob's career in photography successfully expanded into many different areas, but this was his last brush with the world of pop music'. (13)

Over the years, this international award-winning cover has featured in the top echelons of most lists of Top 100 album covers. Martin had mixed feelings about it. 'I don't think it is a great record cover,' said Martin in 1993. (14) He learned to love Disraeli Gears and his later Wheels of Fire. Everybody else did. In 2005 he acknowledged it as his best-known image. He said, 'I am rather proud of them. I was trying to capture that electronic warmth of Cream, which I think I did capture particularly in Disraeli Gears.' (15)

Comparing the cover to other concept covers of the time, Dave Thompson, author of Cream - The World's First Supergroup, sums it up, 'A Martin Sharp collage that took a simple group portrait by fellow Pheasantry resident, photographer Bob Whitaker, and positively overwhelmed it with minute and fascinating details'. (16)

Angie Errico, author of Rock Album Covers, describes Disraeli Gears as, 'Attempting to transform the full kaleidoscopic vision of an acid trip into a one-dimensional album sleeve design defeated the imagination of most artists...This day-glo collage came as close as any design to visually expressing certain aspects of such chemically-induced experiences'. (17)

After printing the cover, the processing company returned the original artwork to Martin, and Martin gave it to Ginger. Ginger treasured it for 32 years. In 1999, while in the process of divorcing his third wife Karen (who had become a Mormon) Ginger explains, '...Karen held an auction to sell off a load of my stuff, including the award-winning artwork for the Disraeli Gears cover, given to me by Martin Sharp, and she kept all the money.' (18)

With Disraeli Gears awaiting release, Cream started planning their third album. That too required Martin to come up with another set of lyrics, plus album cover. Although a 3-piece on stage, the Cream-team now stretched to five, with Martin as their artist and performance-poet Pete Brown writing most of their best lyrics. And then came The Fool.

The Fool comprised Dutch designers, Simon (See-mon) and Marijke. They designed clothes and decorated pretty well anything, like John Lennon's piano, George Harrison's Mini Minor and the Apple Boutique (opened December 1967) on the corner of Baker and Paddington Streets. Martin introduced them to Ginger. Next thing, they were designing Ginger's clothes and then the Cream logo on his drumkit!

Ginger writes, 'Psychedelia was big during 1967 and its influence could be seen everywhere. Martin Sharp did the cover for Disraeli Gears and he introduced us to The Fool, Simon (Posthuma) and Marijke (Koger) and a third member Barry Finch. They were Dutch artists who made far-out furniture and did designs with psychedelic patterns. They made me trousers cut especially short to avoid getting entangled with the bass drum pedals and a purple velvet cloak with a rainbow lining…they also decorated my bass drum with the Cream logo.' (19)

It didn't end there. They also designed Eric's famed SG Gibson guitar and Jack's Fender Bass VI bass.

'I didn't see that Apple place,' said Martin. 'I didn't like those artists, so I never went to have a look at it. Simon and Marijke their names were – The Fool. They were real hustlers from Amsterdam, very clever but really on the make.' (20)

Cream's third album was planned as conceptually different to Disraeli Gears. It would be a double album, the second disc to be recorded live. Martin joined them in July-August, at IBC Studios in London where Cream laid down the first sessions for Wheels of Fire. It was the first time he'd been inside a recording studio. (21)

On 15 August 1967, Belgian surrealist artist René Magritte died.

While Eric was touring and recording in America, Martin designed a metallic-style poster for a 29 September gig at the UFO Club. Featured acts were: Dantalian's Chariot with Zoot Money and his Light Show, The Social Deviants, The Exploding Galaxy, Jeff Beck and Ten Years After. Martin's poster seemed to evoke Pink Floyd. He said, 'I never did one for Floyd. I'd have liked to, but the image I did for Dantalians Chariot was really Floyd's image.'

'Syd Barrett, was a real genius. I haven't found them as interesting since he left. Their leading light I'd say. Pink Floyd was his invention. And then when they got onto what he was on about they could then make it into a product and market it. They'd worked out the formula and they timed it right for commercial success. Without him they wouldn't even be a band, probably. He pulled them together and shaped it, kicked it off. That's what I feel.' (22)

Eric, Jack, Ginger and producer Felix Pappalardi continued their Wheels of Fire sessions at Atlantic Studios, New York City during a break in touring. It must have been an exhausting September and October for Eric. Back at the Pheasantry, his rent was regular as clockwork, paid by the Stigwood management group straight from Eric's Cream account.

Ginger sums up Cream's existence in 1967-68, 'In effect our tour had lasted for a whole year, with just brief breaks now and then in which we'd get a chance to go home'. (23)

Writes Eric, 'Our first American tour lasted seven weeks, culminating in a return to New York to play 12 nights at the Café Au Go Go and a couple at the Village Theatre, where we shared the bill with one of Martin Sharp's favourite artists, Tiny Tim.' (24) Well, he wasn't Martin's favourite artist yet. In fact, Eric was unlikely to have written about Tiny at all, had it not been for events that would follow in Martin's life, one year later.

Tiny Tim was born Herbert Khaury in 1932, which made him about 10 years older than his Rock Music peers. Born in New York, Herbie's father Butros was the son of a Lebanese Maronite Christian priest. Herbie's mother Tillie was the daughter of a Polish Rabbi. Butros voted Democrat, Tillie voted Republican. The arguments never stopped. Their only child Herbie found solace in the music of his 78 rpm records. He stayed in his bedroom and copied the voiceprints of the Swooner- Crooners.

Playing parties, talent quests and small clubs, Herbie's matinee idol image as Larry Love didn't get him anywhere. His out-dated repertoire of Swooner-Crooner numbers barely earned him anything throughout the Rock N Roll 50s. He appeared effeminate in white face make-up and cosmetics. Herbie's first paying gig came in 1959 at Hubert's Flea Circus on 42nd Street, where he appeared as the Human Canary in a freak show. He shared a bill with Estelline Pike the Sword Swallower, Lydia the Contortionist, the Elephant Lady and Destin the Magician who introduced him to his first proper manager, George King. Of his fellow performers, Tiny said in 1992, 'They were freaks of nature'. (25)

The 50s may have been tough, but the 60s welcomed him. George King gave Herbie a Mod look and re-named him Sir Timothy Thames. A New Yorker through and through, Herbie never quite got the British Mod accent. Soon he was back to his comfort zone, which was wearing perfumes and make-up and singing in the high voice. 'Okay,' said Mr King, 'you are now…Tiny Tim!'

From there, his legend grew although Eric had never heard of him when he supported Cream in September 1967. Neither had the audience. Tiny was a few months away from fame.

Spotted at Steve Paul's Scene by Peter Yarrow of Peter, Paul and Mary fame, Tiny Tim signed to the Reprise label and would soon burst onto the charts with one of the most identifiable songs ever, Tiptoe Through the Tulips. But right now, he was supporting Cream and facing a difficult audience because the gig was running so late that the audience from the second session was invading the first.

Someone in the audience chucked a padlock at Tiny's head. In his memoirs, promoter Bill Graham takes the credit for intercepting it. He writes, 'I went to see a Cream concert and the first show was supposed to start at eight and it started at nine-thirty. The audience for the second show came in and there was like nine thousand people in the place at the same time. Tiny Tim was on stage and somebody threw a lock that almost hit him in the face. I saw the thing in the air and I just reached up and grabbed it. That show was absolute chaos.' (26)

That's the first time Eric had anything to do with Tiny. Not that it mattered to him. Eric was more interested – and awed – by the opportunity to jam with the likes of BB King and the Butterfield Blues Band.

The 1967 American tour really consolidated Cream's success. Everything they touched turned to gold. Martin's cover art for Wheels of Fire was about to turn gold – with a silver studio album and a gold live album.

Martin said, 'Eric asked me to do a cover. He was probably touring while I was doing it. It was never meant to be gold. They did that to differentiate the two albums. It was originally a double album, which they later published as two single albums. I designed it as a foldout and that's the front of it. One picture is rectangular - so there's continuity between the folding cover and fluorescent-coloured middle. A bit like a couple of eyes made up – spots.' (27)

Eyes? Spots? Around this time, Martin also painted a picture called Abraxas. Sized like an LP cover, the similar explosion of colour suggests it may have been a Wheels of Fire contender? Likewise the Mighty Baby cover.

Disraeli Gears was released at the start of November to great acclaim. Said Martin, 'I think Cream devised the formula for 3-Rock musicians'. (28)

Martin penned the lyrics for Anyone For Tennis for the Sharp/Clapton contribution to the Wheels of Fire album. Eric wrote a tune but the track was left off the album. It didn't sound like Cream. There was no riff. 'It's about living in Chelsea,' said Martin. (29) Straight away that suggests it's never going to make it in America. Furthermore, it's full of in-jokes like, 'and the Bentley driving guru, is putting up his price…'

Said Martin, 'I remember going out with Eric and his Bentley. He'd got a Bentley and mate of his from school as the driver. They took it out for the first time and ran into another car. We had to walk home!' (30)

Briefly it appeared that Cream's two song writing teams might be Jack & Peter Brown and Eric & Martin. Martin said, 'I thought, "This is going to be it, I'm going to write songs!"' (31) How wrong he was. Martin only ever wrote two more. Do You Love Me? to be performed by Germaine in a film which was 12 months away. And one for Tiny Tim that Tiny never sang. (32)

Late-1967, young Philippe Mora came to London from Australia. Martin invited Philippe to stay at the Pheasantry. Philippe's Mum, Mirka describes Martin as 'kind to my son Philippe in London in 1967'. (33)

Philippe was a bargain. He had the effervescence of a 17-year old, yet was not fazed by famous company, having been brought up in an environment where Melbourne's best-known artists were houseguests.

Notwithstanding occasional Rock stars as drop-in guests, the Pheasantry was essentially an environment for creating visual art. Martin was always painting and there was usually a painter in the downstairs flat until Germaine came. Philippe hit the ground running. Totally broke, he painted frenetically, having no other means of income. He used house paint laced with insect repellent because hardware paint is the cheapest paint you can buy.

For OZ and Big O Posters, Martin produced the Plant A Flower Child poster, and for OZ 9 he submitted intergalactic images redolent of Twice Upon A Time.

OZ was hotting up. Prior to leaving Australia, Richie, Richard and Martin had railed against the Vietnam campaign. As Britain was not directly involved it did not become a frontline issue in London until the Tet Offensive, launched 30 January 1968. This was one of the largest military campaigns of the Vietnam War and gained world attention. It provoked another of Martin's famous OZ covers.

Richard explained, 'A photo from Saigon flashed around the world – the gun-to-the-temple execution of a Vietcong suspect. Sharp splattered this image with bright red ink, put it on our cover and penned the line The Great Society Blows Another Mind. Richie Walsh used it for Sydney OZ.' (34)

Around this time, Richie dropped in on London. Now a graduate with a degree in Medicine, Richie was a 'responsible citizen', married to Sue Phillips. On this visit, Richard was surprised that – probably for the first time in his life – Richie expressed a desire to take a drug. So, Richard whisked him off to the UFO Club, where Richie was stunned by light shows and music that didn't seem like music to him. Meanwhile, Martin scoured the trip dens of Chelsea but was unable to score. Thus concluded Richie Walsh's exploration into drug culture. (35)

In January 1968, Richard decided to take on Malcolm Muggeridge in OZ magazine. Muggeridge was widely considered as a 'sensible' social commentator by Christian conservatives. Richard took him on anyway. OZ was really hitting its straps now. Judged by its ads and lead articles, some thought it smutty, yet it attracted great contributors: leading New York Rock journalist Australian Lilian Roxon, cartoon artist Robert Crumb, Martin, Whitaker, Robert Hughes are just some in a long and brilliant list.

Hughes' The Art of Australia was published in 1966, the book in which he rashly claimed that the first 100 years of the colony produced no good artists at all. That opinion appeared to do his reputation no harm. As a critic, he was supposed to be nasty. His follow-up, Heaven and Hell in Western Art was in the typewriter. Around this time Hughes met Danne Emerson, whom he would soon marry.

In January-February 1968, Cream went back to America to record additional studio material for Wheels of Fire. During those Atlantic Studios sessions Eric recorded Anyone for Tennis on acoustic guitar. Very different from anything else on the album, it sounded more like a Kinks song. Anyone for Tennis never really gained traction until the 1983 release of The Very Best of Cream when it appeared as one of 12 songs alongside Tales of Brave Ulysses, Sunshine of Your Love, White Room and Strange Brew.

Although no one in Martin's circle particularly noticed, in February 1968, the album God Bless Tiny Tim was released. By June, it was high on the on the charts. The hit single from the album, Tiptoe Through the Tulips peaked at No 7 - none of which caught Martin's attention.

Between 7-10 March Cream played San Francisco's Fillmore West. The best takes of Crossroads, Spoonful, Traintime and Toad were used for the gold Wheels of Fire live disc.

In April, Richard and Louise spent 10 days in New York and returned with a string of American underground contacts for OZ magazine including Harvard acid guru Timothy Leary and Yippie countercultural warriors Jerry Rubin and Abbie Hoffman. Richard saw all publicity as good publicity. With Felix now in his ear, Richard was pushing and pushing, especially in New York.

Their New York connection was OZ writer Lilian Roxon, whom they had known from the Sydney Push. Roxon's writings became the foundation stone for serious Rock journalism. She was one of the leading lights of the social and musical scene that centred around a club frequented by the Andy Warhol set. Jimi Hendrix was there the night Lilian took Richard and Louise to Max's. Andy Warhol was at the next table. Richard plied him with samples of Martin's posters. 'Wow,' Andy remarked. (36)

Cream decided to break up in May, a process that would take a full six months. May was the month Anyone for Tennis was released as the B-Side of Ginger's song, Pressed Rat & Warthog. It only reached No 64 on US charts and No. 40 in Britain. Pressed Rat & Warthog showed that Ginger was no Flower Child.

Following the footsteps of his Cream lyric, Martin returned to the Balaeric Islands where he met up with - and broke up with - Anou. 'Do you think I stayed in Sydney too long?' she later questioned Richard. (37)

Martin also flashed in-and-out of Australia where he was not forgotten. Richie had kept his name alive in OZ. Draff's novel Pop had been on sale one year and Craig McGregor's People Politics & Pop was in the shops. In August 1967, Indigenous Australians were granted the right to vote. Well, that was news!

During Martin's London years, Garry and Martin had maintained contact. Said Garry, 'He was doing so well in London! He took off over there, whereas over here we were all struggling. He'd send me London OZs and I'd think Wow! Amazing! Martin would come back every year. Maybe twice – backwards-and-forwards. He couldn't decide if he wanted to live in Sydney or London'. (38)

These were low-key visits. Martin stayed with his mother, called on friends and visited Grandmother Vega, widowed and still living at Wirian. His parents' divorce was done. Henry was planning on marrying Dorothy the following year.

At this time, Garry's career at the ABC was drawing to a close. He was in a relationship with the famous American Civil Rights singer and activist, Odetta. They had met at a party in Paddington Sydney. Martin took Garry and Odetta to Telford, to reactivate old childhood memories.

Martin's mother lived in the Cranbrook Lane house. Said Martin, 'My mother wanted to come to London. I didn't want her to come. She wanted to come and see me but I was living such a different life, I suppose. She didn't come. She would have loved it of course.' (39)

Martin's Sharp grandmother, felt the opposite. Between her and Martin's uncles, there were no congratulations for Martin creating an award-winning album cover design and co-writing a hit song. Martin explained, 'It meant nothing to them. Their world – what mattered – is a respectable job, Royal Sydney Golf Club (which Grandma Sharp enrolled me in), St Paul's College (which she got me into) and Cranbrook School.' (40)

But there was an upcoming generation of younger Sharps, Martin's cousins, several of whom were very proud of Martin's achievements -

Sandy Sharp, Katie Sharp, Andrew Sharp, Russell Sharp and 15-year old Roslyn (Rozzie)...

In 1968 there was an explosion of Art in Pop. Every band wanted a concept album. Every gig required a psychedelic poster.

8.

MUYBRIDGE, VINCENT, MAGRITTE & TINY TIM

Brigitte Bardot called at the Pheasantry. Martin didn't let her in. He didn't believe it was Brigitte Bardot.

PHILIPPE MORA

The credibility of album cover artists ranked right up there with the bands. Matí Klarwein, Bob Seidemann and Robert Crumb stand out. British Pop artist Richard Hamilton designed the Beatles' White Album. Andy Warhol did the banana cover for the Velvet Underground's The Velvet Underground & Nico LP. And Hipgnosis launched a major design group on the strength of their cover art for Pink Floyd, starting with A Saucerful of Secrets. Alas, Album Cover Art was an art form with only about 15 years left in it, before the introduction of CDs shrank the images and 'packaging design' took over.

When hippie tribes reigned, bands from the West Coast of America became famous for their posters, like the Grateful Dead, Moby Grape and Jefferson Airplane. Young people taped them on bedroom walls, even ceilings, creating the perfect environment for listening to trippy music and burning joss sticks. Such posters were available from OZ magazine for 9/6. This was art everyone could afford.

Martin too did 'psychedelic' posters. That was the word used to describe his metallic Big O series. Using similar ideas as Disraeli Gears Martin did a Cream poster. Even though he loathed the image, what is done cannot be undone. It was off-and-running and has remained in circulation ever since. Devastated to see it reprinted as a postcard in 2005, Martin shredded it. 'It's the ugliest thing I've ever seen!' he exclaimed. (1)

More triumphantly - using a similar palette as his Hendrix - Martin did a blue-haired Mick Jagger cover for OZ 15. Behind Mick are little naked running men that were making regular appearances in Martin's 1967-1969 pictures. He found them in a 19th Century book of photographs of the human body, a favourite of art students.

Eaweard Muybridge (1830-1904) was an English photographer, important for his pioneering photographic studies of the human body in motion. His book, The Human Figure in Motion comprises still shots of naked people doing physical activities in a sequence. Like, 18 frames of a naked woman kicking front view – and nine frames of the same woman kicking side view. Or, 16 frames of a naked man batting at cricket. And, 11 frames of a naked running jumping man. (2) Muybridge recorded the time intervals between frames (ie. naked woman feeding a dog, time intervals .222 seconds. Martin gave this book a lot of thought. Ginger chose a painting from this period for his 1970 Ginger Baker's Airforce album, featuring eight frames of a naked running man. (3)

Michael Organ, Manager Repository Services from the University of Wollongong, has catalogued and dated Martin's posters from this period. About the Muybridge characters, he noted, 'A variant of this element of the cover (ie. OZ 15) featured in the design Sharp applied to the shopfront of The Sweet Shop in London during 1968, a clothing and design shop operated by Laura Jamieson.' (4)

Frequented by Twiggy, Jean Shrimpton and Keith Richards, the Sweet Shop sold silk velvet patchwork, appliqué cushions and wall hangings. The 'element' Michael Organ is writing about, is Martin's little naked running man.

Ever a keen book-buyer, Martin kept on reading Vincent's letters and contemplating the history of art. He enjoyed the democratic aspect of art books because, like posters, everyone could have a picture of – say, the Mona Lisa, Vincent's Chair or Man Ray's Lips. Martin explains, 'The images are freely available and I had quite a lot of art books'. (5) So Martin - who was equally comfortable with a pair of scissors as with a brush - starting cutting them up and realigning them, often placing the central image in an unexpected setting. At the Pheasantry, Martin began his earliest explorations into what would become Art Exhibition and Art Book.

Meanwhile, in San Francisco, the posters were certainly magnificent but harder to read. Not that it mattered, the gigs attracted huge audiences through word-of-mouth. However, some posters – for example, Moscoso complicated (and lost) the image as surely as the Abstract Expressionist painters before him. In contrast, Martin sought clarity, which he found in the art of René Magritte (1898-1967).

Said Martin, 'Magritte took over a lot. He put it really clearly because he had such a deadpan style of imagery. He could present any idea by juxtaposing images and combining them. It had a fantastic democracy. He had that style, something that everyone can understand. And people, whether they knew about art or not, had to accept it. It probably had a stronger effect on untutored minds than on the tutored (or equally so).

'If you look at Abstract Expressionism or Cubism, the general public was really thrown. These were really scientific explorations into the concept of Art. The public can't follow that image. They get lost in a maze of modern art. And the public got completely offended by the total loss of the image. Magritte put things so simply, mysteriously - images like anyone would paint - a sign-painter would paint! "Do me a man with a bowler hat" - you know?' (6)

From his childhood Martin reflected on Vincent van Gogh. The print, On the Road to Tarascon was in his father's surgery. And, the biographical novel, Lust for Life was awarded him by Justin. (7)

Vincent van Gogh only sold one picture in his life. He was financially supported by his brother Theo with whom he corresponded from August 1872-July 1890. After her husband's death, Theo's wife Johanna van Gogh-Bonger spent years compiling the collection of 844 letters written by Vincent, of which 663 were written to Theo. First published in 1914, (8) Martin had been reading those letters for quite a while. He quoted them in sketches going back to Formenterra, if not before.

Martin said, 'I was very moved by them. Van Gogh is definitely a saint of painters. He was extremely lonely and spent a lot of time writing. One of his greatest letters to his brother before he started painting was published in OZ, saying he felt he was worth something and that he had maybe 10 years in him, which was true to the year. (9)

'There was an exceptional relationship between the brothers. His brother provided him with the paint and canvasses and he did the pictures. Theo kept every letter that he wrote. So you've got an incredible parallel circumstance.' (10) Martin began cutting up Vincent's pictures and Magritte's pictures. He played around with them, setting them against each other in different combinations. Some, he kept.

There were changes afoot at the Pheasantry, Whitaker moved out and Germaine moved in. She was one of several friends who started writing books. Germaine moved into the downstairs flat and worked on her thesis, a document that would galvanise the feminist movement within two years - The Female Eunuch. Martin remembers her 'crying a lot'. (11) In Notting Hill Gate, Richard was compiling his first book Play Power for which Martin would do the cover. (12) And Robert Hughes was busy writing Heaven and Hell in Western Art. (13)

Martin now had a live-in girlfriend – Finnish beauty Eija Vehka Aho, who had so splendidly assisted with the circles of his Mr Tambourine Man poster. Charlotte Martin moved in with Eric.

But Eric had a lot weighing on his mind. The tensions within Cream were almost too much to bear. Wrote Eric, 'Our gigs became nothing more than an excuse for us to show off as individuals, and any sense of unity that we might have had when we started out seemed to have gone out of the window. We also suffered from an inability to get on. We would just run away from one another. We never socialized together, we never really shared ideas any more. We just got together on stage and played and then went our separate ways. In the end, that was the undoing of the music.' (14)

Exhaustion was another factor, it seemed the promoters were bleeding the band dry on a never-ending tour. Eric, Jack and Bruce took the line of least resistance. They kept going not because they wanted to or even needed to, the only reason Cream didn't disband was that it was easier not to. Dismantling one of the most successful bands of the decade meant the bean counters weren't happy. Nor the fans.

There were rumours aplenty that Cream was finished. Then they'd perform together and prove the journalists wrong. After a six-week tour of America, they made the official announcement: Cream's final concert was billed for November. In theory, Cream was still a unit when Philippe Mora joined the Pheasantry.

Said Martin, 'Philippe Mora arrived and then his girlfriend (Freya Matthews) moved in. It was good. There was enough room for us. Philippe and Eric got on really well, they were great friends I think'. (15)

As a painter, Philippe was pro-active. Maybe he kick-started Martin a bit, as after Philippe's arrival, Martin began to think about exhibiting, whereas Philippe thought about that as soon as he arrived. Martin burrowed through art books and eased back on OZ. Martin explained his sporadic contributions, 'Richard Neville got it together really, I was just there to help. I wasn't so keen, initially and then I got very keen on it for a while. Then I tapered off again. Virtually in the end I was doing nothing for it.' (16)

Better known as an actress (later director) than a gallery owner, Clytie Jessop was quite taken with Philippe's works and she invited him to exhibit in her gallery on The King's Road. Much to Philippe's surprise, the show was a great success. Eric was amongst the buyers.

Philippe wrote, 'Our Pheasantry scene was a kind of cultural catalyst and melting pot. RD Laing would drop in and say we were normal and everybody else was crazy.'

Philippe recalls Martin painting the psychedelic front door, Germaine writing downstairs, being encouraged by Pop Surrealist painter Eduardo Paolozzi and intimidated by curmudgeonly Francis Bacon. He also recalls the first draft of Jim's Sharman's Rocky Horror Show. Philippe wrote, 'When Jim got the original tape of the songs performed by Richard O'Brien he called me over to listen. I was unenthusiastic and thought it was corny – Frankenfurter! – but Jim insisted he could make it all work'. (17)

Through all the visitors, live-ins, drop-ins and all-night painting sessions, Martin and Whitaker found the time to make a short three and a half minute film centred around Germaine. It was screened at the 1969 Sydney Film Festival.

Said Martin, 'I made that little film with Germaine Greer called Darling Do You Love Me?. She was a brilliant performer.' (18)

'A writer called Anthony Hayden-Guest was there, photographer Bill King, Eduardo Paolozzi was in there somewhere, David Litvinoff and Tim Whitborne – who was a sort of painter - and they had some franchise on some prints of the Queen. Tim was a painter and I never actually saw the inside of his studio. That was a floor below.' (19) 'The Pheasantry was a bit like an evolving studio exhibition.' (20)

Around the time Cream's Wheels of Fire was released, Eric recalled David Litvinoff being in an excitable mood. He had scored the job of dialogue coach and technical adviser on the film Performance that was being shot in Chelsea by Donald Cammell and Nick Roeg.

Eric wrote, 'The particular expertise for which he had been hired was his knowledge of the underworld, as the movie, which was basically a star vehicle for Mick Jagger playing a faded-jaded rock idol, was set in the world of London gangsters. He was full of ideas about how he felt the story should develop, and every day he would come and see me to tell me about all the goings-on on set and to fill me in on whatever was going to be happening next day. One night he brought round the director Donald Cammell, who managed to stage a power cut in the flat, and then tried to grope my girlfriend Charlotte in the dark. A peculiar chap.' (21)

'I was sort of involved in Performance,' said Martin, 'I was on the edge of that - not really "involved". I asked my mother to send over a few of my high school pictures, some of the gangster ones. She did and they're in the film'. (22)

'I got on pretty well with Mick Jagger and James Fox. I met them during Performance. I also did some collages in it for Anita Pallenburg. They said, "Do you want the money or a credit?" I said, "I'll have the money" - £300 or something. It was useful at the time.' (23)

One picture in question is Martin's green/orange painting (not the poster) of Max – the Birdman – Ernst. The camera rests on it briefly around the 60-minute mark.

Friends now with Mick Jagger (or friendly, at least), Martin drew him for OZ. It was the first time Martin appropriated Hokusai's Wave in a picture. (24)

Cream wasn't the only band in the throes of breaking up. The Beatles had quit touring and had more time to spend in the studio. In August, September and October they recorded what would be known as the White Album. To date, John and Paul had dominated the Beatles' songwriting. They were so good! George was allowed one composition per album and poor Ringo had a total of two - Octopus's Garden and Don't Pass Me By - on 13 studio albums.

In September, at Abbey Road Studios, George spent a long night struggling with his latest composition, While My Guitar Gently Weeps. The crying guitar was the bit he couldn't get right. In the end, the Beatles scrapped it. Within three days George returned to the studio with Eric. Eric wasn't too sure about this because no one records on Beatles albums but the Beatles. 'Who cares?" George reassured, 'it's my song'. (25)

Wrote Eric, 'We did it in just one take and I thought it sounded fantastic; John and Paul were fairly non-committal but I knew George was happy. A couple of weeks later, George dropped by the Pheasantry and left me the acetates of the double album on which the song was going to appear.' (26)

Martin was seeing supermodel Donyale Luna at the time.

'Luna!' Martin stressed.

Six foot two inches tall, Donyale Luna had replaced Twiggy and Jean Shrimpton as the world's No 1 supermodel. Profiling her for The New York Times, journalist Judy Stone described her as, 'secretive, mysterious, contradictory, evasive, mercurial, and insistent upon her multiracial lineage - exotic, chameleon strands of Indigenous-Mexican, Indonesian, Irish, and, last but least escapable, African'. (27) Martin described her as the Priestess of Chaos. He said, 'I fell in love with the real thing for about a week. That was when chaos struck. It was the bust and everything'. (28)

In early September, Martin's OZ Norman Normal character sprang into unpleasant reality in the form of a cop, Sgt Norman Pilcher of the Drug Squad. Semolina Pilchard dripping from a dead dog's eye is how John Lennon described this guy in the song I Am the Walrus. (29) Semolina Pilchard had already nailed John Lennon, George Harrison, Mick Jagger, Keith Richards, Brian Jones and Donovan. Ginger called the Pheasantry to warn Eric that he had received an inside tip that Eric his was the next name on Pilcher's hit list of Rock stars.

Eric made a judicious exit to North London, where he stayed in a Robert Stigwood house until the heat was off. He didn't think to warn the others because he thought it was all about him. (30)

Martin related what happened next, 'The Drug Squad pressed the doorbell and said, "We've got parcel for you". We had about three flights of stairs and a buzzer for the door at the bottom, and there was a parcel from the Post Office. I got up for the door - having been got up very early and feeling a total wreck – and saw eight policemen standing there, some policewomen as well. They were, of course, looking for Eric - not for me.

'Philippe was there, his girlfriend was having a shower while all this was going on and they didn't know she was there. She's a frightfully nice girl from Melbourne and she came out unaware that Phillipe had been dragged out of bed in the nude and made to stand against the wall.

'Bob Seidemann (who did the 'girl with the aeroplane' cover for the Blind Faith album) was downstairs pressing the button trying to get in! I'm going, "Go away! Police! Run!" They dragged me away and gave me a cuff across the head. He pressed the buzzer again and I managed to get to it. He was so slow to catch on. Bob Seidemann started running and they arrested him. He ran out to King's Road. There's 5000 people out there and he's the only guy running!

'I was totally relaxed about the whole thing. They took me to Chelsea Police Station with Philippe and I just fell asleep because they got me up so early.' (31)

Martin was charged with possession of a small quantity of hashish. He wasn't too troubled by this, neither was his father when Martin wrote Henry, 'The court attitude to hash is becoming more and more reasonable, and the magistrates feel the police should be chasing real criminals and cease wasting time harassing me...us.' Martin's only real concern was that the story might hit the Sunday papers back home, causing more tension with the Sharps. (32)

Peeved that at his Sydney OZ trial, neither Richard, Richie nor himself were required to speak, Martin was not going to let this opportunity slip. Against the advice of his legal council, Martin spoke up. He said, 'I made an impassioned plea from the dock about understanding young people,' said Martin. (33) He also drafted a statement on the virtues of pot and its role in modern society, which he instructed his reluctant solicitor to read to the court. (34)

Martin explained the outcome, 'I got a suspended sentence, which I appealed against. I got a suspended fine or something. The Judge was very sympathetic and dismissed the case. Still, they made an awful blunder - they didn't come to get me.' (35)

Eric took it quite hard. He wrote, 'I felt terrible, because they busted Martin and Philippe, and I had not warned them, thinking that Pilcher would only be interested in me. I will never forgive myself for that'. (36)

Ginger relayed a second message from Pilcher, which was that if Eric got off his patch, he'd leave him alone. Wrote Eric, 'I felt quite ready to move, and as for the first time in my life I now had some money, I realised that I could use it to buy a house.' (37)

Ironically, and to everyone's satisfaction, four years later Pilcher was charged with conspiracy to pervert the course of justice after it was alleged he had committed perjury in a drug-related offence. In 1973 he was sentenced to four years imprisonment.

Eric now spent his time around the Pheasantry reading property magazines, like Country Life. Martin reckoned, 'because I thought music worked like drawing, I used to say dumb things like "Why don't you practice more often?"' (38)

Around this time, Richard reports Martin 'cooling on Rock'. Richard wrote, 'He recalled his boyhood. The long summer holidays at Port Hacking: swimming, fishing on the bay and listening to his mother's 78 rpm recording...the only time the rancour between his parents turned to romance.'

Collections of nostalgic songs of the 1930s and 1940s were being released as LP records. Martin snapped them up – Bing Crosby, Al Jolson, Ruth Etting. And a song by Al Bowlly being played from a shop along King's Road caught his attention, but he only heard it in snatches: Brother Can You Spare a Dime. (39) 'Al Bowlly!' said Martin, 'I discovered him in London.' (40)

Quitting at the top of their game, Eric at last embarked on Cream's final US tour in October. Having caught Tiny Tim's act at The Scene NY and noting Martin's fondness for songs of the 1930s and 40s, before leaving, Eric told Martin that Tiny would be performing at the Royal Albert Hall. 'You like a lot of old songs,' said Eric, 'you've got to go and see Tiny Tim, you're really going to love him'. (41) Years later, Eric confessed he never liked Tiny's singing. He said, 'His voice always frightened me'. (42)

Although the album God Bless Tiny Tim rode high on the charts and his falsetto rendition of Tiptoe Through the Tulips was getting lots of airplay, Martin hadn't heard it. He had only seen publicity pictures of Tiny and knew nothing else about him. As Richard said, Martin had cooled on Rock. He stopped listening to the radio and played records instead.

On 30 October 1968, Richard and Louise accompanied Martin and his date, model Hazel Ganpatsingh, to see Tiny Tim's concert, a sensational performance. Backed by the 30-piece National Concert Orchestra under the baton of producer Richard Perry, Tiny trilled like a Human Canary, got hunky like Elvis, flattened his voice like Sonny Bono and traversed the spectrum of popular song from Al Bowlly & Rudy Vallee to the Rolling Stones & Bob Dylan. He performed duets with himself, singing the female part of I Got You Babe with piercing effect. Surely this was the Douanier Rousseau of Pop! (43)

Martin said, ' I'd never heard Tiny sing until I saw him at the Albert Hall, that's why he blew me away because I thought, "Boy, this guy just knows…!" Brother Can You Spare Me A Dime was a song I'd heard just a snatch of on an Al Bowlly album, just two lines of it. I'd ask people, 'what's this song?' And then Tiny sang it at the Albert Hall and I was amazed. That's when I thought, 'I'd love to work with Tiny'. I thought I could do something for his staging or that whole Paper Moon world of popular songs. (44)

'When I saw Tiny at the Albert Hall and his total command of the whole language of popular song I thought: he is going to be in an absolutely unapproachable position. (45) I thought he would be the absolute heart of show business. Uncontactable. I didn't even try. I didn't even go backstage. And then I did get to listen to God Bless because Eric had a copy.' (46)

Before going to sleep that night, Martin wrote in his journal, 'First Impressions. Did you tiptoe through the tulips with Tiny Tim? To see his

London concert was a revelation. He is the "Spirit of Popular Music", an anthropologist, a mystic, the wise man disguised as a fool. He spans the whole of Pop with such grace and eloquence. He transcends the "campness" of his image and becomes a truly great entertainer (a compliment which cannot be paid to many of our contemporary pop "stars").

'I did see Tiny Tim backed by the London Philharmonic give, really GIVE, a performance that was great, not "groovy" not "gas man" but GREAT!!! He was generous and he loves music and he told me so in such an articulate, honest and open way that I felt the beauty. He sang me the songs that my grandparents were turned on by when they were my age, and he sang me the songs my parents loved, and he made me love them too – and he destroyed my prejudice and created the link between all music and showed me that it is one river of soul and sound and love and pain.' (47)

'It was in this ecstatic state that Sharp sought to take charge of the next OZ and make it entirely visual. Fine by me...' wrote Richard. (48) In the aftermath of Tiny Tim, Martin proposed that he and Philippe should compile a collage of images in the same way that Tiny had presented a collage of song. Continuity was maintained on the bottom third of each page by Eadweard Muybridge's little naked running men quoting or questioning Carl Sagan's propositions about the state of the universe and/or the meaning of life.

Borrowing freely from newspapers and images of people with physical deformities Martin and Philippe also collaged Lee Harvey Oswald, Salvadore Dalí, Vincent, Adam & Eve, Mick Jagger, President Nixon, Little Nemo, Pope Paul VI, Richard Neville, René Magritte, Miss United Kingdom, Queen Elizabeth II, the Duke of Edinburgh, Philippe Mora, Martin Sharp, John Lennon, Yoko Ono, Adolf Hitler, Siamese twins Chang and Eng Bunker, Crucified Christ, Tariq Ali, violent images of the Vietnam

War, a flashback to the OZ 1964 obscenity trial, Hokusai's Wave, a passing reference to 'Eternity' and a muscular Tiny Tim captioned with his song, The Icecaps Are Melting.

What was Magic Theatre OZ about? Was it the purposelessness of life or its quest? (49) Jenny Kee described Philippe as a 'powerhouse of creativity' and Magic Theatre OZ as 'one of the greatest works of the 60s'. Robert Hughes gave it the thumbs up too, describing it as, 'one of the richest banks of images that has ever appeared in a magazine'. (50)

Said Martin, 'It was expressing the experience of collage – running things backwards and forwards – playing with the form of the magazine. I did that with Philippe. I guess it was quite a good expression of the time, just absorbing all the material that was around. Tiny is in that, of course.' (51)

There is continuity between the back cover of Magic Theatre OZ and the front cover of next OZ. Martin's question mark was now a regular feature during this Exploration of Punctuation period, or what he later called Smartiples – visual puns. The front cover of OZ 17 featured a sideshot of Jenny and Louise nude, facing each other with Martin's red question mark as a backdrop. (52)

Using the same palette and energy, during this period Martin also did the cover for Richard's forthcoming book Play Power. (53) A contributor to OZ and a drop-in Pheasantry guest (when he was in the country), author of The Politics of Ecstasy, Acid guru Timothy Leary was enamoured by Martin's Abraxas picture. He requested it as the cover of the London edition of his book. (54) Martin wasn't particularly interested, but he said okay. Publisher, Paladin Granada, borrowed Martin's Abraxas and got a graphic artist to do the Sharp-like lettering. (55)

Abraxas wasn't Martin's only occult image. The previous year Martin had designed a set of 22 Tarot cards (the Major Arcana) for OZ. The Abraxas picture came from that same spirit, musings on Carl Jung's Seven Sermons to the Dead.

Film was a popular vehicle of the times. Martin got a taste for it working with Germaine and Whitaker. Philippe always had ideas. Now, the Rolling Stones were making their Rock And Roll Circus film, involving Eric in a band called The Dirty Mac (ie. John Lennon, Keith Richards, Mitch Mitchell and Eric). (56)

Back in Sydney there was Garry's film and Kingo's films. Albie Thoms was corresponding with Martin, recounting all his latest innovations. Albie's student, Bruce Beresford was living in London and Bruce knew Barry Humphries socially. They talked about government funding for Australian films. Film. Everyone was talking film.

There was movement at the Pheasantry. Eric's reading of Country Life magazine had paid off. A place called Hurtwood Edge was for sale for £30,000 and Eric was buying it.

Eric wrote, 'Next thing I knew, the deal was done and the house was mine. It was an extraordinary feeling. I'd never owned my own home. All my life, I'd been bumming around, from the first day I left Ripley, spending nights on stations or sleeping in the park, or staying on the couch at friends' houses, and then going back to Ripley. The most I'd had was a lease at the Pheasantry, and now I had Hurtwood…I moved in very quickly…'. (57)

He has owned it ever since

9.

ART ABOUT ART

Martin began to disappear after the Magic Theatre OZ, Richard was very happy to accept advice from Felix Dennis or me.

JIM ANDERSON

Scene: the Pheasantry – the flamboyant red oxide and white Louis XV façade and triumphal entrance: Eric Clapton moved out and Nigel Waymouth moved in.

One of the three proprietors of the Granny Takes a Trip boutique, Nigel was also a third of the graphic design and musical avant-garde partnership known as Hapsash and the Coloured Coat that designed posters, contributed to OZ and were described by writer, George Melly as 'Nouveau Art Nouveau'.

Said Martin, 'When Eric left I shared it with artist Nigel Waymouth. The Pheasantry was a great studio, I think one of my most creative studios. One tried to apply that lifestyle - the combination of music and art - to the Yellow House, it's pretty much the same feeling I think – different scales'. (1)

Ah, the Yellow House – partly conceptualized but unlikely to have been named at this stage. As he read the Letters, Vincent's dream of a studio of artists in the sunny south was beginning to resonate with Martin, who was itching to get back to Sydney. An all-art environment was an ambitious project. Martin was swapping ideas in his correspondence with Albie and conversations with Philippe.

'Philippe was doing a sensational series of paintings,' said Martin, 'he was only 17-18 or something. So sophisticated. Really great works. The opportunity was there at the Pheasantry, I guess. It was a good atmosphere – art and music. He was so young and he came from a very talented family.' (2)

Extending his interest in collage, after Magic Theatre OZ, Philippe got the idea to make a film from the off-cuts of Performance, the bin pickings of the film. Trouble In Molopolis was financed by the unlikely combination of Eric Clapton and an Australian artist living in London, Arthur Boyd. The drummer of an Aussie band in London, Tony Cahill of the Easybeats, handled the music with Arthur Boyd's son, Jamie. Robert Hughes lent his apartment as a location, Richard was PR man and Jenny Kee appeared as Shanghai Lil. (3)

Meanwhile, Cream was winding down. Commencing 4 October 1968, the band played its goodbye American concerts before returning home and bringing their last two years to a close at the Royal Albert Hall. The final concert was anti-climactic. Eric, Jack and Ginger left the stage without saying much to each other. They just wandered off. Ginger explained, 'When Cream died - it died. Short of murder, we couldn't solve a problem between us'. (4)

After the concert, the band's demeanour was called into question. Some said Eric was arrogant. Others reckoned he was depressed. Martin said he was self-effacing, 'Eric was incredibly modest. He'd didn't face the audience on stage at the Albert Hall. They're all up there and he's playing into the speakers with his back to the audience because he wasn't singing. Jack Bruce took over all the singing. Eric had lost his voice in a way, because there was beautiful singing on that first Cream album'. (5)

Eric was more candid, 'I'm an ego-manic with an inferiority complex. So I like attention and I don't like the attention.' (6)

Eric retreated to his Surrey estate. Charlotte partnered with Led Zeppelin guitar hero Jimmy Page, Eric took up with Alice Ormsby-Gore and what followed in the 70s were bleak years for Eric, battling his addictions.

Said Martin, 'Eric vanished. He went to live in the country back where he grew up. It's a terrible thing when popular music becomes an industry and puts so much pressure on people. At the Pheasantry we were smoking and maybe tripping a bit. I didn't know about any heroin. That happened afterwards, not at the Pheasantry - not that I had any knowledge of. But heroin has never been an interest of mine and never will be.' (7)

Jim Anderson arrived in England in 1963. A dropped-out lawyer and would-be writer, he met Richard Neville at the 1967 Legalise Pot Rally in Hyde Park but was not drawn into OZ until more than a year later. Jim worked with Richard on the book and shaped it into Play Power. He dropped into the Pheasantry one evening and met Martin and Philippe, drawing/collaging together at the time. That's how they met.

Sensing Martin's interest in OZ peaked with Magic Theatre, Richard was seeking other collaborators. OZ on its own was a big enough workload, to which he added the pressure of publisher Jonathon Cape's formidable book deadline. So Richard was pleased to involve Jim - his Play Power writer/researcher/editor - in OZ as well as Felix Dennis who had ideas for music reviews and – well – ideas for all sorts of things. Says Jim, 'Martin began to disappear after the Magic Theatre OZ, Richard was very happy to accept advice from Felix or me.' (8)

Jim's influence on the magazine became obvious in OZ 23, the Homosexual Issue resulted in Felix and him being hauled into Scotland Yard for a severe finger wagging. The warning was blithely ignored, leading to OZ 28 the infamous School Kids Issue and the subsequent Conspiracy and Obscenity Trial of 1971. (9)

Jim joined OZ and Martin went to Sydney. On this trip, 26-year old Martin was more businesslike and public. His visit coincided with the The Last OZ – the last Australian OZ. Richie was changing it into a political newssheet, the OZ Newsletter – 12 issues, $2.40. (10)

'OZ is dead', Richie headlined before signing out. He wrote, 'Australia has changed a good deal in the six years we have been in publication. We have passed from the arrogance of Menzies to the larrikinism of Gorton: from paternalism, through incompetence, to improvisation. The country has passed from a pathetic state of inferiority to a brutal kind of jingoism. We like the new mood and the new leadership no better than the old.' (11)

Martin was much chirpier. His Wheels of Fire-style OZ cover announced in tiny lettering, 'Sharp has returned…but not for long…ho ho ho'. Titled Martin Sharp: Expatriotism, his centrefold was a kangaroo evolving wings over nine stages then flying off overseas. Signed: 'Bye bye See Ya! Martin'. (12)

Despite responding cheekily to the subject of expatriatism, Martin was actually in the process of coming home for good. His peers were doing well in Australia and he was certainly impressed with cultural developments in his homeland. Ubu Films - Albie's film group - was at the forefront of underground film screenings. Ubu shows had become Happenings and Ellis D Fogg's Psychedelic Lightshows were as impressive as what was going on in Swinging London. The English underground press picked up on it. An article called 'The Sydney Scene' published in IT (International Times) wrote, 'Nothing much happens in Sydney, but Ubu is the major centre of what does happen'.

To welcome Martin back from London and filmmaker Aggy Read back from New York, an underground dance was staged at the Paddington Town Hall. It featured a new band, Tully. Writes Albie, 'What resulted from this combination was a psychedelic sound unlike anything heard in Sydney, mixing rock and jazz with the new electronic tones of a Moog synthesiser. The crowd of about a thousand stood awestruck as lights splashed over them and on to the surrounding walls, realising this was music to listen to rather than dance to, and Lightshows came into their own as a creative medium'. (13)

Over the next two years, Tully would regularly perform not-to-be-missed shows with compere Adrian Rawlins and light shows by Roger

Foley (Ellis D Fogg). Said Roger, 'The first concert where we used Tully was in the Roundhouse and that's what really blew me away because 1000 people came to the show and the Roundhouse shut the door – no more people – and another 1000 people were standing outside looking through the windows. The other thing that blew me away was all the people inside, instead of dancing to the light show and the bands, just sat down and watched them.' (14) Martin, like many others, saw a connection between what Tully was doing and what Pink Floyd had lost.

It was indeed a significant Sydney visit. Martin stayed with his mother, worked again with Richie Walsh, caught up with friends and family, checked out Greg Weight's photographic studio on South Dowling Street, found out what Garry Shead was doing, got to know Roger Foley a bit better, figured out Adrian Rawlins' role, met a young enthusiast - George Gittoes and, with the assistance of Peter 'Charlie' Brown, made arrangements for a Martin Sharp exhibition at Clune Galleries.

Family life had a few changes in store. Martin's father Henry married Dorothy Muller in 1969, meaning Martin now had a stepmother.

During this visit, Grandmother Sharp caught up with her errant grandson with his shoulder-length hair and velvet suits. Martin reeked of Swinging London. 'She was great', said Martin, 'I was doing the series of silkscreen lithographs. She took a keen interest. She wanted to see what I was doing. She saw the one with the cock and I was very embarrassed. Don't Leave Me Here Standing All Alone was its title. She said, "Oh! That's the engine that drives the train!" She was very frank.' (15)

The cock (Don't Leave Me Standing All Alone), the nipple (Boo Zoom), the exclamation mark (Exclamation), the egg (Float) and the question mark (Wot!) were part of Martin's series of archetypal symbols that he called Smartiples. Some he painted in Sydney, others in London, but – like Eadweard Muybridge's little naked running men - they provided a bank of simple images that he would constantly dip into in composing larger works.

Of this series, Carl Williams wrote in Apollo magazine, 'I see them as a counter-cultural version of Picasso's Demoiselles d'Avignon, an attempt by Sharp to go beyond what was expected of him, to stretch the psychedelic poster genre to breaking point and create a new visual language.' (16) Williams may be right. Martin was certainly simplifying what the Psychedelic poster artists were visually complicating.

Meanwhile, in the northern hemisphere where Martin was about to return, Tiny Tim had met Vicki Budinger at a signing session for his book Beautiful Thoughts. (17) Martin celebrated Miss Vicki in a full-page OZ magazine collage in which he quoted Tiny describing his perfect love, 'She is between 15 and 25 and is always with me. I guess I always need an audience and back in those very hard times when I first started to sing, I had to invent one. When I met my future wife I knew I had seen her before… she had come to me in a dream as a fairy princess. I fell in love with her. I shed a little tear and put it in an envelope to keep.' (18)

And Eric teamed up with former Spencer Davis Group multi-instrumentalist Stevie Winwood, Ginger Baker and the bass player from a band called Family, Ric Grech. They formed Blind Faith. Their first and only album (titled Blind Faith) was released in July, with the controversial Bob Seidemann cover of a bare-breasted pubescent girl holding a silver spaceship. The young girl was a London suburbanite, who posed with the consent of her parents and for a fee. ('An absolute genius work!' said Martin, 'It was the innocence…!') (19)

Steve Winwood has a different view. He said, 'I had nothing to do with it at all. It is what it is. If someone suggested that get put out today, I might have something to say about it'. (20)

Eric's contributions continued to be reticent. Not totally confident about song writing, Eric re-arranged the Buddy Holly song Well All Right and wrote one song, a hymn - the majestic and mysterious, In The Presence of the Lord. (21)

Tiny Tim's Second Album was released in January 1969. It did not duplicate the glory of the first. Martin had met Tiny fleetingly at the

Speakeasy Club, but in August 1969, when Tiny played Caesar's Palace in Luton (north of London), Tiny Tim's stars had tumbled to a point where he was at last accessible to his public.

Martin talked Louise and Richard to accompanying him to the venue. After the concert, all three went backstage. In his hand Martin carried a borrowed recording device and he taped everything Tiny said. Unfortunately Martin held the microphone too close and it came out quite blurred. After effusing about Tiny's genius, Martin asked Richard to 'get the gift'. Richard returned hauling an enormous picture from Martin's Exploration of Punctuation period. Said Martin, 'When I went to see Tiny at Caesar's Palace I took this lovely picture I'd done with an exclamation mark and gave it to him. It was a very nice picture.' (22)

Richard remembers it by its weight. He wrote about bearing the burden backstage, 'where it was presented to the astonished warbler'.

'Oh, what a shame, Mr Sharp,' said Tiny, 'It doesn't fit into my shopping bag'. (23)

Back at the Pheasantry, Nigel Waymouth kept painting and Philippe kept on working on his film. Philippe got the idea to paint on animation cells, where the finished image is on the reverse of the film/glass or Perspex. Philippe explained, 'You draw the image in a black line and then paint in the colour. Mart immediately picked up on this and expanded the concept by buying huge Perspex pieces and painting on them in the same process. Voila!' (24)

One day, while reading Jorge Luis Borges' memoirs, Martin came across a passage about Borges' meeting with the Spanish poet Federico Lorca. Mickey Mouse was discussed. Martin explained, 'Lorca could see Pop Art simply by understanding an image. He said, "Mickey Mouse is a symbol of America. I can read what's happening to America by studying Mickey Mouse". It's like an iridologist saying, "I can understand your health because I know what your eye is all about".' (25)

While Eric was living at the Pheasantry, Martin had done a picture of Mickey Mouse stepping out of a picture frame. He had also done a cut-back version of Vincent On The Road to Tarascon.

Perhaps Martin's parents were in his subconscious. Mickey Mouse - from Jo's trinket cabinet and Vincent's picture - from Henry's surgery?

Martin explained what happened next, 'I was doing a picture of Mickey Mouse. I was also doing a simplified version of Vincent On The Road To Tarascon and they were sitting next to each other. I had the sheet of Perspex 6 x 4 and I just put it over the two of them, traced it off and put them together. (26) 'Two girls were assisting me - Andonia and a friend. I've always liked to have some help in the studio, not always, but sometimes I do and they were a big help.' (27)

Martin was in the process of 'lifting' famous archetypal images. Fancy Our Meeting became strongly identified with Martin. Before the year was out, it would be transported to Sydney and exhibited in the Sharp Art Exhibition at Sydney's Clune Galleries. It was also a Big O poster, best explained by Michael Organ of the University of Wollongong. (28)

The juxtaposition of two familiar images in an unexpected setting led Martin to continue his experiments with art-on-art. He said, 'I'd been tracing out of art books. One of the first ones I did was Vincent Van Gogh's head coming out of the green chair and I thought, "Well, the purest thing is to actually cut up the image".' (29)

At the Pheasantry, Martin started creating his Artoons – published in 1972 as Art Book. (30) Snipping his way through art books of works by De Chirico, Magritte, Bonnard, Cezanne, Warhol, Degas, Holbein, Hamilton, Gaughin, Dalí, Arp, Duchamp, Vermeer, Ingres, Botticelli, Picasso, Signac, Goya, Whistler, Munch, Bacon, Man Ray, Monet, Piero Della Francesca, Mantegna, Matisse, Ernst, Seurat, Lichtenstein, Mondrian, Hokusai and especially Vincent, Martin laid the foundation for the Yellow House (1971), Art Book (1972) and Art Exhibition (1973). Some of these images – especially 'Matisse/Magritte' (known later as Pentecost) remained with Martin for life. (31)

Martin believes the very first example of appropriation is the picture painted by René Magritte in 1957. Said Martin, 'Magritte was an inspiration in the way that he would take a simple object and transpose it to another setting. In fact, he did use a figure from Primavera, in Ready-Made Bouquet – it's Botticelli's Primavera coming out of the back of a man with a bowler hat who is looking at a forest.

'I don't think I actually saw that before I started to do it, but looking at it now I see it as absolutely the first exploration of that area - using another art image in a Pop completely deadpan way. You're not altering it in any way, just a straight reproduction.' (32)

Although Martin's London years established his reputation as a great poster artist, lyricist, album cover designer and one of the OZ set, he found it tricky to exhibit his paintings. Other than Clytie Jessop's gallery and the Sigi Krauss' gallery, Martin describes his occasional exhibits as '...not in the sort of gallery I would have particularly liked to have exhibited in'. (33)

'I did try to get a few exhibitions going', he continued. 'Clytie Jessop was great. She used to show our work. She had a little gallery on Kings Road. Philippe had an exhibition there and I exhibited a few pieces there.

'And Sigi Krauss, where Michael Ramsden worked. Sigi opened this gallery in the West End and I had my collage show there Artoons. It became Art Book. That was just before I left. I suppose you can say about London - Performance – that movie – happened and I think things went a bit sour then. There was certainly a negative impulse from it - dramatic – exciting!' (34)

Certainly David Litvinoff got nervous. The Kray Brothers had been sentenced to jail some six months before the film, but not before noting that Litva had done too a good job as 'technical adviser' to the film. He was reputed to have betrayed underworld secrets. After Performance, Litva got jumpy and fled to the Philippines. Mr Jumping Jack Flash – god, he got mileage from that!

In March 1969 Martin had held his second solo exhibition Sharp Martin and his Silver Scissors at Sigi Krauss Gallery in Covent Garden, featuring collages based on famous works of art.

Then Martin attended two memorable concerts. The first, the 1969 Isle of Wight Festival held 29-31 August. The Festival attracted an audience of about 150,000 to see the Moody Blues, Bonzo Dog Band, Joe Cocker, Free, the Who and most of all Bob Dylan, who had not been seen since his near-fatal motorbike accident in July 1966.

Eric arrived the day before Dylan was to take the stage, so did John Lennon, Ringo Starr, Keith Richards and Charlie Watts. The sealed VIP area was reserved for Beatle wives and celebrities like Liz Taylor, Richard Burton, Jane Fonda, Roger Vadim, Syd Barrett, Donald Cammell and Elton John. Richard was in there somewhere. So was Jim. Towards the end of the concert, Martin got to the very the front of the stage.

'Front row!' said Jim, 'I was a few rows back. Richard was, maybe not the front row, but he was up there too. I went separately with a friend of mine, we did get quite close but it was an effort to get there. I didn't have any privileged sort-of situation.' (35)

Martin was so close that when Dylan sang his second-last song, Who's gonna throw that Minstrel Boy a dime…? he plucked a coin from his pocket, flicked it onto the stage and it went tink. Martin swore he could hear it on Dylan's 1970 album, Self Portrait.

Who's gonna throw that Minstrel Boy a dime…?

Tink.

'That's me!' Martin exclaimed. (36)

Richard remembers the concert too, he writes, 'Martin Sharp came tiptoeing through the slush, attired as a harlequin, "If only Tiny Tim was here," he said, "he's the one who can link up all the generations, a true minstrel of the age, ambiguous, multi-voiced, an immortal innocent, the most incredible songbird in captivity…". Yes Mart, yes. Ever since the night at the Albert Hall, this is how Sharp had been speaking'. (37)

The second-last concert Martin saw before coming back to Sydney was the Incredible Songbird himself at the London Palladium performing for Princess Margaret's Command Performance in November. Martin didn't make it backstage, though Princess Margaret did - after all, it was her concert. There's a famous photograph on Google Images of the Princess greeting Tiny Tim, singer Lou Christie and a rather uneasy David Bowie in the queue, awaiting his handshake. (38)

Martin came home before the year was out, though not before placarding Tiny's genius in Hippie Atrocities OZ No. 25 (December 1969). By this issue, the fresh influence of Felix and Jim was felt in both artwork and text. OZ 25 featured the Fabulous Furry Freak Brothers, Dylan's Great White Wonder bootleg LP, Elvis and Martin's two-page centre spread. It seemed like this was to be Martin's exit card before arguing with Richard about Tiny Tim and heading to Sydney. (39)

Jim Anderson recalls it this way, 'Richard was apologetic about handing over Martin's Tiny Tim b/w double spread for inclusion in OZ 25. He felt Martin had gone a little cuckoo and it would get OZ laughed at. It didn't worry new designer David Wills and me who were putting the issue together. David had already laid out his brilliant double spread on Elvis Presley, my favourite singer - before Bob Dylan and the Beatles turned up. Tiny Tim was just another welcome piece of magic for the hippie mix. Martin was lucky I did not hand-colour his b/w Tiny Tim masterpiece. David and I both thought about it.'(40)

Surrendering to Tiny Tim's unquestionable visual potential, Martin said, 'I used to try and talk people, Are you going to make a film about Tiny Tim? He's amazing!' Unable to stimulate interest Martin didn't give up. He said, 'So I did that cartoon in OZ, the double-page one…'. (41)

The one that proclaims a great talent has arrived. Hear ye, hear ye, the bluebird of happiness, the Prince of Song. Tiny Tim - The Spirit of Popular Music past, present and future, welcome to my dream.

Why did Martin return to Australia? He said, 'Artistic and romantic reasons. I didn't have the resources to live over there. You've got to be realistic. It wasn't like I was earning a lot of money. It was so easy to come back, some people leave it too long and they never come back. Luckily I managed to come back and bring back a lot of the stuff I'd been doing there, to do something interesting with it.' (42)

So goodbye London, and goodbye the 1960s.

'I still link into that period pretty strongly', said Martin in 1993. 'I think the 60s were a success - a big change, anyway. I'm still working with ideas I discovered then. I guess it's got a lot to do with smoking and thinking. To me, going to London was like going to university or something like that. Luckily meeting people and them being very open. They really were friendly times. Every door was open. It was the prime of one's youth as well. I'm just an interesting character who seemed to be somewhere at a certain time.

'I learned a lot but I couldn't have lived there. I wasn't together enough. I needed support. I just had a better chance of surviving here (Sydney). You can see how things work over there. If you're not born into it you'll never get it. I could have become a part of it I guess. I'm still remembered by some people as part of that 60s time - through OZ and stuff. (43)

About the time Martin was moving out, a lion called Christian was moving in.

Anthony (Ace) Bourke and John Rendall from Australia moved into the King's Road and bought a lion from the Harrods department store for 250 guineas.

A lion.

The three of them lived as flatmates. The lion called Christian became a King's Road celebrity. Then a book, a film, a youtube sensation, but more significantly for our purposes, this same Ace Bourke curated Martin's Martin Sharp – Sydney Artist exhibition at the Museum of Sydney in 2010. (44)

10.

UNDERGROUND MEETS UNDERWORLD

Martin asked me to photograph work that he'd brought back to Australia. I photographed them and he wanted to keep the ball rolling so we made prints, little frames. It was called The Incredible Shrinking Exhibition.

GREG WEIGHT

In the late-60s, Sydney's Kings Cross was Australia's Montmartre-cum-Greenwich Village. It had evolved into the place where the hippies met the hipsters.

Although tiny in size, Kings Cross is a densely populated locality. A short walk in any direction takes you to another suburb - Darlinghurst, Elizabeth Bay, Woolloomooloo. Or Potts Point - where Martin eventually located at 59 Macleay Street, a short Mini-Moke ride to Wirian and a short walk to almost every other happenin' thing in Sydney central. Jazz, poetry, Rock music, theatre, restaurants, the best coffee and the best tobacconist in town, all with a European – or cosmopolitan – beat.

Plus there is an Art history to the Cross. Poets Christopher Brennan lived thereabouts, Kenneth Slessor lived here. Artists, Sir William Dobell, Donald Friend, John Olsen and so on…

Kings Cross was a layered community. Depending on what you wanted - it wouldn't chase you but you could find it.

The Forbes Club was an illegal gambling joint frequented by Sydney socialites. Rev Ted Noffs ran the Wayside Chapel, a street church with a small events theatre. Atheist/anarchist John Webster from Speaker's Corner the Domain, carried his soapbox provocations into the broadly tolerant Wayside Chapel, where Noffs welcomed and debated him. Stripper Sandra Nelson made front-page news when she bared her breasts strolling Darlinghurst Road in mid-afternoon sunshine, wearing a Rudi Gernreich topless designer-dress – the very latest shocking thing from Europe.

The Piccolo Bar in Roslyn Street was another hangout. Run by Italian migrant Vittorio Bianchi since the 40s, it was, 'a meeting place for cabaret performers, prostitutes, hippies, punks, poets and nuns…denizens of the Cross', describes Roger Foley. (1)

Not far away was Clays Books, one of the few Sydney bookshops to stock books by the Beat writers. And that brought you up to the main strip where Owen Lloyd, the Bird Man of Kings Cross busked at the El Alamein Fountain, encircled by his enormous flock of budgies.

There was a smattering of hookers on this stretch, stoned but never whacked. Hare Krishnas chanted along the pavement. Buskers, spruikers and Jesus People too. Bouncers – big guys with folded arms – guarded the entrance of the Paradise Club, famous because of Sandra Nelson. And a row of motorbikes lined up outside the Pink Pussycat Strip Club. That's where a biker called Snake hung out, so named because he had a 6ft Diamond Python wrapped around his waist under his leather jacket. American troops in bars were a reminder of the continuing Vietnam War.

Sure it sounds rough, but unless someone did something incredibly stupid, like touching a stripper or something, people were rarely beaten up. Well, perhaps in the side streets but not too often on the main drag.

Located near the top of William Street, El Rocco was the most famous jazz venue in the country. Inside, TV people brushed shoulders with suburbanites, blue-collar workers, fake beatniks – anyone. When the Sydney production of Hair was staged at Kings Cross' Metro Theatre, the bandleader and percussionist was John Sangster from El Rocco. Tully, was the house band. And Albie Thoms ran the lights.

In the back streets of Kings Cross-Darlinghurst, John Bell and Ken Horler were seeking to locate their Nimrod theatre company. Ethereal poet Pip Proud wandered the streets in a cosmic haze. Kings Cross had it's own newspaper, the Kings Cross Whisper. Heck, this place even had its own witch. (Rosaleen Norton)

59 Macleay Street was the former Clune Gallery, run by Frank, Thelma and their son Terry Clune. The gallery had famously exhibited many breakthrough artists – such as John Olsen, Robert Klippel and a young Robert Hughes. It would become the Yellow House and continue to be a haven for artists. The Clune Gallery had been a major advertiser in early-60s Australian OZ, with Martin sketching their pen-and-ink ads. But the building was on the real estate market now.

This location was the closest Sydney had to the King's Road Chelsea, that's for sure. 'The Pheasantry was without a doubt the precursor to the Sydney Yellow House', wrote Philippe Mora, who lived with Martin when Martin was forming his earliest Yellow House ideas. (2)

In the late-60s there was a lot of talk about communal living. From the squatter movement to hippie collectives, London OZ was full of it.

In the summer of 1967, co-founder of OZ magazine's underground rival, International Times (IT) Jim Haynes, started an art-and lifestyle venture called the Arts Lab. Located in Drury Lane, Covent Garden, the programs were as freeform as the events – performance, dance, plays – 'happenings' they were then called, running late into the night. Legendary for a short time, the Arts Lab closed its doors in 1969, though not before inspiring some 50 other 'non-institutions' scattered around Britain. Martin knew about them, in the pages of OZ for starters. (3)

During his late-Pheasantry period, Martin had turned his attention to the subject of Art itself. Pre-eminent in his thinking were the works of René Magritte and the letters of Vincent Van Gogh in which Vincent idealised a 'studio in the south, in the sun'. That certainly couldn't happen in London.

Martin envisaged his Yellow House as a lot further south. (4) He said, 'I found London artistically challenging enough! The Yellow House was an idea that came out of London'. (5)

With a head full of Vincent, the Pheasantry and the Arts Lab (that he never mentioned) Martin began swapping ideas with underground filmmaker Albie Thoms and a keen young artist, George Gittoes. Martin had clear ideas about the general direction of the visual art on walls. And with a background in experimental theatre and film, Albie had ideas for the kind of happenings that could spring the place into life, especially at night.

Wrote Albie, 'I found it an engrossing idea, envisaging film screenings and music concerts among the paintings. So I agreed, promising to return after I had completed my engagement in Amsterdam'. (6) A sign of things to come? Albie's ongoing relationship with Martin would subsequently always be dotted with other film and theatre engagements.

Returning to Australia in April 1969, Martin took residency upstairs in the Clune Gallery along with 'protected tenants' ie. long term residents who could not be moved on until the property was sold. Meanwhile, Ian Reid, a young farmer from Captains Flat decided to buy the premises, therefore – in theory – everyone had to move out, leaving the premises vacant.

Pre-settlement, Ian arrived at his newly acquired property where he was unexpectedly greeted by Martin and two others. Ian had met Martin at the Pheasantry and on meeting him again agreed to allow 59 Macleay Street to continue as an exhibition space. Said Ian, 'I did it because it seemed like a good idea at the time and because I could. It became an early step in a journey of 1000 miles.

'I was a cattle farmer and came into some money. My lawyer said, "The Clunes Gallery and their property is for sale. Why don't you invest in real estate?" I said okay. I handed over a cheque, borrowed some, signed some papers and took a wander up Macleay Street to see my new premises. The atmosphere there was glum. I had purchased the property vacant possession but was greeted by Martin, Terry Clark and Charlie Brown and a lot of paintings in packing boxes. Having sold their property, the Clunes couldn't hold Martin's exhibition - so all that was up to me. And so the show began.' (7)

With the assistance of mutual friend Peter (Charlie) Brown, Martin presented Paint Your Own Gallery, an exhibition of his Pheasantry pictures along the lines of the cover for the newly released Ginger Baker Airforce LP record. For years afterwards, this is exactly what Martin's audience – fans – wanted from him. The egg. The toothy-smile. Eyeballs. Exclamation marks. Swirls. Little naked running men. Mickey Mouse meeting Vincent…but that was then. In 1970 the world was more serious than the hippie idealism had had preceded it.

With Australian forces directly involved in the Vietnam War, Sydney was extremely politically conscious. Martin did a b/w poster for the 1969 Vietnam Moratorium. Borrowed from the children's book Le Petit Prince, Martin appropriated Antoine de Saint-Exupéry's picture of the Little Prince which he captioned, 'We are them…they are us…Moratorium!' He created a sense of horror by replacing Saint-Exupéry's star with a skull. (8)

Held 3 May 1969, the University of New South Wales Vietnam Moratorium is where Martin first heard Jeannie Lewis sing. She could sing everything - folk, blues, jazz and opera.

Jeannie began her musical career in Sydney University revues in 1960. She sang with the Ray Price Jazz Quintet, was a semi-regular singer at the Sydney Baby Push (the name given to the second generation Push) and also at the Gas Lash. Jeannie was arrested in a demonstration in 1964 at Wynyard and helped convene the folk singers for a fundraising concert for the Freedom Ride, leading to civil rights for Indigenous Australians. At the 1969 Music for a Change Moratorium, Jeannie Lewis blew Martin away.

He said, 'I went to the Roundhouse at the University of New South Wales for a Moratorium - or something like that - and there was this incredible band with this wailing chick who was singing - like the best woman I'd ever heard sing. I thought, "Who is this? Where did this band come from? Is this what's been happening while I was away? This is as good as anything I've seen in the world!"' (9)

To organise the return of his paintings, it was back to London again briefly for Martin. In his absence, Philippe's subject matter had shifted to Degenerate Art. Subjects like meat (beef and pork chops) and religion (Jesus Christ). Steeped in 'artoons, Tiny Tim and anti-gallery art, Martin was initially unenthused.

Philippe struggled to get the visiting Martin involved, 'I had a hell of a time encouraging Martin to exhibit in a fine art gallery', Philippe wrote. 'For political reasons he shied away from it and preferred posters and cartoons ie. mass market and non elitist. I was in the same place but enjoyed galleries because of my background in galleries and parents but it all reached a climax for me with the Degenerate Art Show aka Crucifixion Show I curated with Sigi Krauss which included my anti-art Meat sculpture.

'I finally got Martin to contribute a painting in glass which was exhibited on the floor. I remember Mart at the Sigi Krauss gallery smashing the glass on his painting on the floor. Broken glass! Anyway, Mart enjoyed Sigi and the atmosphere. Sigi's Gallery was really the most avant garde place in London at the time. Stanley Kubrick came and used art from it in A Clockwork Orange – dancing Jesus figures and giant phallus.' (10)

There, Martin was exhibited alongside, 'Mora, Powell, Ramsden, Strawheim, Shamask, Philadelphia and other Neurotic Perverts'. (11) A member of the public took offence at the images and threw a brick through the gallery window. The idea of broken glass and broken windows captured Martin's interest. He made it a feature in his Incredible Shrinking Exhibition - photographs of his first show re-exhibited in small mirror-frames, which he worked on when he came back.

While Martin was gone, Tiny Tim played a 10-night stand in Sydney where he made a terrific impression at the Chevron Hilton, but Martin wasn't there. Ted Markstein was. He said, 'I saw Tiny Tim at the Silver

Spade at the Chevron. Half empty. Two hours. The most astonishingly versatile knowledgeable exponent of music I have ever seen in my life. Fucking fantastic. And the audience totally lacking comprehension as to what this master was illustrating to them about music!' (12)

Meanwhile, Greg Weight established his career as a photographer. From his South Dowling Street Redfern studio he did photo shoots for classy magazines, publicity and portfolio shots. Greg was regularly published in fashion magazines and the Sydney Morning Herald, which is where he surmises Martin may have spotted his name and remembered their old times together.

Said Greg, 'I'm working in my studio, the phone rings and it's Martin. He's back in Sydney. He came over. Very interested in the fact that I'd done photography. Asked me to photograph a lot of his paintings immediately. It was work that he'd brought back to Australia that he hadn't sold in the UK.

'I photographed them and he wanted to keep the ball rolling so we made prints of those. He made little frames (or had frames made). It was called The Incredible Shrinking Exhibition. The anticlimax that I'd felt at the end of our relationship when he went overseas was completely repaired by him coming back. I also realized that he hadn't forgotten what we'd done together. He wanted to reconnect.' (13) And so it has ever been with Martin and Greg.

Paint Your Own Gallery and The Incredible Shrinking Exhibition preceded the Yellow House. Most of the key players in what was to become the Yellow House attended – and were inspired by - that exhibition. The energy enticed a small team of key players. It was a rallying call of sorts. Roger Foley bought a picture. (14)

Questioned about his pre-Yellow House hopes, Martin replied, 'I wanted to create a place in which everyone could participate. I wanted to get something going, to give it a start, use it as a lubricant. I wanted to get paint, to be able to paint the whole place, to fulfil the fantasy perhaps and try to bring it into reality. A lot of people helped. There was a fantastic feeling, a magic atmosphere and a very high level of communication between the people who were there and the people who came into the place. It was expanding all the time'. (15)

Having generated a powerhouse of energy, Martin was well positioned to actualise Vincent's dream of an artist's community in the south, and Albie caught it from the start. Says artist Peter Kingston, 'It was Albie and Martin who started the Yellow House'. (16)

Albie already had his team. Filmmakers Aggy Read, Bruce Beresford and Peter Weir; film student Phillip Noyce; light artist Ellis D Fogg (Roger Foley); theatre director Jim Sharman and all those Contemporary Theatre Production Company, Theatre of Cruelty and Ubu Film people with whom he had done productions, projects and films.

Martin too had a team, though not as clearly defined. Around this time, George Gittoes, studying Arts at Sydney University, shared ideas with him as to how the Yellow House might proceed. (17) Richard (Dicky) Weight – Greg's older brother - was another cornerstone. He knew Martin from the National Art School and had applied to the Sydney City Council to paint the Sydney Harbour Bridge yellow. He painted the Yellow House yellow instead. (18)

Said Martin, 'As far as I knew this wasn't being done anywhere else at such a grass roots level. I brought back my London paintings. I had an exhibition all ready, which I'd done on my own, all arranged by the Holdsworth Gallery. A friend of mine, Peter 'Charlie' Brown was managing it. By the time I got back in the country he'd had a row with the lady running it and was no longer managing it. I was loyal to him, pulled out of that and I had to find somewhere else. What was to become The Yellow House was offered to me – but at that time it was just Sharp Art Exhibition. We started painting the walls to make it more interesting.

'I remember turning round to Terry Clark - my Maths Teacher at school - just a bit older than me - he was there helping, and his friend Charlie Brown who was a focal energy point. One night I can remember painting upstairs and some kids from Cranbrook turned up, lent a hand

and got into its spirit. They said, "Great atmosphere, boy this is fantastic - you can really do something here!" With this enthusiasm you can really make art work. There was an obvious need for people to express themselves. If you could just provide the context, then you could direct it. (19)

'I love exploring different mediums, so I'd take an idea from a collage-to- a-painting-to-a-cartoon or whatever. I was very open-minded as far as what medium I worked in. I find the commercial gallery scene pretty restrictive because really they're like boutiques – stores that sell art and have a different show every so often. Within that context you can put on a good exhibition and explore certain ideas, but you really don't have much freedom because it's too restrictive. So Paint Your Own Gallery, which later became the Incredible Shrinking Exhibition which became the Yellow House – got free of all that.' (20)

Martin organised both shows while living upstairs on the premises. At the very start, Martin lived almost alone, supported by a few companions, confidants and consorts. 'A few friends lived nearby. They started moving in as various people came and got involved with it. It was amazing to have a place that you could do what you like with. It was probably expected the building would be bought and pulled down, but it wasn't.' (21) Ian Reid comments, 'That was in some ways true. I'd bought the place because I could. I had no experience in real estate, I had no interest in real estate but somehow I found myself doing it, which is one of those things that you do in innocence.' (22)

Gradually the whole thing gained momentum, shunting – at this stage – to what would it would become within six months. Says Martin, 'It was a community of artists working together in the south.' (23)

Martin wasn't at 59 Macleay Street when Albie called to see him to lay ground plans. Dicky Weight was there and showed Albie the main gallery where he was painting the walls in the manner of Magritte's skies. But no, Martin wasn't present. He was at Palm Beach where he had rented a house to decamp. Albie roamed the empty rooms and found George Gittoes painting walls, ceiling – everything. Seeking Martin, Dicky pillioned

Albie (on Aggy Read's motor bike) to where Martin was staying with his secretary Bliss and a couple of assistants.

Brett and Wendy Whiteley were staying in a house nearby and invited everyone to dinner. Other guests included Peter Kingston, Mick Glasheen, and Peter Wright. (24)

Whenever he'd had enough of Yellow House preparations, Martin would head to Palm Beach, which can't have been totally relaxing. Whiteley's biographer writes of an irritating 'powerplay' between Brett and Wendy.

Add Martin's presence.

Since the Tate Gallery London established Brett's international reputation by buying his Untitled Red Painting in 1960, he and Wendy had done every cool thing there was to do. They had travelled the world, connected with Francis Bacon and lived in New York's Chelsea Hotel, a place where the cultural underworld hung out. Brett was the darling of the Sydney art set. Now - here was Martin, the homecoming king. Not just a friend but a rival also.

Seagull, the artist in a downstairs studio at the Whiteley's Palm Beach place said, 'Two camps would form, with Martin Sharp and his young friends at one end of the room indulging in a bit of grass, while the heavy mob – Brett, me and our friends – settled into serious drinking at the other'. (25) Serious drinking indeed. Jonny Lewis, who would later tag along with Martin, recalls drunken Brett and drunken Peter Wright coming to blows - the extraordinary thing being that 'Brett was fighting and painting at the same time!' (26)

From that time on, perhaps before, Brett always kept a challenger's eye on Martin's projects. From their angry co-efforts in the Yellow House to Brett's publication Another Way of Looking at Vincent Van Gogh (27) many felt Brett was constantly trying to outsmart Mart. It's something Martin strongly denies, 'I wasn't aware of any camps...!' (28)

At that initial Palm Beach visit, Albie recalls Martin showing no urgency about making things happen at the gallery, where the opening of the Incredible Shrinking Exhibition was scheduled for April Fools' Day 1971, less than a fortnight away.

Some, including Martin, speak of this exhibition as if it was the start of the Yellow House. It certainly attracted reviews, some hostile, which Martin snipped out of the newspapers and collaged in his Catalog – the collage and sketchbook that he was working on at night, in his comfortable apartment at the end of the building, overlooking Challis Avenue. The Catalog idea is a continuation of Magic Theatre OZ, only more personal. Less Robert Crumb and more Cranbrook.

Some journo wrote a review of Martin's exhibition: 'Sharp, with one eye a satirist and full of contempt for the young Bohemians he serves and exploits, confronts the viewer with repetitious vulgar lithographs in stark red and blue abounding in ghastly assemblages. In his homages to Van Gogh, his lack of comparable ability is crassly apparent and in their ways they are just as sickly as his pornography'.

Martin clipped that one for his Catalog and pasted it on an image of the Le Petit Prince blinded by a moonglow - the same Little Prince image as the Moratorium poster.

Another review: 'Martin, in his black velvet hat crammed down over his black locks – on his gnashing teeth smiling at the river of remarks – was supported by his velvet trousers and two-tone shoes, close to the echoes of his mind. Visit at your peril.' On this one, Martin pasted an Eadweard Muybridge naked male figure swinging a baseball bat. The hostile, over-stated, reviews kept Martin in laughs. (29)

Albie's 'review' is much closer to the spirit of the times: 'Martin's Incredible Shrinking Exhibition opened on April Fool's Day with Little Nell (Laura Campbell) tap-dancing in the Cloud Room to the sound of Bing Crosby singing Irving Berlin's 'Blue Skies'. It was a glittering occasion.' (30)

Little Nell was Martin's new girlfriend. She had appeared tap dancing behind Tiny Tim in the one-hour Channel 7 TV special A Special Tiny

Tim, filmed when Tiny toured the country in Martin's absence. (31) Martin spotted her tap dancing in a city arcade. Jonny Lewis filmed her.

Jon (Jonny) Lewis lived with his mother and brother Mark in Wylde Street Potts Point, a short walk from all this action. His friend, Bruce Goold knew of Martin's exhibition and he was up for crashing it. Of his sensational meeting with Martin, Jonny says, 'We wanted to crash it and crash it we did. That's where the paintings were knocked off…'. Yep, Jonny and Bruce stole two of Martin's pictures and inveigled them into the Women's loo. From there, to Jonny's mother's car and off they drove. Says Jonny, 'I started thinking, This is terrible, we shouldn't have done this!' So they backtracked, entered through the back gate, leaned the pictures against a tree in the garden and ran off.

Said Jonny, 'All we wanted was attention. Next day we thought we'd better go back and smooth things over. So we came back and there was Mal Ramage and Charlie Brown. So us two boys rolled up and I said, "We've got something to say. We're the guys who took the paintings, we're a bit sorry…". Charlie Brown said, "That's funny because we found them in the back yard". I remember a distinct smile came over Martin. I think they were all smiling. They thought we were good. So that was our entré and we started hanging around the place. And of course Martin wanted everyone to paint walls.'

In this way Jonny Lewis joined the pre-Yellow House collective and eventually moved in. According to him, he didn't actually contribute anything. 'I just absorbed it all, that's all I did'. Roger disagreed, 'Jonny helped everybody!' (32)

After this, preparations for the Yellow House began in earnest. Dicky helped Martin prepare the building. George started creating his Puppet Theatre room.

Came a time when it all became official, Albie went around assigning rooms. He took a top-floor room for himself. Peter Wright was next door. Colette St John moved in with him and assumed the role of cook. Musician Nic Lyon also moved in. And so on. Bliss also moved into a room on the top floor - next door to barrister and former Sydney University actor, Mal Ramage. Said Mal, 'I lived in the Yellow House for a period of time. I was the Straight Man in the Yellow House. I had to go and bail people out if they got into trouble and things like that. There used to be two mime characters, Julian (Jewellion) and his girlfriend Moth. And Julian got arrested one day. The Telegraph quoted me as saying that it was disgraceful that someone should be arrested just for making people laugh!' (33)

Thinking at first there would be no room for him, Jonny got genuinely excited when Albie crammed him in a tiny room in the mezzanine area, just big enough to throw a mattress on the floor. Having installed a parachute in his bedroom, Jonny reckoned, 'Everything was fantastic after that! This is where I got my education. I thought these people are great, these are the people I want to be with. I felt absolutely comfortable'. (34)

Others visited daily, with Peter Kingston (Kingo) opening a tearoom in the backyard so that visitors could sit and chat after experiencing the show. Kingo, who was one year behind Martin at Cranbrook School, got to know Martin when screening the film Who Lives in a Little House? at an architecture convention in the ballroom of the Hotel Australia. Martin just happened to be walking past, so Kingo said, 'Come and have a look at our film...!' The friendship went from there.

Said Kingo, 'Martin was at a crossroads, whether to go to New York and live there? Warhol and all those were very evident then in New York and Martin would have mixed in well there. But he chose to come back here and his life took a different turn. It would have been very different if he'd gone to New York. We're very glad he came back here because he got the Yellow House up-and-running with Ian Reid.' (35)

Dicky's brother Greg was also popping in-and-out, but this wasn't the Yellow House yet and Greg was yet to get fully involved.

Some spaces were totally vacant, except for Martin's large paintings left over from his previous show. He explained to Albie how these rooms could be converted into exhibition areas similar to the Cloud Room on the ground floor. Says Albie, 'where Magritte's puffy clouds on an azure sky were to provide the background for his next show'.

Martin and Albie discussed events, theatrical performances, film screenings and concerts. Albie immediately thought of London's Arts Lab – but 'getting it right'. He writes, 'Ours would be clean and colourful, in contrast to that place's dark and dusty spaces, a haven where we could celebrate the delights of living in Sunshine City'. In his book My Generation, Albie describes all his dealings with the Yellow House in this sort of detail.

Albie developed a program of activities to accompany Martin's exhibition: Filmmakers' Cinema on Thursday nights, soirées on Friday nights, screenings of old movies on Saturdays and cabaret on Sunday. Albie also wanted to establish an art school. He writes, 'As there was a didactic purpose to it all, preparing the audience for our further explorations, I suggested we call the enterprise the Ginger Meggs Memorial School of Arts, since it would be exploring Modernism from an essentially Australian perspective. Martin liked the idea...'. (36)

Jonny Lewis enrolled as the first student in the Ginger Meggs classes, which began with a Filmmaker's Cinema screening of Marinetti. This was followed in subsequent weeks by films by Garry Shead, Mick Glasheen and Peter Kingston.

Everything was taking shape and going to plan, so Martin scribbled a postcard to Richard Neville in London, 'What an incredible trip, a mind-blower – come and see Little Nell do the shimmy!' (37) But Richard was otherwise engaged.

Richard, Felix Dennis and Jim Anderson were fully pinned on an Obscenity charge. The date of the OZ trial was 22 June 1971, so they had plenty of time to prepare themselves and drum up publicity, which is unusual for a court case. The previous significant literary/obscenity charge had been the 1960 'not guilty' verdict for Lady Chatterley's Lover by DH Lawrence. It was contested and won, on 'literary merit', which put the OZ accused on thin ice, because a lot of people thought OZ had zero literary merit.

Dubbed the Schoolkids Issue, it wasn't FOR schoolkids. It was BY schoolkids. Get this difference to understand the trial.

Jim Anderson had been left in charge of OZ while Richard was in Greece or thereabouts. Jim foolishly – or brilliantly - depending on how you see it – let the schoolkids have their head. Unrepressed kiddie smut suddenly burst out of nowhere. Like, depicting Rupert Bear with a stiffy. For the first time ever, schoolkids had editorial control.

And the cover!

Says Martin, 'I wasn't involved in that issue. I certainly felt that it was a brilliant idea to give it to schoolchildren. It launched a new generation of kids. That's why it shocked so much, because kids spoke out and it just went like a bombshell, just the first time they'd ever been given the freedom of speech in the press!

'This Schoolkid's Issue was the sort of rage expressed exactly from the position they were in at the time. And the lawyer was John Mortimer, a famous playwright, and Geoffrey Robertson, a star of the law!

'So that was Richard's Production, that whole court case - sending out gilt-edged invitations inviting people to the OZ trial. His dress rehearsal case was in Sydney but his big show was defending himself at the Old Bailey.' (38)

By August 1971, the three accused were convicted of obscenity and given sentences ranging from 9-15 months, but released on appeal at which the trial judge (Judge Michael Argyle) was severely reprimanded for misdirecting the jury. Phew. All this was happening in London while Martin was 12,000 miles away.

And Jumping Jack Flash? Directly from Bali, Litva suddenly arrived.

David Litvinoff claimed to have upset London's East End underworld by revealing too much of their operations for the Mick Jagger film Performance. 'You're a big smiler,' said one of the Kray Bros, producing a carving knife and cutting a 'big smile' into Litva's cheeks, the scars of which he now bore. Although nobody quite knew how much to believe, Litva said he was a Talk Man for the Krays. That was his job. Litva called on problem-people, suggesting a quick resolution…'because the next guy to call is a whole lot bigger and won't be so patient'.

Although the Krays were in prison now, they still had their avengers on the prowl and - shit-scared - Litva came to Sydney (via Bali) to check Martin out. He frightened everybody. Says Roger, 'He absolutely terrified me'. (39). Says Greg, 'David could be very scary'. (40) Says Tim, 'He was a crazy man that one. Whoah!' (41)

Litva surfaced when Tim and Jonny were ambling past the Chevron Hotel. Martin parked his Mini-Moke and out leapt this firebrand dressed in shorts, sandals, Balinese shirt, dark glasses and smoking a 3-paper joint shamelessly on Macleay Street.

He walked straight up to Tim and Jonny and unleashed a torrent of words, 'Wut's these two gay boys doin walking down the street like this? You boys, going anywhere? Who do you think you are? I've seen people like you in the London streets…and anyway you can all go to fucken hell as far as I'm concerned!' Then, abruptly nice, 'Are you coming to the Yellow House boys?' (42)

Not that there was a Yellow House yet and not that he had even seen the premises, having come straight from the airport. 'That's what I mean about Litvinoff being mercurial', says Mal Ramage. 'I suppose he was a manipulator of people. I don't think he frightened me but I was wary of him, I was aware that he could turn very quickly. I think he had a great intellect actually.' (43)

Proprietor of the In Shoppe men's wear, Ted Markstein, lived opposite the Yellow House. Ted says, 'He was an evil bastard. They were mincemeat to someone like that. They were very naïve at the Yellow House. They had limited life experience. Maybe because they were young they lacked that natural self-protective suspicion.' (44)

Martin said, 'David came to the Yellow House. He was the main force, in a way – a terrific example.' (45)

11.

THE YELLOW HOUSE

The Yellow House morphed out of Martin's exhibition.
It was a continuum. Nothing changed.

IAN REID

Martin was running the pre-Yellow House by day. Albie was running it by night. Martin directed the walls. Albie directed the shows. Litva was added as a sort of manager-provocateur. His main jobs seemed to be putting out the garbage, sifting visitors and shaking up every proposition.

The 'Martin Sharp Gallery' at 59 Macleay Street was now shared.

Said Martin, 'The Yellow House was conceived as: the more artists involved...! And everyone was given a space they could work with. It was just totally starting off something, rolling and seeing how it went. Once I saw what happened I realised that's how you could do it. It was a big discovery that people are out there, willing to get involved and enjoying it'. (1)

At the outset, only a handful of name-artists were involved - Martin of course, and Brett. And - although few Sydneysiders had actually seen his films - Albie Thoms was a well-respected underground filmmaker. Those who cared to read the photographic credits in newspapers and fashion magazines would have noted the name Greg Weight. Posters plastered all over town told you about the Ellis D Fogg lightshows combined with

Tully concerts, where the ubiquitous performance-poet Adrian Rawlins took the role of slightly annoying compére.

Adrian was a Melbourne poet, performer, organiser, promoter and raconteur - probably best remembered simply as a 'character'. Adrian's art piece was himself. Performances were impromptu. He interviewed Brian Epstein when the Beatles came to Australia in 1964 and connected with Bob Dylan on his 1966 Australian tour, after which Adrian convinced himself that Dylan was a Christ, sacrificing himself. (2) Adrian (like the band Tully) was a follower of the silent guru, Meher Baba.

How did Sydney people get to hear all this was happening?

One medium that spread the word into suburbs was the ABC-TV program at 6.25. Each weeknight GTK (ie. Get To Know) was squeezed between the Six O'Clock News and the soapie Bellbird. From 1969-1974, GTK would broadcast a daily snippet of Pop-culture. It was usually a band, but sometimes art happenings, light show events, interviews with opinion-makers, etc. One evening the Burbs were treated to Adrian Rawlins laughing for five minutes. Just laughing.

During the 18 months since Martin had made 59 Macleay Street his domain, his lesser-known contributing artists were maturing fast. Under Martin's general umbrella and lessening influence, each was developing his/her own concepts. There was sufficient energy afoot to require art spaces (usually rooms) to be formally assigned by the newly formed Yellow House collective that gathered around the kitchen table. Their discussions took place against a constant background of recorded music since all rooms had been wired for sound by John Bee - a Kings Cross disco deejay. Tiny Tim was heard lots – as was Bob Dylan's Self Portrait LP - interspersed with vintage tracks from Al Bowlly and contemporary Rock.

Greg recalls, 'Everybody attended Yellow House meetings where laws were passed and secretaries took notes: Martin, Albie, George, Dick, me, Brett Whiteley occasionally. We were all talking about one thing and another thing and about where we were going to get the paint from when Brett got so bored with the conversation that he said, "Fuck man, you've got to jump on the kangaroo's back before it leaves the ground or else you're going to end up with a face full of dirt!" It rang home and we thought "Let's not talk about it, let's just do it". So Brett cracked it: "Dick get the paint, so-and-so do this, so-and-so do that, all meet here on Monday, we'll designate the rooms, get cracking and DO it!"' (3)

The artists treated the ceiling, walls, floors – everything – like an artist's canvas. What followed was feverish activity interspersed with evening theatre, film or musical events. 'Happenings' was an often-used word.

Some of the work had already been achieved, like Dick Weight's Cloud Room and Peter Wright's Spookyland, (so named by Arkie Whiteley). But most had to be created from scratch, like Martin's Fantomas Hall, Franklin Johnson's Stairway, Dick Weight's Tribute to Hokusai, the Infinity Room (Greg Weight and Julia Sale), Rembrandt to Magritte (Brett Whiteley and Martin's interior), the Magritte Room (Bruce Goold, Tim and Martin), the Bonzai Room (Brett Whiteley), George Gittoes' Puppet Theatre, Peter Wright's Ultra Violet and Kinetic Light Installation, the Capsule Room (Roger Foley) and the Yellow Room with a team comprising Martin, Peter Powditch, Philippe Mora, Peter Wright, Vivienne Pengally and Tim Lewis.

Says Roger, who lived close by, 'I used to constantly get called to come and repair the Capsule Room because people were bonking there all night. A lot of sex was going on in the Capsule Room. It was very comfy. All padded. Foam. We also had half-filled inner tubes underneath the floor so every time you moved it went down and somebody else would go up'. (4)

Germaine Greer's The Female Eunuch had only just been published, a book that would revolutionise everybody's thinking about women's issues, especially in this place. Many of the players knew Germaine from the Sydney University, the Sydney Push or even in London. (5)

Later, it would suit everyone to rewrite the history of the Yellow House as a non-sexist environment, though in reality, with few exceptions the art was left mainly to the 'boys'.

Says Adrian Rawlins, 'People were able to be in the Yellow House as either artists or appreciators if they wanted to be. The only criterion was their own genuine interest in what was actually going on. There were far too many runaway girls who were there because Martin had other ideas for them. In the back room there was a long refectory-type table and there would be Martin and 6-7 girls who painfully couldn't draw, patently had no visual perception whatsoever - but they were pretty, so they were there'. (6) Proprietor, Ian Reid describes Martin as, 'blessed with good looks, education, confidence, creativity, money and a magnetic personality'. (7) Female contribution was often secretarial and menial duties, or what may euphemistically be called 'assistants'.

Clearly Jeannie Lewis was not one of those. She was a major talent in her own right and Martin knew it. Martin had met Jeannie at the Roundhouse, University of New South Wales. He says, 'She was singing a song called Save the Country. It was so full of passion. It made me feel there's no need to go anywhere else when there are stars of the first magnitude here. I asked her to come and sing at the opening of the exhibition I had before the Yellow House'. (8)

Martin was so impressed that - if it can be said the Yellow House had a house band - Jeannie was it. She and her band regularly performed there every week and Martin paid them. At the end of the long and happy run, Martin thanked her and told her to take any painting she wanted. Jeannie chose the Vincent van Gogh, the one with the cartoon bubble and the words, 'I have a terrible lucidity when nature is so glorious….'. (9)

'But Jeannie,' Martin exclaimed, 'it's just a poster!'

'No it's not!' She replied. (10)

Greg Weight lived in his own South Dowling Street studio and regularly dropped in. Martin asked him to put a room in the Yellow House for the Spring (opening) Exhibition. Greg says, 'I'd gone to Cronulla and the sand dunes were, to my great delight, in pristine condition. Virgin. I shot a couple of rolls of film. When Martin invited me to be involved, I showed them to him and he said, "Let's make this a room, what will we call it?" There's nothing in the world more infinite than particles of sand so I ended up calling it the Infinity Room. That Infinity Room was also a suitable venue for one of Julia Sales' sculptures, which was a feathered chair and table - a total contradiction!' (11)

Greg's Infinity Room inspired Jonny Lewis to take up photography. First, he needed a camera, which he didn't have until Martin handed Jonny his paint-splattered Nikkormat before returning to London.

As a country boy, coming to terms with some of the events at the Yellow House wasn't straightforward for Ian Reid. An example was Jon Lewis' loop film of dolphins surfing. Says Ian, 'It was attractive - dolphins playing across the surface of an aquamarine wave before a golden beach. This was Art – but perhaps I couldn't recognize it as that at the time. Why the fuss? The point was that a young man had gone out, caught the magic of this scene on film and exhibited it. With hindsight it was a beginning for creative expression. It was a good and brave thing for him to have done.' (12)

The Stone Room was the first room to be completed. It was created by George, his mother Joyce Gittoes and Peter Kingston. Some saw it as the crown of their creation. Says regular visitor Ted Markstein, 'What blew me away was the creation in real life of the Magritte paintings, I thought that was fucking wonderful - the Stone Room!' (13) Says Jonny, 'The Stone Room that Kingo worked on day-after-day-after day, was extraordinary. There was nothing like it!' (14) In time, Greg's photo of the Stone Room became the cover of the catalog for the 1990 Yellow House Retrospective. (15)

Cinema nights continued, one was an amazing screening of George Greenough's Innermost Limits of Pure Fun. No one had ever shot footage inside the curl of a wave until Greenough figured out how to do it. Martin included a tribute to Greenough in the Stone Room in their version of Hokusai's Wave. He added a mirror ball on the tip of its spume, providing a fish-eye reflection of the installation, similar to Greenough's innovative technique. (16)

Says Mart, 'A number of people worked on it but the Stone Room was my idea. It was taken out of a Magritte painting which has a stone room with a table and all these items on the table. The door was open with a stone landscape. The difference is the Hokusai Wave in the doorway.' (17)

Hokusai's Wave created tension between Martin and Brett. Greg recalls, 'Brett Whiteley was back in town. Brett was intrigued by the Yellow House because he was really the star of the Sydney art world and now there was this other thing taking the spotlight, so he had to get close to it to find out what it was about.' (18)

Jonny remembers Martin and Brett working together on the Wave. Jonny describes their differences, 'Don't let Brett near oceans because he started turning the spray into ejaculate! Every night Martin would come and see this. He would paint over it and put back the Hokusai claw. Next day Brett would come over, look at it and say, "something's wrong here" and he'd paint the sperm back in. This went on for about a week.

'Bruce Goold, me, Brett and Martin were in the room when Martin threw a hammer across the room at Brett. Thankfully it missed. Brett was very shaken. We all were. I remember removing myself discreetly from the room and seeing Brett downstairs pacing up-and-down, smoking very nervously and saying, "He's lost it! He's lost the plot! He's gone! I tell you – he's lost it!"' (19)

To Brett, a master-painter, being over-painted was a real insult. To Martin, Brett was simply being a smartarse at the expense of the total concept. 'I think all the paintings in the building were directed by Martin' is how Roger Foley – Ellis D Fogg – sees it.

After the success of his show in Watters Gallery (an environment called WOOM credited to 'Ellis D Binns and Vivienne Fogg' – to indicate the close collaboration between artists Vivienne Binns and Ellis D Fogg), Albie said, 'Hey Foggy, you've got to come up here, we've got a room for you!' Martin already knew him from the First No Pinky 1966 show where Roger had brought Martin's cartoons the life on the stage.

'And that's when I built the Capsule Room in the Yellow House,' says Roger. 'I didn't live there, ever. I've always been an independent sort of fellow. It was certainly Martin's place, but it was Albie's too – because without Albie it wouldn't have been a "fun" place.' (20)

Sundays were set aside for multi-media music performances, starting with a Thirties Cabaret that Albie and Peter Wright put together. Borrowing tables and chairs from Juillet's restaurant next door, they converted the Cloud Room into a Thirties nightclub. With lights borrowed from Ellis D Fogg and a small stage set up at the end of the room, it featured Little Nell tap dancing to footage of Fats Waller performing Ain't Misbehaving. Actor Gillian Jones joined the performance too.

Writes Albie, 'It was a magical evening that hinted at the mixed-media explorations to come. During this Nell began tap dancing to the music, with the film projected over her. Bruce Goold joined in, wildly whirling around the tiny stage, before crashing into the sheet we were using as a screen, so that it fell over both of them. They continued to dance under it, and Albie projected the film onto the writhing result, creating a kind of kinetic Christo'. (21)

Another Sunday night, Adrian Rawlins read a spirited 21-minute rendition of the Allen Ginsberg poem Howl. Singer/guitarist Greg Quill performed with his band, Country Radio. And highly regarded bands Co-Caine and Sun made a musical contribution for the Yellow House crowd.

But most Sundays nights were lower keyed. Folksingers protested Vietnam. Nic played Japanese koto music. Or maybe Jewellion the Mime (Julian Greig) gave a performance. Martin spotted Jewellion dressed as Pierrot, performing with Jeannie somewhere. So he invited him to perform in the Yellow House. Jewellion moved in with his partner Moth, another clown. They camped in the corridor behind George's Puppet Theatre and busked daily on Bayswater Road. That's where Jewellion got busted and Mal Ramage had to barrister him out of trouble. Jewellion eventually found his way to France to study under Marcelle Marceau. There was a fundraiser. All the Yellow House people helped.

The musical line-up kept growing. Dubbed by Albie, the 'Dylan of the Domain', Peter Royles was a Kings Cross busker, usually located near the El Alamein Fountain.

Peter explained how he got involved, 'I hitchhiked to Sydney from Victoria in 1969. I came to Kings Cross and played guitar in the streets and coffee shops for a few years. I was playing the Domain's Speaker's Corner when David Litvinoff and Bruce Goold asked me to come and play the Yellow House, so I came along and became part of the music with Nic Lyon'. (22)

Peter pitched a tent in the roof and moved in, singing his Dylan songs and accompanying himself on twelve-string guitar and harmonica.

Meanwhile…

…in Eltham Melbourne, Marcus Skipper had formed a country blues band with his brother, classical guitarist Sebastian (Seb) Jorgensen who had returned from London. Seb was a bit of a legend. He'd won an international music award in Italy and shared the same bill as Jimi Hendrix at London's Festival Hall. Both Marcus and Seb were raised at the Montsalvat artist community near Eltham, founded by their father Justus Jorgensen. Ian Reid had visited that community and knew Seb. (23)

Writes Marcus, 'I was fronting a country blues band called Reuben Tice Memorial Band. Sebastian stole it and rebadged it the Oz Band, promising great things'.

The Incredible Oz Band declared their support for the editors of London OZ in their impending trial. Richard, Felix and Jim – the Second Triumvirate – were charged with Obscenity. And while Martin's former associates grappled with the law, the Yellow House crew continued its preparations.

In 1971 before Australia's 3rd Aquarius Festival was held in Canberra (the famous one was 1973, Nimbin NSW). The Incredible Oz Band took the Canberra stage by storm. Their performance was unstructured, confronting and loud. Marcus Skipper pulled down his trousers and dacked the drummer. Next, Adrian Rawlins joined the band for what Marcus described as, 'the longest, biggest, deepest, throatiest OM that ever stirred a solar plexus'.

Marcus continues, 'Adrian was made for the Theatre of the Absurd. He was going to bring style, poetry and charm to spruiking in Macleay Street. He joined our bunch of merry fellows and we bussed up to Sydney, into Kings Cross and the Yellow House. It was too small for our performance potential, so we broke up in bits. The rhythm section played the Magritte Room, the backup and singers went upstairs, Adrian worked the front door and hall and Seb shared the couch with Martin'. (24) Within 18 months Seb would be running the place.

The opening of the Yellow House was planned for Spring. In the interim, and with owner Ian Reid's tolerance, they moved into the next-door premises (No 61) that Ian also bought. Both houses would be joined by a hole knocked in the wall – featuring Lichtenstein's Whaam! and united into an artistic environment with Herman Hesse's Magic Theatre concept very much in mind – ie. price of entry – your mind'.

Money was a constant problem. To help keep the show on the road, Martin put up for sale his personal collection of works by 19th century cartoonist, Livingston Hopkins. Hop, as he was known, had been an influence on Martin from childhood. There were few buyers.

Away from it all, his own upstairs suite, in what Jonny calls Martin's 'salubrious' apartment, Martin was finalising his Catalog. Started in the pre-Yellow House period, this 32-page b/w American quarto-sized visual diary is a collage of his day-by-day gleanings and redolent of Magic Theatre OZ.

Pictures of/by Vincent, Tiny Tim, Robert Crumb, The Phantom, Von Mora, Munch's Scream, early high school Sharp, Magic Theatre Oz, the burning monk, Peanuts, OZ friends and little naked Muybridge figures skipping throughout the pages. Plus words, plenty of words - quoting Vincent, the press, his own diary notes, reviewers, Erich Fromm, an 11-year old boy and a passage about Abraxas. Enter The Little Prince. (25)

Just like the pictures, the writing was a smattering of wherever Martin's thinking was at when he picked up his pen, scissors and glue.

Said Martin, 'The Catalog - you could dive in anywhere, there were no rules as to what you read next. It's a great way of doing a book. I used other people's material. I didn't pay much attention to copyright. I started when we were getting the Yellow House together, while the 59 Macleay Street Exhibition was on. It was something I'd work on every night. I would cut up some quotes, stick them in, do a bit of embossing. It was that multi-level sort of thing'. (26)

The Yellow House was a buzz of activity as everyone involved themselves in preparations for the Spring Exhibition. Visitors chipped in and helped. Says Greg, 'There was this intense 3-4 months preparation, nobody was getting paid, you just had to get in there and do something, paint walls and do things. That concept surprisingly came off. The place just looked like a Christmas tree!' (27) Martin's mother Jo visited the place and said, 'Darling, it's getting more beautiful every day!' (28)

Now living at Lavender Bay, Brett, Wendy and Arkie Whiteley painted one of the rooms white and installed a miniature Moreton Bay fig in its centre, with photographs by Greg on the walls. Brett called it the Bonzai Room. David Litvinoff moved in with the Whiteleys and got pretty close to Brett. Says Jonny, 'Brett adored him. The eccentricity, it was so out there. I think that friendship was so intense that it possibly imploded.'(29)

Ted Markstein adds, 'David Litvinoff introduced Brett to smack. He told Brett that his pictures lacked "a sense of evil", which is not a good thing to tell someone of feeble mind - like Brett'. (30) The dark side of Litva is what that Martin and Eric Clapton never really saw, nor ever faced.

Painter, Antoinette Starkiewicz arrived from Melbourne. Sculptor, Tim Burns landed from Perth. The Sydney University Architecture students who were sent to do assignments on the place were co-opted into painting walls. Roger installed special effects lighting throughout the house. Sue Ellen cooked meals of brown rice and vegetables. Arthur Karvan, who had returned from a year in the US, was co-opted as financial manager and set about the impossible task of trying to raise funds.

Spray guns were brought in to paint the walls and sanders to polish the floors. Works from Martin's collection were added to the show. Among them were Scottish sculptor and artist Eduardo Paolozzi lithographs that Martin offered for sale at $200 apiece. Paintings by Peter Powditch, Philippe Mora and Michael Ramsden were hung. Visiting British fashion designer Zandra Rhodes helped Martin develop an all-white room where he displayed his Van Gogh-inspired drawings, Footsteps on the Road to the Yellow House.

The Ministry of Arts and Culture was a portfolio created in 1971 and Martin invited the new Minister to attend the opening of the Yellow House. He was arriving at 10.00pm. Driving everything to a last minute climax was becoming customary for Martin's openings and this one was no different.

The Yellow House was located next door to Juillet's restaurant, operated by French chef, Patric Juillet and his wife Chrissie Brett. Ian Reid helped kick-start this restaurant where, gangsters, socialites and artists ate at adjacent tables. Poet Allen Ginsberg ate there one evening in company with Brett Whiteley and other Yellow House people. A constant stream of pre-Yellow House and Yellow House stories are set in this restaurant. It was around the corner from their old haunt, Vadim's.

After staying up all night working on the Cloud Room, Infinity Room, Bonzai Room, Puppet Theatre, stairs and every other installation and mural, the exhausted crew staggered to Juillet's for a well-earned bowl of breakfast soup. They noted that the dawn western sky was filthy yellow. Before their last coffees those clouds broke and Macleay Street witnessed a dramatic hailstorm. Everything turned white in 10 minutes. Back at the Yellow House there was roof-drama. The Bucket Brigade galvanized into action while that staircase, so lovingly painted by Bruce Goold just a few hours before, needed major touch-ups. No sleep, now this.

They did it all, of course, with aplomb.

At 10.00pm the government car pulled up outside No 59. Someone from the Yellow House opened the car door and out stepped the Hon George Freudenstein, Minister for Arts and Culture. He walked to the front door to a small fanfare of music led by Nic Lyon on viola. Martin had placed a ribbon on the door, which the Hon snipped before entering. Once inside, there was wet paint everywhere. The combined fumes of the different paints they'd acquired free from the various paint companies hit the nostrils. Said Nic, 'It was pretty hard to walk in there. I don't remember what happened after that. I think we all went to bed. It was all a bit of a blur from then on.' (31)

Albie stayed awake. He recalls the night as a spectacular success, 'The Spring Exhibition at the Yellow House opened with an enormous party that brought Herman Hesse's Magic Theatre to life. As well as the artworks on the walls, Nic Lyon, Seb Jorgensen and Peter Royles provided live music. George Greenough's film was screened and George Gittoes performed a puppet play, while Jewellion's Pierrot glided from room to room. Other Yellow House residents appeared in fancy dress, hired from the Elizabethan Trust, with me choosing a Harlequin suit.

'Our massive installation quickly proved popular with the public, with parents bringing their children and people from the suburbs braving the demimonde of Kings Cross to see the show. It reversed the basic premise of Pop Art. Instead of turning popular imagery into fine art, we turned fine art images into popular art, exemplified by Martin's painting of Mickey Mouse meeting Van Gogh on the road to Tarascon.

'The critics' responses were varied, with the enthusiasts having reservations and the knockers outrightly dismissive. One described it as a "Mardi Gras of Jumping Jack Art" while another thought it "gay, crazy, and full of a mad sort of optimism…a festivity rather than an art exhibition". Another described it as "a continually disrupting and disorientating blend of the serious and unserious, the sophisticated and the slapstick, the vulgar and the nice", and one perceived that it "uses the past almost nostalgically for a statement about the present and the clichéd for an evocation of the new".

'Also damning was Ross Lansell in Nation, who claimed "serious artists have to discard such crutches as togetherness, pleasant though this immediately may be; they have to fight tooth and nail to forge their own various artistic identities, to take the creative process further than they can comfortably bear".'

In a letter to the magazine, Albie responded to Lansell's accusation that the artists were doing it in comfort. Albie wrote, 'we live without money, on one meal a day, with the roof over our heads uncertain, begging, borrowing and stealing materials for our art, ignoring legal restrictions that would have prevented us making it, and promulgating a lifestyle at variance with community standards'. (32)

Despite the newspaper critics, the vast audio-visual environment was attractive to television reporters. The ABC-TV show GTK filmed there on several occasions.

Jonny recalled one slightly edgy occasion, 'I remember Martin saying on GTK about the Yellow House, "It's the greatest conceptual art piece in the world." It was very arrogant of him in some ways – and he regrets it – and I'm thinking, "what does he mean?" I learned that it was Vincent's dream in the south. I still think that's extraordinary, that you would take the dream of one of the greatest artists in the world and recreate it as young people in the south, in the sun. That's fantastic!'

GTK sent a film crew to the opening. They caught up with Litva who was wearing a mask. 'He was fantastic,' says Jonny, 'because they asked "What's the Yellow House?" and Litva said, "There's 325 sexual deviants all living together here and we're making art." He's eating an apple while he's saying this. And I'm thinking, "I'm not a sexual deviant!" But it sounded good.' (33)

The Spring Exhibition continued to attract audiences, paying a dollar-a-head admission with an option on the Catalog for an extra 50c. Martin wrote on the cover 'It should be free'. They took turns on the door to collect the entrance fee, which some visitors objected to paying because the monitoring was inconsistent. One day it might cost $1, next day the doorkeeper had wandered off.

Clayton Simms, who worked at nearby Garden Island, was one visitor, straight off the street. He said, 'I didn't know what the fuck it was, I just thought, "These people want to live in a house with this great painted ceiling…" that's what I thought. It took a long time before I woke up that it was a gallery. I went there one Sunday night and suddenly someone asked me for money. I thought, 'That's it – it's a gallery!' (34) Ian Reid adds, 'I say bullshit – I think he got it right to start with! It was a house with a painted ceiling! If it was a gallery it would have been run like a gallery!' (35)

At the time, Martin poured out his dream to at least one interviewer. He said, 'The only thing we now lack is the people aren't with us. There will come a time when the people are with us. People may come in here who have never painted before. We'll just give them a brush or a musical instrument and they'll suddenly become interested. If this environment can become free enough to make them lose their inhibitions about being creative, and if everyone sang a song, or wrote poems, or drew a picture, or took a photograph, then each of these people would have found a way of understanding life – a way of looking at reality from a disciplined point of view. It's like looking through the lens of a camera, it opens you up'. (36)

The success of the exhibition surprised many but it was not built to last. When the property failed to sell at auction, Ian Reid decided it was time it paid its way with rents. On hearing this, Dicky was furious and Albie stormed out.

Albie writes, 'With Martin in agreement, and Arthur and Mal Ramage supporting him, Ian Reid came up with a proposal for the rental of its residential spaces to people prepared to pay a premium for the privilege of living there. Though I was grateful for the opportunity to have lived and worked in the place, I felt this was an attempt to profit from our labours, without any recompense and I said so at a meeting called in Arthur's apartment to discuss the plan. Martin responded that the Yellow House was his idea and that it was up to him to decide its future, which offended me deeply, since I, along with the others, had contributed so much to its final form. Furious, I stormed out, packed my bag and departed, leaving behind the environment that had taken over my life.' (37)

Said Ian, 'I didn't take on the responsibility of everybody's lives. If an expectation of dependence on me had developed in the Yellow House that was a mistake. It was a greater mistake to think that I had profited from their presence. What I did was provide the place where people could do things. I'll just say that if I asked the people to pay rent – well good on me! The party had to end some time. And if Albie says he stormed out, well – he stormed out. I was thinking, "This has gone far enough".

'Although it kept going with Jorgensen etc – I don't remember what the financial arrangement was (if there was one). That was okay, my life was going in a different direction at the time.' (38)

Ian was a responsible husband and father. He had married Martin's cousin Katie, who he met at the Yellow House.

For 'romantic reasons' (ie. Little Nell) Martin returned to London. Says Martin, 'I wanted to close the place, I didn't witness the last phase. George Gittoes said to shut it down. I felt it was getting too mad, so I shut it down. Sebastian wanted to keep it going.' (39)

Minus Martin, the remaining Yellow Housers took an around-the-kitchen-table vote, and Seb took on the leadership, management or whatever. The tenant proposal was not implemented. It was another eighteen months before the building was sold. In the interim, it was allowed to function as before, with younger artists replacing those who had left.

Albie's film and experimental theatre was replaced by music. Where films like Garry Shead's Ding A Ding Day were once screened, Seb was more interested in musicians. So was Nic Lyon.

Carrl Myriad and Janie Conway played there. Nikki Madden played there. Possibly every notable musician of the time played there. They'd go from playing PACT Folk – Sydney's primo music venue of the time - to the Yellow House. And if Seb or Nic thought they were passable musicians, they'd jam with them.

There were some magic moments. Mic Conway and the Captain Matchbox Whoopee Band played there. Seb asked them to. (They were only 12 months from their hit song My Canary Has Circles Under His

Eyes.) There were six band members plus partners. Mic Conway recalled British comedian Marty Feldman loving the band and hanging around for a day or so. (40) Others recall members of British psychedelic group, Pink Floyd, marvelling at the Stone Room and George Greenough's film. Some see traces of Greenough's influence in Pink Floyd's after-work.

Though the Yellow House continued to attract audiences, its open-to-the-public activities became fewer and less frequent. Some of the rooms were changed, not for the better. One of the original Yellow Housers was Roger Foley whose seniority made him 'responsible'. After Sebastian, he assumed the role of consultant.

Says Roger, 'Some of the young residents were very good artists but they were very young and innocent and could not look after the place. I lived just around the corner and I was happy to do that.

'These were people who lived their art form and were keeping the 60s spirit of peace and love alive. Most of Martin's Art was still in situ as Martin had walked out and gone to London, so Sebastian Jorgensen ran the House for a while, mostly as a live music venue which I continued to support as well as maintaining my Capsule Room environment in the house. One day Seb visited me and said he was returning to Melbourne and could not look after it anymore and gave me the keys to keep an eye on the place as my installation was also still there. I told him I did not want to manage the place but that I would be happy to advise and assist the residents from time to time.'

Roger continues, 'I sort-of became responsible. I had two rooms going, one was the Laser Infinity Room, which used a lot of mirrors and Perspex to create a sense of being in outer space. I'd drop in to see what was going on. "An electricity bill's come in Foggy, what are we going to do?" I said, "You've got to collect money at the door haven't you!"

'I was asked to add another room to fill in some empty space and built The Laser Infinity Room - a high tech take on Greg Weight's Infinity Room. David Ahearn organised a performance, an underground newspaper The Five Cent Joint found a home. Tim Burns was the only other member of the original group still involved, with his 'Road Smash' installation remaining on view.

'A very young Asco Sutinen (now Axel Sutinen) wanted to print a poster for what they were calling The Yellow House Chapter III and asked me if I wanted to be mentioned on it as Chester had asked me to build another environment - now called an 'installation'. I said "terrific" so he gave me a draft copy for me to add a credit about my contribution. There was no space left except on the side of the very busy psychedelic style poster so I quickly wrote a suggestion on the edge thinking that he would rearrange the text to fit it in. I was bemused and then pleased that he just printed it as it was with my writing on the side. Later. I realised that apart from Albie and Dick's Catalogue/Poster for the Spring Opening of both houses in September 1, 1971, and a couple of flyers from Martin and Albie, this was the only poster the House ever had.

'The group, now calling themselves 'Space Environment' included Christine Koltai and Phillip McKeon - now Phillip Arts - running touch and sensitivity classes, Chester Harris who had worked for London OZ - he illustrated Germaine Greer's essay on "Cunt Power" for the Female Energy OZ 29 July 1970 issue - and was now teaching art and continuing to draw extraordinarily graphic erotic works and selling them on the Macleay Street out the front. Also Ian Hartley and Asco Sutinen continued making new art.

'Later in Sydney I got a call from Chester saying there was an electricity bill they could not pay - it seemed no one was collecting the $1 entrance fee. I put together a small arts grant application to pay for a benefit concert at The Cell Block Theatre called Rock Ballet Fantasy, which included the world premier of Christine Koltai's ballet The Dolls, Albie Thoms films, Drum Majorettes, a Highland Pipe band, the Fogg Lightshow and the first public performance of my then girlfriend Gretel Pinniger as Madam Lash, with everyone contributing for free. We were all chuffed that Robert Helpmann came and praised the bizarre collection of performances, however our show did not draw a big enough audience and the electricity bill remained unpaid.

'Local kids started climbing over the fence late at night, stealing artwork including some of my light sculptures. And sadly, and unknown to me at the time, an embittered and inebriated ex-resident would return from time to time and smash artworks in an effort to close the place down.

'I felt like a bit of a Dad sometimes. Eventually people would come in off the street or over the fence at night and were stealing out of the rooms, Martin's pictures started to be smashed and vandals were attacking the place.' (41)

'It seemed as though the place would run down very quickly because of the lack of direction inherent in communal decision making - what we called the 'nice guy' problem - and also through this vandalism and lack of electricity. So I took it upon myself to inform the residents that unfortunately the place would have to close. I believe Ian Hartley rescued some of Martin's work that was still intact and took it to Wirian and closed the door. Some residents were very unhappy about this decision, the end of the dream, but they offered no solutions. I didn't know how to contact Ian Reid so I had to say, "Sorry, you people can't look after it properly, we're going to have to close". I left a message for Mal Ramage and sealed up the place best I could.'

'While collecting my own work I gathered more of Martin's stuff that was lying around damaged, including broken pieces of Abraxas that luckily all still fitted together - how did that get so broken I wondered? I took it all to Jo, Martin's mother who looked aghast at the state of it, put aside a few things and said if I liked it she would sell the rest to me. I offered her $500 for which she gave me a receipt. It seemed a very fair price to me as Martin had sold his Hendrix painting done in the same style as Abraxas to Jim Sharman for $500.' (42)

Over approximately a three-year period the Yellow House went through four phrases, each quite different from the others. All were under Ian Reid's protective ownership umbrella:
- 1970-1971 - pre-Yellow House exhibitions, all Martin.
- 1971-early/1972 - the period generally seen as the Golden Period, with artists under Martin's instruction by day, performers under Albie Thoms' baton by night. The house band was Jeannie Lewis et al, all under Arthur Karvan's general management.
- 1972 - musician Seb Jorgensen ran the place and an emphasis on music replaced the emphasis on film.
- 1972/early-1973 - young people moved in until Roger Foley closed the place for keeps.

The Yellow House Catalogue is one of the Yellow House's few in-house publications. It lists the following names as artists/contributors: 'Ian Reid,

Bliss, George Gittoes, Bruce Goold, Karen Hobby, Peter Kingston, Jon Lewis, Nic Lyon, Moth, Mal Ramage, Peter Royles, Sue-Ellen, Martin Sharp, Albie Thoms, Greg Weight, Peter Wright, Dick Weight, John Bee, Tim Burns, Bob Daley, Ellis D Fogg, Lyn Fuller, Franklin Johnston, Slavka Jovic, Arthur Karvan, Kaleidoscope, Tim Lewis, David Litvinoff, Aggy Read, Zandra Rhodes, Jim Sharman, Brian Thomson, Brett Whiteley, Wendy Whiteley, Julie Clarke and Trisha.' (43)

Maybe 1000 people painted, performed or helped in some way around the Yellow House. Maybe more.

Tim Lewis is among the unlisted artists. He was friends with Jonny Lewis, Bruce Goold and Dick Weight and lived with his parents at Double Bay. Tim says, 'I didn't finish East Sydney Tech because I went to the Yellow House instead. I certainly wasn't a prime player. I helped with Magritte Room.' Within a couple of years Tim would be working side-by-side with Martin, as Greg had done previously. (44)

Says Ted Markstein, who lived directly across the street, 'From my observation the Yellow House was absolutely incandescent for about seven months then it started to fall apart. Given the players, I'd say it was amazing it got seven months!' (45)

Ian Reid commented that he watched the Yellow House disintegrate, 'When Martin left, the creative energy and funding to pay the bills dried up. By the time the doors were closed it was 10 minutes past the hour. The properties were in a mess. It was costly to remediate and should have ended sooner.

'The role of patron isn't easy. While it's rewarding to support creativity, it's a failure to create dependence. At the end of the day, artists succeed if they have talent - and hopefully a "start" helps them along the way. With the wisdom of hindsight things might have happened differently but the Yellow House was a "happening". It provided the venue and I'm proud to have done so, it's become a part of our history and I have no regrets.' (46)

When the Yellow House was over, 57-61 Macleay Street became a boarding house until sold.

12.

YESTERDAY'S PAPERS

Sharp's grafts, looking simultaneously so familiar and extraordinary, help to recharge the originals.
GEORGE MELLY

Four years before, when London OZ launched its very first issue, the names usually associated with the publication were Martin, Richard and an under-acknowledged Louise Ferrier. Her leading role in OZ has seldom been fully credited. Some say that's because Louise is not a person to seek attention. Others say it's because women's contributions were consistently underplayed in those early pre-feminist days. In establishing OZ, Louise was involved in everything from business decisions to cover girl. She allowed the use of her premises and played the part of secretary as needed.

When Martin returned to London in 1972, Dr Germaine Greer's book The Female Eunuch had been around long enough to seep into cultural attitudes about women's rights. Published in October 1970 by MacGibbon & Kee, within its first six months the book was reprinted six times and translated into 11 languages. (1)

Greer reasoned that though women do not realise it, men subconsciously hate them and so women are taught by society to hate themselves. Groups who formerly saw themselves as politically correct were branded as guilty as the rest. Liberationist groups, participants in the Sexual Revolution, acid-eaters, American Beats, the Sydney Push, the Baby Push, Yellow House artists (designated a 'Men's Club' by participant Juno Gemes (2)), even the ideology-proud OZ editors, were shocked to read of themselves as having reenacted the sins of their fathers!

When Martin returned to London a different OZ trio was in the public consciousness, one that would famously always be associated with London OZ – charismatic gadabout Richard Neville, former OZ street-salesperson Felix Dennis and enthusiastic newcomer Jim Anderson. The three had created one helluva kerfuffle while Martin was gone.

Going back to January 1969 – OZ 17 – featured Jenny Kee and Louise's nude cover photo with Martin's Question Mark as background.

OZ 19 – Germaine cheekily unzipping Viv Stanshall's fly – ie. Viv from the Bonzo Dog Doo Dah Band. Thus far, with Richard peppering his endeavours with overseas trips, OZ editors Jim and Felix were traveling quite well.

Next, Hells Angels OZ, followed by OZ 22, an issue Jim Anderson would rather forget. Martin's Moon & Mickey Mouse cover restored confidence with readers in OZ 23 – 1969 the year of the Moon walk.

Then came Homosexual OZ with a cover photo of two of Jim's friends, a black guy and a white guy in a naked embrace - cock-to-cock as it were. OZ was right up with the times. Gay Liberation was on the move with spontaneous, violent demonstrations by the gay community at the Stonewall Hotel in Greenwich Village NY. Jim welcomed the subject, Felix didn't.

'Who's going to buy it Jim?' questioned Felix. Felix had cover-ideas of his own. He wanted to use Bob Seidemann's picture of a barebreasted adolescent girl holding a silver airplane. It wasn't the Blind Faith album cover yet.

Says Jim, 'Felix fought really hard to have it on the cover. I had my first experience of coming up against the brick wall that was Felix Dennis. Felix did react very poorly. He banged my head against a brick wall. Felix was so strong – that's why he became a multi-millionaire in his wheelings and dealings with other people. You couldn't handle him.

'He gave way eventually so my cover was on – it sold out immediately. When the police realized what it was, they came around immediately and seized 25 copies of what we had left. Everything else was gone. Richard was away, he was always away…'. (3)

Although the OZ team didn't take it seriously, they were under police surveillance. Jim explains his casual approach, 'It was a warning but we were just treating it as a joke. We just did what we did at the time. We were part of the cultural upheaval, the anti-establishment feeling, the revolution. That's all it was. It was part of the territory. It was all around. We weren't more provocative than anybody else, we were just a bit more popular – we were distributed nationally – we were more dangerous in the eyes of the government.'

Then to Felix and Jim's dismay, two issues later in Women's Liberation OZ, Richard wrote, 'We are feeling old and boring at OZ…' and he asked schoolkids to contribute. Says Jim, 'Felix and I laughed when we saw that because we were not old and boring, we were the brand new boys at OZ full of enthusiasm and raring to go! When we were left alone, we exercised things to the max - I suppose - with our newly-found freedom – with Richard away. He was quite shocked with what happened with Schoolkids OZ!' (4) Richard Neville shocked. Now…that's a thought.

Next - Acid OZ, using Timothy Leary and an outrageous Robert Crumb cover with an acid-eater's eyes popping out of their sockets. Jim explained how this led to a big disagreement with Martin, 'For the Acid issue Martin sent us something from Sydney - which was a Mickey Mouse. In the Mickey Mouse frame was a blank space like a television screen with nothing in it. David Wills and I were looking at Martin's b/w illustration. I said, "David we can't have a black and white thing in a psychedelic issue, everything else is psychedelic, what can we do?"

'I said, "We can put in something in that blank space" and so I put in *Acid is good for you*. David and I did it together. Martin hated it. He never said anything to me directly but he really felt insulted by that. It seems that was the origin of a certain distance that always existed between Martin and me.' (5)

The next issue, OZ 28, May 1970, was the infamous Schoolkids Issue. Martin had nothing to do with it. Robert Hughes had an article in it. Thirteen months later – 23 June 1971 - Richard, Jim and Felix fronted the Old Bailey on charges of publishing obscene material and sending indecent material through the post. Nobody had ever been sent to jail for that before. What followed was the longest and most entertaining obscenity trial in history.

In support, John Lennon wrote the song God Save OZ. (6) Yoko wrote Do The OZ. Later came an off-Broadway production The Trials of OZ, a one-hour television film called The Trials of OZ, and a book by Tony Palmer also called The Trials of OZ. The trial cost British taxpayers £80,000. (7)

At the sentencing, there was something spiteful about Justice Michael Argyle's closing address, describing Felix as having limited ability and being a dupe of the other defendants. That insult cut Felix and probably motivated him to show his detractors he was second to none. The three accused were convicted of obscenity and given sentences ranging from nine to fifteen months imprisonment. They were released on appeal, at which the trial judge was severely reprimanded for misdirecting the jury.

All this happened while Martin had been running the Yellow House in Sydney.

Robert Hughes was appointed art critic for Time magazine in 1970 and had moved to New York. Eric had formed Derek & the Dominos, released a double album, retreated to Hurtwood Edge and sought privacy. Performance had been released to some sort of acclaim. Syd Barrett wasn't well. The Beatles had officially broken up. Philippe's film Trouble in Molopolis had been screened to positive reviews. Granny Takes a Trip had opened a branch in New York. And King's Road had made the shift from Bohemia to conspicuously fashionable. Said Martin, 'After the Pheasantry things started to go. Kings Road had a big tourist thing at that stage. You'd walk out in the street and they'd be taking snaps of local bohemians. You get a bit sick of it.' (8)

The whole scene had changed. Says Martin, 'King's Road Chelsea was still there but it was all over, disseminated, died or whatever.' (9)

Martin went in search of Little Nell, who had moved to England with her family. Nell got her toehold working the Portabello Road street markets. Her stall was next to Freddy Mercury's stall (later, singer of the band Queen). A couple of years had passed since Jim Sharman had shown Richard O'Brien's draft for the Rocky Horror Show to Philippe. What may have seemed like a corny idea back then was rapidly turning into a brilliant show in need of a tap dancer.

When Martin caught up with Nell in London, she was shaping up for the Rocky Horror role of Columbia in the West End stage show and – although nobody knew it yet – also the film. It was Nell's big break.

Actor Lex Marinos feels aspects of the Rocky Horror set design and costuming was more influenced by Martin than is generally acknowledged. Looking back, he said, 'I think Rocky Horror owes a lot to Martin, a lot of that imagery. It's brilliantly done but I can't help feeling Martin's influence was enormous on that show'. (10)

Little Nell's Mickey Mouse ears in the Toucha Toucha Touch Me sequence certainly seem like something Martin might have suggested. For a short time, almost everything Martin touched went a bit Mickey Mouse.

Those ears showed up again the following year when Martin designed the costumes for a stage show called Kaspar in which all characters wore Mickey Mouse ears.

Martin says, 'After the Yellow House I went back to London, with no money in my pocket, to see Nell. I had to get out of Sydney. I'd been writing to Nell a lot. I was in love with her, which - through the letters - was wonderful. I got there, we stayed a night in the Ritz and the money was gone.' (11)

Returning to his Kings Road haunts, Martin found people talking about other things, like Glam bands. Forget the glory days of Cream, Martin said, 'That scene had passed and another scene had taken over'. (12) King's Road was full of New Romantics who were evolving into Punks. A short walk from the Pheasantry up King's Road took you to No. 430 where Vivienne Westwood and partner Malcolm McLaren opened a boutique called Let It Rock. It would be better known in its next incarnation under the name SEX - selling bondage clothes as Punk streetwear. That's where Chrissie Hynde, later the singer of the band the Pretenders, would work as a shop assistant and where the Sex Pistols formed.

Martin stayed with friends, socialised and attempted to gather the possessions he had left after his previous stay. He said, 'I returned to London for romantic reasons but I was broke at the time and I really wasn't in a position to go anywhere. London was different, the people I knew were yesterday's papers and there was a new crowd in. I didn't have the Pheasantry anymore. I stayed with the Campbell sisters who were very kind to me. I worked for Big O Posters and did another exhibition'. (13)

He also ransacked small print galleries looking for affordable works, particularly by Magritte, which he found, purchased and brought back to Australia. He was also looking for Hokusai prints.

Martin's central project was continuing Art Book collage experiments that he had started at the Pheasantry. Martin felt as comfortable with scissors-and-paste as with a paintbrush. He was never shy about snipping pictures out of expensive art books if he had a worthy idea. Martin cut up pictures by Old and New Masters, reconfigured the images and glued 74 familiar fine art images in new and unexpected contexts. In time, art critics called his process 'Appropriation'.

In 1990 Martin admitted, 'I still don't know what Appropriation means, but I knew I was onto something with those collages and cutting up the art books. It was like I was going around looking for a parking spot and there's a spot in a crowded area – Oh, I'll just zip in there! It was as simple as that. It was real hard work but it was as simple as that'. (14)

At the time, they were a quiet success. The pictures were launched and celebrated at Sigi Krauss Gallery, Covent Garden. (15)

Jazz and Blues singer, critic, writer and lecturer, George Melly reviewed the show under the title Double Exposures. He wrote, 'Superficially, the fascination of the pictures comes from Sharp's skill at combining very unlikely images which manage to gel instantly and convincingly'. His conclusion gave Martin the thumbs up. 'I find these works more than simple aesthetic experiments. What most of his sources share originally is the fascination of icons, but modern icons tend through constant reproduction to lose their magic. Sharp's grafts, looking simultaneously so familiar and extraordinary, help to recharge the originals. His title is well chosen.' (16)

Publishers of Martin's Art Book, Mathews, Miller and Dunbar had made a name for themselves through their much-loved Art Deco-style book The English Sunrise. (17) That format explains the striking design of Martin's book, its simplicity, clarity and lots of white space. A significant difference is The English Sunrise is 8x8 where Art Book is 6x5. 'It's a wonderful book,' said Martin. 'I thought Art Book should be in that same small format. I think they should re-run it!' (18)

Martin described his process, 'Popular Song was a big part of it, collages about music and migration of images through painting through reproduction. It came at a moment when reproduction had moved far enough from the original images for us to be free with them. I started to cut up my art books, so Gauguin figures in van Gogh landscapes, Magritte figures in De Chirico landscapes. This inter-twining, as if the barriers had broken down between the individual world of painters and all the characters were inter-mingling in each other's pictures.' (19)

What to do about Tiny Tim was also constantly on Martin's mind. Tiny's second album had been less well received. (20)

Tiny's star had tumbled quite a bit since the Albert Hall Concert. He had enjoyed two huge moments only, 17 December 1969, his TV wedding to Miss Vicki's aired to an audience of 40 million people on the Johnny Carson Show. And he stole the show at the Isle of Wight Festival held 30

August 1970 before 600,000 people. The stadium was cramped, the sound appalling and the toilets disgusting. There were fights, broken fences, a prevailing sense of menace and lots of mud.

Joni Mitchell demanded respect. 'I'm an artist' she bleated to a barrage of cans. Jimi Hendrix had equipment problems, re-started, apologised, tried again and thanked the audience for their patience. Miles Davis found it pointless. Donovan and Ralph McTell felt the same. And then, like a ray of sunshine, out came Tiny Tim with his little ukulele, bassist and a light drummer.

In 2004 Q Magazine listed what followed as one of the Top 10 live performances in Rock history – Tiny Tim singing a medley built around Rule Brittania and There'll Always Be an England to an audience whose mood suddenly changed from mean to…singing along with Tiny Tim! Those were the only two great Tiny Tim moments since Martin had seen him in Luton.

On the other side of the ledger was the release of the high camp, low quality, bootleg LP titled Concert in Fairyland. It was a collection of studio demos - including On The Good Ship Lollipop and Animal Crackers - recorded back in 1962 way before he was famous.

The album lacked dignity. The cover art was crook. Tiny's fans thought it really was his third album. Was Tiny Tim some kind of joke? (21) A joke Tiny himself encouraged on his many television appearances, most prominently Rowan & Martin's Laugh-In. Sometimes he stole the show for all the wrong reasons but at the time, singing in the high voice and camping it up for a giggling public paid the bills, at least.

Tiny's management didn't seem to know what to make of him. Instead of giving him swooner-crooner songs that had worked so well in the past – unbelievably they followed the direction of that terrible bootleg and had Tiny sing On The Good Ship Lollipop, Oliphant the Elepant, Mickey the Monkey, I'm a Lonesome Little Raindrop and other puerile tunes. (22)

Turning Tiny Tim into a children's act was a silly idea. Tiny was more relaxed with cross-dressers than with children! None of this seemed to bother Martin. He saw beyond the joke. Martin had seen him at his glorious best and wanted to make a film starring Tiny Tim, who – despite ups-and-downs – was still one of the most famous faces in show business.

Martin said, 'I would have been always angling for it. The idea for the film came from the desire to work with Tiny ever since I saw him at the Albert Hall. When I saw him I thought he would become huge and I was looking forward to following his career. So I followed his career, but it started to vanish, I got worried about it, so I started to talk to film industry people.' (23)

Film was the medium of the time. Film and performance art had welded the Yellow House together in the evenings: Albie Thoms, Peter Weir, Garry Shead, Peter Kingston, Ellis D Fogg, and psychedelic surf filmmakers George Greenough and Paul Witzig. Also, while attending Armidale University, Martin's cousin Sandy (Alexander) Sharp co-wrote a script called Private Collection, a 1972 film featuring Pamela Stephenson, Grahame Bond, Noel Ferrier and Michael Caton. Sandy's brother Andrew (who had helped at the Yellow House) had been a child star playing the stage role of the Artful Dodger. Film was everywhere. Even Brett Whiteley shot film.

Meanwhile in London, Rocky Horror was on its way up. Bruce Beresford's The Adventures of Barry McKenzie was a big success. Having succeeded with his Trouble in Molopolis, Philippe Mora was working on his next film Swastika - controversially about Adolf Hitler's home life. Though banned in Germany, it would be released in 1973 to critical acclaim in the United States, England and France. Martin knew all this. And having worked on the edges of Performance, Martin had quite a few film industry contacts of his own.

Donald Cammell was Martin's first contact. Martin gave him a copy of his failed attempt to tape Tiny Tim. The tape was probably unlistenable and did nothing to capture Cammell's interest. But Sandy Lieberson, who founded the British production company Goodtimes Enterprises, saw a future in musical film starring the pop stars of the times. Lieberson was formulating plans for That'll Be The Day (1973 – David Essex and Ringo Starr) followed by Ken Russell's Lisztomania (1975 – Roger Daltrey). Lieberson was keen to hear Martin out, but Martin had no script, no contact with Tiny, just a general idea and a lot of enthusiasm.

Martin also approached Pete Townshend who was flush with the success of his Rock Opera Tommy. Townshend was sympathetic. He even offered the use of his home-studio facility. Martin explained, 'Pete Townshend has always had a very soft spot for Tiny. I think he felt guilty when they appeared together at the Scene in New York and Tiny had to follow the Who between major acts. Pete promised to introduce him with a big flourish but the boys in the band pushed Pete into another direction. He neglected it and he always remembered that as the time he let Tiny down.' (24)

As well as Art Book, Big O Posters, the last days of London OZ and discussions about filmmaking, Martin also looked up designer Zandra Rhodes, who had visited the Yellow House where their friendship began. She wrote, 'Martin Sharp, painter/cartoonist had his exhibition at the Yellow House and this was a great inspiration to me. He stayed with me in London, becoming a good friend'. (25)

Zandra invited Martin and Nell to model her first jumper for a Vogue magazine fashion shoot. Wearing pink, green, blue with bat sleeves and ducktails – Nell nibbled Martin's ear with Martin looking suitably sheepish in a striped top. (26)

Then from London to Paris, where Martin stayed with Matí and Sophie Klarwein, whom he had known since Pheasantry days. Matí's fame had grown through his album cover art. His Miles Davis double album cover, Bitches Brew and Santana's Abraxas were almost as famous as Disraeli Gears. Matí and Sophie also knew Salvadore Dalí.

While hanging out with people-who-knew-people (or at least knew where they lived) Martin decided to look up Man Ray who resided in Montparnasse. Martin admired Man Ray enormously. He had combined

Man Ray's 'lips' with an Edvard Munch bridge scene in Art Book. Martin didn't have a contact. It was a cold call.

In November of the previous year Man Ray had received massive acclaim in a monumental retrospective of 278 works at the Boymans-van Beuningen Museum in Rotterdam. The show was then to tour Paris, Denmark and finally, in triumph, to the Philadelphia Museum of Art. But at the last moment the Philadelphia Museum of Art changed its mind claiming it did not have the funds to bring the show to America. (26) Whether this was on his mind when he met Martin, we don't know, but it was a disappointing encounter.

Martin describes the meeting, 'Man Ray was with his wife, the model for many of his pictures. He was most upset that he'd never been given the accolades as a painter. I thought he held his own in photography alone. He took Magritte into the realm of photography. Beautiful simple images. I think he created some the greatest Surrealist images.

'That was what was bothering him. There was something that wasn't right as far as he was concerned - he hadn't been honoured. Complaining about Picasso getting so much money - something like that. It was a bit disappointing. I gave him an OZ magazine.' (28)

Martin's encounter with Salvadore Dalí was much more colourful.

With views of the Tuileries Garden, Le Meurice has been ranked among the most elegant hotels in the world. Each of the seven floors has a distinct style, with suites decorated in the style of Louis XVI and exquisite Italian marble bathrooms. Le Meurice was Salvadore and Gala Dalí's usual residence when staying Paris. They would arrive like royalty, with entourage, courtiers, performers, the works.

The Dalís were hosting the smart young people, the demi-mode, regulars from Dalí's Port Lligat studio/residence, transgender performer Amanda Lear, the Miles twins - who appeared in Performance as velvet-wearing Baudelarian figures carrying a Magritte painting, and the well-connected Spaniard Carlos Lozano. Sophie invited Martin to accompany her.

'Sophie was like a Matisse painting,' Martin describes. 'She was pure nostalgic Paris. Not many people in Paris had an idea of Pop Art but she did.' And so Martin came to meet the artist who counted The Great Masturbator (1929) amongst his Surrealist masterworks, 'Dalí was enthroned. This was his court. Incredible Spanish dancing, fantastic singing, flamenco guitars, stamping feet. And then it was upstairs to his room. It was the young and beautiful people - a sort of soirée going on. Sophie and I were about the oldest there.

'Dalí would come in, pair them off and send them into this room. Gradually pair-by-pair they were called into another room, and eventually all that was left was Sophie and I left outside. Then he came in again and took us to meet Gala. Gala was lying in bed. Both talked to us and then he showed us out.

'The next day we found out that he'd set up this orgy – extraordinary! All these people were involved in this orgy - about 20 people. There was this beautiful brother and sister from Morocco. One of these handsome Miles twins was fucking this guy's sister from Morocco. The brother dragged the Miles boy off and made love to his own sister. This was the quintessential thrill for Dalí – incest - this bizarre chemistry. He'd set the whole thing up. What an amazing memoir!' (29)

Martin walked the streets of Paris in his spare time, checking out art shops. He described one defining moment, 'I was very interested in Japanese prints. It was my hobby, I'd see if I could find any anywhere, because they were still rather cheap. In Rue de Banque I found this little shop that sold Japanese pictures. There was a big pile on the floor. I was looking through 200 of them. I was particularly interested in Hokusai. I recognised some by Hokusai, various other prints, and right at the bottom there was this fantastic picture, the best by far of the pile - which was full of excellent material. It was this abalone diver.

'Abalone divers are always women. They used to work from boats, dive down, cut the abalone off the rocks and come up again. And here's this most graceful Arabesque figure, a beautiful print. The shape of the hair reminded me of the curl of the stars in Starry Night. I thought, It looks like Utamaro. I asked her how much it was, it was 200 francs. I didn't have the money at the time but when I got the money I went back and picked up the print. I was very thrilled with it.

'I took it to more up-market Japanese print shop. I showed her this print and she said, Oh, this is by Hokusai! I couldn't believe this stroke of amazing luck finding a Hokusai - and one that I'd never seen before!

'I finished the mural, did one more in a shop somewhere, went back to London and took it to the Victoria & Albert Museum. Walking in with it wrapped up under my arm, people were reacting in a strange way to me as I was walking through the corridors, as if they sensed that I had a very rare picture under my arm.

'I wanted to get it identified. The guy in the Oriental Art section turned up a reference to it in a book called Decorative Arts Of Japan by an American woman published in about 1920. He said he knew the great English expert on Hokusai, Joseph Hillier. He said he'd check with him. (30)

'I went back some weeks later. He said he checked with this scholar and it might be a drawing after a painting by Hokusai or a print after a painting by Hokusai, but it wasn't a Hokusai. He offered me a small amount of money for it, which I refused. I brought it back to Australia.' (31)

Andy Warhol and his entourage came to Paris to film L'Amour around the same time as Martin discovered the picture he now dubbed The Lost Hokusai. 1974 had been a watershed year for Warhol. His outrageous 60s were shifting into his entrepreneurial 70s. Warhol's films had received both desultory and acclamatory reviews. He and his gang of assistants and hangers-on flitted between New York and Europe rounding up new rich patrons for portrait commissions. Martin was curious. Andy and Paul Morrissey were doing a film shoot in fashion designer, Karl Lagerfeld's apartment.

'Some Swedish girl was going to interview him,' said Martin, 'she took me along. He was making a film with Paul Morrissey - swept back hair, strong jaw, glasses. We went into this house. Joe Dellasandro and people were making the picture. In the central room of the house Andy Warhol was sitting knitting this dark green scarf, which was about 15 feet long.

'Very quiet and I thought very interesting. If he weren't there, nothing would be happening. He's the eye of the storm, sitting there calm, meditating. He provided the stillness so all the action could happen. I thought that was pretty impressive.' (32)

Martin returned to London, gathered his Magritte prints and the Art Book pictures, came to an arrangement with Big O Posters and wondered why his Tiny Tim film project was being greeted with indifference. As for OZ? He didn't quite drop OZ nor did he drop in. Editor Jim Anderson doesn't recall ever seeing him during this period, yet Martin continued to send occasional contributions.

One of Martin's most significant spreads came in OZ 43, A Letter From an Idle Fellow by Vincent to Theo in 1890. The letter affirms Vincent's belief that everything good comes from God and goes on to question one's métier or 'calling', from which Vincent sadly concluded that he was probably seen by society as 'an idle man of the worst type'. The article is illustrated with seven of Martin's pictures, including his Double Vincent collage, later to appear in Art Book. (33) Ten years to the day of writing this letter, Vincent van Gogh committed suicide.

Then, right out of the blue, came a commission that would affect Martin for life, 'I was down & out in London when I got an invitation to repaint the entrance to Luna Park, from Leon Fink!' (34)

In April 1969 the remaining six years of Luna Park's lease and contents had been sold for $750,000 to a consortium of business people called the World Trade Centre P/L, which included Leon Fink and partner Nathan Spatt. World Trade Centre P/L applied to construct a $50 million International Trade Centre on the Luna Park site. Approval was refused after which Leon Fink and Nathan Spatt formed Luna Park Holdings P/L, and they continued to run the place as an amusement park. In 1972 they announced a general program to upgrade the whole park. (35)

Leon's wife Margaret Fink had known Martin from early-60s university days when Martin had shyly checked out the Sydney Push where she, Margaret Elliott then, was a regular. Not as daunting as Germaine – but daunting.

'Leon Fink's wife Margaret knew me as an artist and cartoonist,' wrote Martin. She made the connection between Fairground Art and Pop Art and suggested that Martin would be the right artist to redesign the Face of Luna Park.

Martin took Leon's offer extremely seriously. He wrote, 'I approached it not as a sign painter or a person of the carnival, but as an intellectual artist. Like many people, I knew Luna Park as a permanent part of our landscape. I had never particularly liked it as a child but when I was a cartoonist for OZ magazine I did draw that smile as an image, which I also used in painting. (36)

'I suppose I could be described as a Pop Artist, drawing on the landscape of popular culture for imagery. Luna Park was very much that - the largest sculpted image of a face in Australia and entering through a huge mouth (certainly a Medieval image of the Gateway to Hell) one found a world of artistically primitive, but nonetheless powerful images, comic and grotesque.' (37)

13.

COUNTERCULTURE GOES MAINSTREAM

I left Australia in September 1967 and I didn't come back until 1971 and I was amazed in that brief period of time - 'Goodness me, something's happened!'

GARY SHEARSTON

After 23 years of Conservative rule, the close of 1972 saw the Australian Labor Party win government and the new Prime Minister Gough Whitlam speedily push through a raft of reforms that would radically change Australia's economic, legal and cultural landscape. Most urgently, the new Labor government abolished conscription and completed the process of disengagement in the Vietnam military campaign. The universities were no longer battlefields of protest.

Whitlam embarked on a wide-sweeping campaign of social reform that included healthcare, social security, education, Indigenous Affairs, Foreign Affairs, Women's issues, national symbols, environment, heritage and cultural affairs. The Family Law Act 1975, with its no-fault divorce, is one initiative that Martin would have welcomed a decade earlier, having witnessed the injustice that his mother was made to endure through the old system of lumping the blame on one party or the other. (1)

Change is what Martin came back to. A cheeky soapie called No 96 was a popular TV favourite, the critically acclaimed film Wake in Fright introduced brutal realism into Australian film and the Aboriginal Tent Embassy was erected in front of Parliament House (now Old Parliament House) to represent the political rights of Indigenous Australians.

Weirdly (for some) counter-culture had merged with the mainstream. Almost everyone under the age of 25 had smoked marijuana and skinny-dipped at least once. Young people didn't dress up - they dressed down. Bank clerks grew their hair and schoolteachers quit wearing ties.

On Australia Day 1972 the Sunbury Music Festival was held on a 620-acre farm outside Melbourne. Forty-five thousand hippies showed up. Adrian Rawlins was co-compere. Then a second antipodean Woodstock captured headlines when ten thousand alternative lifestylers converged on the little north NSW town of Nimbin for the 1973 Aquarius Festival. Many remained and set up communes. Now, back in the country – Richard and Louise were right on the spot. (2)

During Martin's absence, the Yellow House crowd had dispersed. Its legend had grown. A fully-fledged 'Yellow House person' was a highly credible thing to have been.

Greg had married Suzie Cuthbert – Suzie who introduced Martin to Eric Clapton and prompted Martin to scribble the lyrics to Tales of Brave Ulysses on a serviette. Bruce Goold concentrated on linocuts and woodblocks of Australian flora and fauna. George Gittoes experimented with holograms and computer-generated images. Garry Shead enjoyed artistic pilgrimages to Toyko, Paris and the United States. Roger Foley-Fogg could be spotted flashing around town in an open-topped car with girlfriend Madam Lash (Gretel Pinniger). Jonny Lewis was establishing his reputation as a photographer. Peter Royles headed north. Adrian Rawlins was emceeing major Rock festivals. Jeannie Lewis performed shows and joined the Music Board of the Australia Council of the Arts.. Nic Lyon was working in theatre and Arts Festivals. Jenny Kee opened the Flamingo Park fashion boutique in Sydney's fabulous Strand Arcade with designer-partner Linda Jackson. Brett Whiteley was a Sydney art legend. In a way they all were. And David Litvinoff was planning to return England. (3)

The Australian Council for the Arts, informally known as the Arts Council (established 1967), was strengthened under the Whitlam Government. Albie Thoms was a beneficiary of a $5000 grant from the Experimental Film and Television Fund to make Sunshine City a film to mark his return to Sydney from Europe. (4)

The strengthening of the arts in an official sense marked the demise of the arts in an unofficial sense. All those slightly chaotic inner-city amateur poetry readings, agitprop theatres and 'Happening' events were forced to either step up or close down.

The standout venue at this time was the Old Stables Theatre, a small, austere building more than one hundred years old, which had previously been a stable, taxi garage and gymnasium. There, actor/director John Bell, director Richard Wherrett and entrepreneur Ken Horler formed the Nimrod Theatre Company, which strove for excellent Australian content. Many of their connections linked to early-60s Sydney University revues.

Nimrod gained growing support from Australia Council - from $6500 in 1971 to $33,200 in 1973. (5) During that period attendances more than doubled from 18,763 to 44,550. (6) Using only the best playwrights and best actors, Nimrod gained a formidable reputation for staging quality Australian plays.

In his book, See How It Runs, writer Julian Meyrick sums it up, 'Throughout the course of its artistic life Nimrod flirted with pieces that evinced qualities opposed to its usual fare: productions that were dark (not light), interior (not exterior), spiritual (not social), difficult (not accessible), silent (not convivial).' (7)

Another change was Folk Music, which had carved itself a niche in the mainstream. From its beginnings as convict ballads and Labor songs sung in pubs, the movement had transformed into an articulate political voice. Artists like Jeannie Lewis, Margret Roadknight, Don and Marion Henderson, Michael Driscoll, Pat Drummond, Black Allen Murawalla,

Gary Shearston and John Ewbank were regulars at the old Corn Exchange building in Sussex Street named PACT House. Many of these singers had performed at the Yellow House. (PACT Folk moved to the YWCA Building in Liverpool Street in 1970.)

Jeannie was Martin's principal contact with this group - but there were others as well. 'Black Allen' Murawalla was the first Indigenous Australian that Martin got to know. ('Same for me,' said Jeannie, who had known him from the folk circuit, 'Black Allen was my first Aboriginal contact personally.') (8)

Gary Shearston was another folkie friend. With a poke at the Australian OZ trial, Gary had a 1965 hit with his song Sydney Town. Gary struck out for England and America in 1967 and came home to a very different country. Amazed by the difference Gary exclaimed, 'Goodness me, something's happened!' (9) Around this time Gary wrote the song Dingo, a song that Martin would see as fraught with symbolic meaning (10)

That's the kind of Sydney to which Martin returned thanks to Gough Whitlam, Australia Arts Council, Nimrod Theatre, PACT Folk, Germaine Greer, the OZ trials, the Aboriginal Tent Embassy and the nearly completed Sydney Opera House. Innovators like Albie Thoms, Garry Shead, Brett Whiteley, Greg Weight, Ellis D Fogg, Black Allen Murawalla, Jeannie Lewis, Seb Jorgensen, Dicky Weight, Philippe Mora, oh – such a long list. They all had a part to play in chipping down the Alfs and the Norman Normals. It's fair to say: OZ won.

Martin's parents were now eight years separated and divorced four. In an attempt to reconcile with his father, Martin chose to live with Henry and stepmother Dorothy for a time. He intended to paint his next exhibition – Art Exhibition – at their harbourfront place in Shellcove Road Neutral Bay. Dr Henry Sharp was now a Fellow of the Australian Medical Association with a string of honorariums, notably the Royal Alexandria Hospital for Children, Eastern Suburbs Hospital, Prince of Wales and Prince Henry Hospitals. He was a Macquarie Street dermatologist who explained his job to Martin as, 'You can't kill them and you can't cure them!'

Martin explains what happened when he moved in, 'I was going to live in the boatshed, have a studio there, do my exhibition there. I took over a few pictures that were important to me and put them up. I particularly liked a Peter Powditch one.

'My father came down and looked at them in a disparaging way and I felt, "I can't create here, this person doesn't respect that I'm hanging up my own pictures in a space I'm meant to be living in!" So I wasn't made welcome. As soon as he disapproved of those pictures I'd hung up I realised that his territorial imperative was so strong. I came back with Mum.

'I think when I held on for Wirian, (ie. heir apparent) that was the turning point because I didn't go to my father's side, I stayed with my mother's. He said to me that night, "That could cost you your patrimony!" – meaning - by hanging on to Wirian.' (11)

And so Martin went back to Jo. Back to Cranbrook Lane. Back to his playroom with the Hornby train set that he used to crash when his parents fought. Back to where he and Greg had painted the Art for Mart's Sake exhibition in 1964.

Martin used some of his Art Book collages as studies for the 10 pictures that he intended to return to their original medium as completed paintings. Over the next three months Tim Lewis assisted in what started out slowly, before peaking as all-night sessions. Said Martin, 'It must have been hard for Tim because the original designs were mine but we became a unit beyond ego in order to do a job.' (12)

Twenty-two year old Tim Lewis was a former Cranbrook student who was in Form One when Martin was completing his final year. He too was a product of Justin O'Brien's art classes. Tim learned to love Martin's art when he attended East Sydney Tech from where he soon found his way to the Yellow House. Said Tim, 'Jonny took me to the Yellow House. Martin was there. Martin said, Here's a paintbrush – go for it...'

That's how they met.

After the Yellow House, Tim moved to Double Bay and continued with his own paintings of geometric abstractions. Tim gave one of his pictures to a friend, Colette St John. Said Tim, 'Martin saw my painting and was blown away! He'd just returned from London where it was gloomy and cold. He came back to this blazing typical Australian summer and I'd done this painting, which had that intensity of that Sydney summer.

'Martin liked the painting and asked me to help him with his next exhibition - Art Exhibition. He was gathering people together to paint his book – Art Book. I think he had a concept of doing something like a Yellow House, getting a group of people together to help him paint but he only ended up with the two of us painting it - Richard Liney and another guy Victor Rubin - a good painter. They were only there at the beginning.' (13)

Tim worked on all the pictures. For the Matisse/Magritte picture (later repainted and re-titled Pentecost) Martin painted the room and Tim painted the bird. They both signed every picture.

Initially they stretched the canvases with help from drop-in friends. When that didn't work out, Tim introduced Martin to people who stretched canvases to a professional standard. Tim also introduced Martin to Liquitex paints, which Martin used for the rest of his life. (14) That Cadmium Yellow used in Film Script – the yellow that's half an inch thick – that's Liquitex. Naphthol Red Light, Bright Aqua Green and high viscosity Light Blue Permanent are all Liquitex - straight from the tube.

'That's where I got to know him,' Tim reflected. 'I was very young and naïve, and for me to be in this room with Martin - and then all of a sudden Richard Neville dropped in and got onto the typewriter. Brett Whiteley would pop in. He'd look at the paintings we were working on, "Oh wow man!" Then he would dart off. Jean Shrimpton popped in one day when we were painting. I was the young guy, starry-eyed and all that sort of stuff and here are my heroes!' (15)

One evening at the end of February Martin announced, 'We're going to a concert'. It was a Rolling Stones concert at the Sydney Showground. 'A really fab concert,' said Tim. 'Nikki James, Richard Cobden and I were in the Moke and we arrived at the top of William Street.

"Where are we going Martin?"

"We're going to a party for the Stones." Oh, okay.

'I thought we'd get out at the party. No, we go straight up to the penthouse - Nikki, Richard, Martin and myself. And then: "Is Mick there…?" – heavy bodyguard "…it's Martin Sharp…"

"Oh Martin – yeah – come in."

'There's Mick and Charlie. Mick was sitting there eating fish and chips. He welcomed us and asked nothing about the concert but about cheaper airfares and those sorts of mundane things.

'I had a packet of Drum. Mick said, "What is it? Dope?" I said, "No…" but Nikki James had just come back from India with a nice bit of hashish. So she packed a chillum and we had this really lovely conversation. Charlie asked us, "Does anyone want a Cold Duck?" (Cold Duck was the fizzy bubbly of the day.) So we had this amazing chillum with Mick and then all of a sudden – bang - it was over. We were downstairs at the party. Taking us to meet the Stones was an example of Martin being full of unsuspected surprises!' (16)

Then it was back to work.

Through Martin's studio Jo developed new friends, somewhat like the young bohemians she had known at Merioola, only wilder. Sometimes Tim stayed overnight. Brett swam nude in her pool, Colin Lanceley talked non-stop Art, former-Yellow House people were constantly dropping in. And, before his exit back to Britain, Jo also enjoyed the company of David Litvinoff.

Towards the end of March, Roger Foley-Fogg dropped by and filmed Martin and Tim at work. Roger's film shows two handsome young long-haired artists, smoking and deliberating over their 'takes' on Picasso's Demoiselles D'Avignon and de Chirico's Song of Love. Viewers also see Anne Kelly looking over the architectural plans for the face of Luna Park – Martin and Tim's next project. (17)

Jo sometimes cast her eye over Martin's paintings. Martin described her comments, 'My mother wouldn't have understood the metaphysics of

Reprise Of Giorgio De Chirico's Song Of Love, but she'd say to me, "Oh darling, that sky needs a bit more blue in it..." or something. She had a very good eye. It wasn't an intellectual eye but she was a Pop Art person and I was too - even though I was a Sharp'. (18)

Art Exhibition was held at Bonython Galleries in Paddington. 'Martin does like to work on tight deadlines', said Tim. 'I remember the opening, driving up in a Mini-Moke. Jo was in the Moke, Martin was in the Moke, Nikki James was in the Moke. We got to the opening. I saw all the people and I just freaked out. We hadn't slept for about three days. My head was on the Moon somewhere and I ran off. Someone chased after me and dragged me back to the exhibition.' (19)

Art Exhibition was well received. The National Gallery Canberra bought The Unexpected Answer (ie. Whaam), English model Jean Shrimpton bought a picture and someone else bought Botticelli/Picasso The Birth Of Venus. Commenting on the latter Martin said, 'That's been sold for quite a lot but it's worth it because the ideas behind that picture were ahead of the ball game. If you check Europe or America or anywhere I think they were on par and equal with what was happening there - but they didn't know that here at the time, they thought they were "amusing" ideas.

'Art Exhibition had some very valid ideas in the language of art which were paintings about paintings. But that was 1973 and years later it's become Appropriation – but it grew out of Magritte and Pop Art. Our environment was art books, so let's make pictures out of art books, cut them up and keep the images flowing through time – powerful images which already had resonance established – it was just a matter of having the nerve to play around with them, make new pictures and then paint them.

'After the Yellow House I couldn't look at an art gallery. It was very hard but I had to. The Yellow House exploded art galleries and to go back was a retrograde step as far as I was concerned, unless one can make a very esoteric comment using an art gallery as a theatrical setting for an idea encompassing the gallery – hence calling it Art Exhibition!' (20)

After seeing the exhibition, Nimrod director Richard Wherrett invited Martin to design costumes and sets for his production of Peter Handke's play Kaspar towards the end of the year.

But first, the Face of Luna Park.

Soon after Art Exhibition, Martin moved into the chauffeur's quarters of the two-storey Wirian garage. He set up his studio on the top floor, spent a week living downstairs and said, 'That's where I started – in that garage. I would have lived in the car if it had been there! It was very nice to sit in, as a kid'. (22)

Martin also acquired 'Bloke' - a red setter named after CJ Dennis' Sentimental Bloke and shifted into the corner room in the servants' quarters of the main house. A toehold.

Both Martin's grandmothers were sick. Grandmother Vega, Wirian's proprietor, was in a nursing home. Caretaker, Albert Peck was a legacy from Martin's grandfather. He checked the place, mowed the lawn and did maintenance duties. After a time, Tim followed Martin into the servants' quarters. And Richard and Sharon Liney moved in too. Tim explained, 'Martin was always funny about moving into the main house while his grandmother was alive'. (23)

Martin, Tim and Richard Liney started work on the Face of Luna Park in April, one week after Art Exhibition. The Sydney Opera House was to be formally opened by Queen Elizabeth II on 20 October 1973 but in the interim, the Opera House Committee had incensed Sydney's art community by their shabby treatment of the brilliant architect Jorn Utzon. Martin, Tim and Richard supported Utzon. (24)

The Face of Luna Park was, in a sense, a straightforward job. The main mission was to create a face in sync with Luna Park's previous five faces, especially the last one by Arthur Barton. Instead, Martin approached his task more 'scientifically'. While painting Art Exhibition with Tim, Martin took time out to study the mythological meaning of the Face of Glory.

A 9th-century Mahayana Buddhist Temple in Central Java was of special interest. Its name was Borobudur.

Martin said, 'Researching the history of the face, the earliest legends we could pick up were at Borobudur. We found out it was the Face of Glory, which is like the Luna Park face even in expression, guarding the Buddha. Inside Luna Park was a real Buddha, a real effigy in marble and gold leaf - not plaster and paint. It was the Real McCoy, surrounded by this court, which is the Endless River.

'So in Borobudur there's this Face of Glory guarding the Buddha and in Luna Park you've also got the Face guarding the Buddha.' (25)

But the main thing - for Martin, Richard and Tim - was to work with the Arthur Barton design. At this stage, Martin's personal involvement had less to do with the park itself and more to do with Arthur Barton's art, the artist he'd seen painting billboards at Sydney's Royal Easter Show in his teenage years. Martin said, 'After I got involved a lot of people thought it was the nostalgia that I got into. I can hardly remember Luna Park as a kid. I probably didn't like it that much as a kid - but later on in life, it became a passion. (26)

Arthur Barton was the Luna Park artist for a total of 35 years until he retired in 1970 due to failing eyesight. In 1968 he created the iconic Face with exuberant colours. Said Martin, 'Arthur Barton put the happy face on Luna Park. It was pretty sour looking before him. He was the best. He put a great big smile on its face. His works gives Luna Park its real spirit and if it wasn't there it wouldn't have been as exciting for us.' (27)

Luna Park would ever remain a central theme in Martin's art. This core group of artists and others who joined with them, would continue to venerate Barton's works and attempt to restore them years after their commission was fulfilled.

In his book Luna Park, Just for Fun, author Sam Marshall described the situation at Luna Park around the time of Martin's commission. He wrote, 'In 1972 the Park was opened for year-round operation, no longer having a three-month winter closure when rides were thoroughly overhauled and maintained. Time was closing in.

'A general program to upgrade the Park was started. Maintenance intensive rides such as the Spider and the Tumble Bug were removed. Plans for the Zipper, Hurricane and Astrospin were secured by Rod Earle and built in Australia at a cost of $90,000 each for introduction in December 1973. When these were installed at the front of the Park, the area resembled a parking lot for mobile rides. A lack of bridges accentuated this.

'Margaret Fink, then the wife of major shareholder Leon Fink, made the connection between Pop Art and Luna Park. Artists armed with paint and imagination were commissioned to revitalize the Park. Martin Sharp, having completed a colour scheme for the Dodgem Building, repainted the face with the assistance of Tim Lewis and Richard Liney who were also interested in Pop Art. They applied a zigzag motif topped by geometric clowns' heads and acrylic mirror to the towers. At a cost of $28,000, it was completed in June 1973 to coincide with the opening of the Sydney Opera House. Ha-Ha was painted on the tower bases. On the back of the face a mandala with a giant psychedelic eye was painted to keep an eye on the park.' (28)

Precarious and frequently stoned, Martin, Tim and Richard Liney sometimes painted from a high scaffold, with Tim scared of heights. Tim said, 'We started off painting the entrance. We had scaffolding up on the towers. The whole thing was scaffolded. Then Richard wanted to spray the lips with glitter – we did that. The mirrors on the towers were also Richard's – we did that too. Martin did the Ha-Ha. The Face itself was on a deadline. Again, no sleep for two nights before and all that of stuff, but we pulled it off!' (29)

Interviewed by Cleo magazine about Luna Park and Sydney Opera House, Martin said, 'They are Sydney's two great sculptures. We were working on the face when the Opera House opened.

'As we were not very happy with the way designer Jorn Utzon had been treated and his interior reinterpreted by other people, we widened the face's smile and painted Ha-Ha on the two flanking pillars. We made the entrance a cartoon laughing at the Opera House'. (30)

One crisp winter's morning in June a French tightrope walker - who was given this idea at Nimbin's Aquarius Festival - walked a high wire between Sydney Harbour Bridge's two northern pythons. It was an important moment for Martin, Tim and Richard who watched spellbound from below. Important because in the 1890s circus daredevil the Great Onzalo (aka Alfred Rowe) crossed Sydney Harbour on a tightrope where the Bridge now stands and Martin knew all about it.

'They built the Bridge over his footsteps,' Martin wrote about the Great Onzalo. 'In 1973 Philippe Petit on another tightrope strung between the northern pylons, formed the Cross high above Onzalo's path. That very moment two metal flake spray painters were increasing Luna Park's smile…Luna Park smiled when Philippe Petit crossed the wire.' (31)

Martin contributed to The Last Issue of London OZ published June 1973. He said goodbye to it all with a collage of Superman set against Vincent's Starry Night captioned with 'Please Clark – don't walk out on me! You're the only secret identity I've got!' An uncredited poem about death featured on the opposite page.

The last OZ also carried an ad for The Rocky Horror Show at the Kings Road Theatre. Little Nell's stars were beginning to sparkle. (32)

With the closure of OZ, Jim Anderson was immediately offered a contract with Harcourt Brace & Jovanovich to write an account of his 60s experience. Shaken by the OZ Trial, he sought anonymity instead. Jim's travels took him to Bolinas, a little town in California where he remained for years. (33)

Not at all shaken by the trial, Felix emerged with lots to prove. A dupe, indeed! From the ashes of OZ, Felix used his experience and contacts to lay the cornerstones of what would become Dennis Publishing, his publishing empire.

While all this was going on, the two Richards joined forces over a new publication, Living Daylights. Richard was editor and Richie the publisher. This offering was less counter-cultural and more cultural than their previous offerings. One of their great discoveries was cartoonist Michael Leunig.

Martin also contributed. One of his memorable cartoons was 'a land of sweeping plains' with Hal Gye's Sentimental Bloke sweeping the Central Desert. Another is Boofhead at the crossroads of life, puzzled by it all.

Not quite as whimsical, Martin also drew a dramatic Mickey Mouse with a death's head for Living Daylights. It intermingled with Martin's design theme for Richard Wherrett's coming Kaspar production at the Nimrod Theatre.

Said Martin, 'I did a drawing of Mickey Mouse with death's head - You Know Who I Am! It was a warning. It had Muscle Man in a Mickey Mouse costume with a death's head face. I did it intuitively - like you can feel death stalking. Richard Neville published it. But George Gittoes said I was wrong. He said it was an evil image and I shouldn't have brought it forth. I thought, there's one way of bringing it forth consciously - with a purpose - to give a warning!' (34)

Before the close of 1973 Martin became associated with Mickey Mouse like – say – Andy Warhol with Campbell's Soup. Fancy Our Meeting probably started it, Death Head Mickey seemed to confirm it, Kaspar would seal it and the Dream Museum collection enshrined Mickey as a permanent part of Martin's novelty collection.

Martin's novelty collection started when Martin purchased a little Mickey Mouse figure that he kept instead of giving it away. In his travels through London, Paris and Sydney, Martin was constantly popping into bric-a-brac shops looking for treasures. He said, 'I used to like buying them. I used to give them away as presents.' (35)

One day he found a heritage Mickey that he decided to keep. Placing it alongside several Mickey Mice from his childhood and several others, visiting friends kept giving them to Martin, which added to the growing collection, which Martin enjoyed. He also contemplated its sad side. Martin said, 'Kids always play with their toys, so the ones that you get are always the ones where the children haven't played with their toys. The children died or something like that.

'That led onto Kaspar. It was 1973, about the same time as I was doing cartoons for the Australian and Living Daylights, trying to get a flow between them so they interrelated.' (36)

About Kaspar, Martin said, 'It's one of the best things I've ever done.' Tim helped him paint the props. (37)

Kaspar was a play written by Austrian writer Peter Handke. It was about the Kaspar character acquiring language. Martin's poster featured a horrified Mickey, head on a stool, blocking his ears from the torrent of Ha Ha Ha Ha Ha Has. Cast members – who each played a variation of Kaspar – all wore Mickey Mouse ears.

Directed by Richard Wherrett, Martin's cousin Andrew was in the cast, along with Philip Sayer, Richard Cobden, Chris Haywood, Berys Marsh and Lex Marinos.

Lex writes, 'Kaspar came with an immense European reputation. Complex in style and lacking in narrative, it is loosely based on the true story of an autistic youth, Kaspar Hauser. Apart from the central role, there is a chorus of prompters, including Chris Haywood and myself, who present logical and illogical blocks of dialogue in a variety of tones and styles. It was funny, shocking and moving'. (38)

Lex further explains, 'It was quite an abstract play with one central Kaspar and other secondary Kaspers - who are the voices in his head, the voices outside of his head or whatever. We were all in formalwear, white clown face and Mickey Mouse ears. Martin's ideas, of course.

'It was a genius piece of design. It's not a big stage but Martin stripped the theatre back to the brick wall and started to paint the walls. It was a wonderful design to work in. All those swirling, wild brushstrokes emerged as a perfect metaphor for what was going on in Kaspar's mind.

'We were rehearsing and Martin would be on the stage painting. It was extraordinary seeing it take shape. One of the themes that he returned to continually in his work was Van Gogh's Crows Over the Cornfield. That tortured Van Gogh fantasy world was exactly right for the sort of mental anguish that the character was going through. One extraordinary day, Martin had the M-shaped or V-shaped crows flying. There's a line in the play where - at a point of seemingly awareness and recognition - Kaspar says, "Why are all these worms flying about?"

'We were rehearsing that scene while Martin was painting and he suddenly put a little squiggle into one of the crows and turned it into a black worm flying! It was just inspired. It was such a light-bulb moment where the set and the script came together!' (39)

There remained one big project before the year was out. Again with Tim's assistance, Martin painted a big (683 x 1024) portrait of Tiny, which was commissioned by Macquarie University. With a ukulele-playing Tiny Tim centerpiece, Martin painted Eternity in this major work. Martin shrugs off previous inclusions with 'I might have put it in some cartoons.'

At this stage Martin knew only what the press had written about Arthur Stace, the Eternity Man - that Stace was an alcoholic who had turned up at St Barnabas' Church Broadway in 1956, got impacted by a sermon and quit the booze. After this, he slipped out in the dead of night, most nights, and chalked the single word 'Eternity' on pavements from Martin Place to Parramatta. Martin wouldn't fill in the blanks about Mr Eternity's life until the publication of Keith Dunstan's book Ratbags in 1979. (40)

Said Martin, 'There are all sorts of images sourced in the big one of Tiny, just bringing together a whole lot of different worlds: Starry Night, Hokusai's wave, Tiny from his album cover, Eternity, Al Jolson, His Master's Voice dog, the Southern Cross, the Bluebird of Happiness, the landscape from the Little Prince (the most beautiful landscape on earth). The idea was to bring all those elements together and use the resonance of them as elements of making a new picture. That was done in 1973 - a big year of working with Tim Lewis and Richard Liney.' (41)

Tim added, 'The garage was lovely because there was a studio. That's where the Macquarie University's Tiny Tim was painted.' (42)

14.

OUT & ABOUT IN PARIS & LONDON

Mr Sharp saw me at the Albert Hall in 1968 in England. Later on when I came to Australia he followed me around.

TINY TIM

Martin had spent his past five years flagging Tiny Tim to all who would listen: filmmakers, visitors to the Yellow House, influential people and people who had no influence at all. On his 32nd birthday - 21 January 1974 - Martin went to see Tiny perform in a Worker's Club in Newcastle, north of Sydney.

Said Martin, 'By this stage I'd realised that I was going to have to do something about Tiny because he'd completely slipped from the top and was in the orbit where I could reach him.' (1)

They had previously met in London's Speakeasy club in 1968, which Martin recorded on a borrowed cassette player. He held the microphone too close and the sound was distorted. Richard and Louise were present at their second meeting in Luton where Martin again less-than-successfully attempted to tape the maestro. Determined to get it right this time, Martin purchased a state-of-the-art Marantz recorder, drove to Newcastle and unknowingly started his lifetime's work of recording everything Tiny said or did that was within his ambit.

Still one of the Top 5 most Famous Faces in the world, that famous face seemed like all Tiny had. He was facing a major career slump. Notwithstanding a Grammy nomination for his For All My Little Friends album, Tiny was dropped by Reprise Records and never again signed to a major label. He was also facing another kind of slump. When Martin met him, Tiny was just 48 hours away from heading back to New York where Miss Vicki would end their marriage.

It was a devastating collapse. Plucked from obscurity just six years before, Tiny had rocketed to stardom – the Top 10, best venues, best orchestras, best everything, plus the biggest celebrity wedding ever televised. Gradually it had all slipped away. Miss Vicki was slipping away too and taking their daughter Tulip with her. Not too many noticed that Tiny had reinvented himself as the New York-style defacto man, a religious one.

Martin described the circumstances of the Newcastle meeting, 'the grand stage was removed from him. The record deals were removed and he was exiled to the very outer suburbs of show business, which is where I saw him in 1974 in a Leagues Club. I wasn't feeling too fantastic at the time. I got a little tape recorder and dragged myself up there. He didn't really know me at that stage but I got a fantastic welcome'. (2)

Martin reintroduced himself in Tiny's dressing room, hit the recording button straight away and taped Tiny confidently and spontaneously. Martin explained, 'It seemed like a totally natural thing. That's what I was there for. It was like he was waiting for someone to come.' (3) 'I got to sing with him on the first song I recorded, "Miss you since you went away dear, miss you more than I can say." I just picked up the melody. I was like the audience meeting the singer again'. (4)

Martin presented Tiny with a copy of his newly published Art Book. Tiny flicked through the first few pages, then paused thoughtfully on the Hamilton image of a brown-hued negative of Bing Crosby against a surreal De Chirico street corner. Tiny exclaimed, 'Oh, it's Mr Crosby!'

Martin felt the connection had been made. He explained, 'about the same time as I was doing collages, Tiny was doing with songs what I was doing with images. That's why I clicked with him. I understood scientifically that he was really on an edge. And Tiny could get into Art Book, which was interesting because he doesn't know fine art.' (5)

Tiny reciprocated by signing a copy of Charles Dickens' A Christmas Carol to Martin, 'To my dear friend Mr Sharp, a pleasure meeting you, Tiny Tim 74'.

And so, from the dressing room to the stage. In those days, club audiences often treated Tiny's act with indifference – a curiosity more than a minstrel. Martin didn't care what the audience thought, starry-eyed from the warmth of their meeting Martin found Tiny equally impressive on stage. 'He was like a prophet', describes Martin, 'standing there, holding the microphone stand, doing Heaven Is My Home ad lib'. (6)

Before going their separate ways, Martin penned a note, which he handed to Tiny: Anything I can do to help, I really love what you're doing. As far as Martin was concerned, he'd made a promise and the note sealed the deal. 'It started from there I guess,' he explained. (7)

From now on, Martin's two great subjects were Tiny Tim and Luna Park. There were others too – Vincent, Mickey Mouse, the Southern Cross, the blue groper, the Little Prince, Boofhead, Hokusai's Wave, Indigenous Rights, crime, corruption and spirituality. Leaving the Luna Park assignment in the capable hands of Tim Lewis, Martin returned to London for seven months to fulfill two Zandra Rhodes commissions - set designs for her exhibition based on her 1971 and 1973 trips to Uluru, and a staircase mural in her house. (8)

What Martin found in London did not entice him to settle in. OZ magazine was long gone and everyone had moved on. Robert Hughes, Germaine, Richard and Louise – all gone. Eric was housed up in LA at 461 Ocean Boulevard, the name of his second solo album. And Philippe was in Europe screening his film Swastika at the Cannes Film Festival.

Pop Art was being written about in the past tense. Publisher, Thames & Hudson included Martin in the John Walker book, Art Since Pop. It was a compliment on one hand, but it was wrapping up an era with the other. The book featured Martin's vibrant Vincent collage, the original of which Martin had gifted to Jeannie. (9)

Plant a Flower Child was eight years ago. 'Peace & Love' were the watchwords of the previous generation. Kill a Hippie became a gag-line, a song and a board game. Punk Art reigned, not Pop Art. Artist Jamie Reid was about to cut a swathe with his image of a safety-pin-through-QE2's-nose for the Sex Pistols' God Save the Queen record. They mightn't like the connection but Punk artists owe two things to Martin: day-glo poster colours and - although Punks probably didn't go for silver scissors – it was still scissors and glue.

Martin painted Zandra's mural, re-read Jung's Synchronicity: An Acausal Connecting Principal (10) revisited The Hokusai Sketchbooks by James A Michener. (11) He also copped his first bout of kidney stones in London. At first, he didn't know what it was. These attacks would continue to dog him intermittently throughout his life.

Martin continued flagging the idea of a Tiny Tim movie to film and Pop people. Other than massive enthusiasm, at this stage, Martin wasn't offering them much more than three or four indecipherable tapes. 'I wouldn't say I was confident of their support', he said. (12)

He looked up Pete Townshend, a friend who had agreed to transfer the tapes from reel-to-reel to cassette in his home studio. 'There's some pretty good talks on them - as well as some preaching...', is how Martin described the content. 'Townshend did a lot to transfer early Tiny tapes in his studio. He probably has the mintest copies of the talking tapes and the first singing ones.' (13) These tapes have never surfaced, so who knows what Townshend thought of all this? Martin is fondly remembered in Townshend's autobiography. Tiny isn't mentioned. (14)

Sandy Lieberson knew Martin from Performance. He was working with Ringo Starr and David Essex on the film That'll Be The Day. Lieberson wasn't interested in Tiny but he got Martin a second commission. Said Martin 'I got a job in Paris through Sandy Lieberson to do a mural in his friend's house, I forget which Rue it was. The mural was Vincent on the Road to Tarascon with Starry Night in the background and it went down a 3-stepped stair. (It was quite a modern house.) I repeated the figure three times with the Starry Night in the background.'

Foraging through those Parisian bookshops, Martin found some film scripts, which he read and was struck by the idea of a remake of the 1927 film The Jazz Singer with Tiny taking Al Jolson's role, the son of a cantor who wanted to sing popular songs. (The idea was worthy enough for Neil Diamond to pick up on it in 1980 for his film of the same name.) The Jazz Singer was Martin's first idea for the Tiny Tim film. But it was the next idea that stuck.

Martin said, 'I started looking through scripts and came up with a Tin Pan Alley version of Orpheus and Eurydice. That became the feature film idea. I was getting the idea on the Metro in Paris.' (15) It surely would have made a wonderful animation (an animator like Eric Drooker). Tiny Tim aficionados would have loved it!

Martin's story opens in Luna Park where Orpheus (Tiny) is a singer and Eurydice is the magician's assistant. One day Orpheus begins to serenade her with I Got You Babe. A journalist hears his talent and organizes a concert at the Sydney Opera House. Later that night the journalist takes Eurydice to a nightclub where Mr Big is impressed by her performance. After being attracted to her, he introduces her to heroin. (Martin was increasingly aware of heroin casualties, both in London and in Australia.)

The Sydney Opera House Concert is a great success. Eurydice fails to take her bow. Mr Big rushes backstage to find that she has gone. The search for Eurydice is on. Orpheus joins the search. Time passes. Disguised as a street singer, one day Orpheus is surprised that someone – Mercury - throws Eurydice's button into his hat. He chases after Mercury who runs into a railway station. In lieu of a ticket Orpheus sings Brother Can You Spare a Dime and starts his downward journey led by the disappearing figure of Mercury.

His decent continues through the River Caves, until he finds himself directed towards the Ghost Train. Wildly he twirls his way through the

Hall of Mirrors to find himself in a huge empty theatre – the yet-to-be-renovated Floating Palais. On seeing him, the stage manager announces, 'You're on!' The pianist strikes up Begin the Beguine. Eurydice responds. The producer turns to Orpheus and says, 'You're on – but don't look at her, never look at her'.

Martin wrote, 'It is a terrible struggle but he forces his performance on. He stands at the footlights starring out at the audience…the comedy is ended. The curtains close, Eurydice rushes forward trying to embrace him. He rebuffs her. The curtains open for curtain call. Orpheus steps forward to tumultuous applause. The audience clamours for Eurydice. Orpheus turns toward the curtain, his hand raised to herald her. The curtains open. She steps from the darkness to a wild thrill of adulation.

'Orpheus, his eyes shining with love and pride cannot keep from glancing admiringly at her. Their eyes meet. Horrorstruck they are rooted to the spot. The curtain closes between them. Orpheus, downstage, rushes toward it but to no avail. Instead of pliant velvet he finds the curtain as hard and unyielding as stone.' (16)

Looking back, he said, 'The idea became real, the film we actually made, though in a documentary way.' (17)

About his state of mind at the time, Martin wrote, 'Confused by living between Sydney and London, trying to write a film script for Tiny Tim who had plummeted from World Fame to Obscurity, and who I considered then, and know now, as the most wonderful artist in the world. I saw him do a modern Orpheus and wrote accordingly.' (18)

While in London and Paris, Martin had left Tim 'holding the fort' (as Martin called it) at Wirian and Luna Park. Albert kept an eye on the Wirian and Tim worked on his own exhibition as well as the exterior colour schemes for the Floating Palais, Icy Mountains, Coney Island and Pirate Pete. Every day, with no driver's license, Tim drove from Bellevue Hill to Luna Park and back. No scaffolds necessary this time, he sat at a desk, worked off the architectural drawings and instructed tradespeople – invariably painters. (19)

Said Tim, ' I'd mock it all up, give it to the painters and they just painted it. Martin went to London leaving me with a Mini-Moke and Bloke - his red setter dog. By this time we'd moved into what used to be the servants quarters - Colette St John was there for a brief period of time. The rest of the house was curtained off because Martin's grandmother was in a nursing home. As she was still alive, I guess he thought, "I can't really move in – it's not appropriate …".

'When Martin was away for those months, the garage was my studio. I painted my Self Portrait show there. I got on very well with Jo. She liked me for some reason. But Martin had left me with this dog, which tended to wander, and this mad caretaker Albert. You never knew when Albert would show up. He maintained the place but he wasn't living there. He was living in Edgecliff.'

One day Bloke took off and never came back. Martin was in England at the time. Tim had to contact him and awkwardly explain that he'd lost him. Shortly before Martin's homecoming, Tim exhibited his Self Portrait at Coventry Galleries, which was well received. (20)

After seven months away, Martin moved back into Wirian. He also returned to work at Luna Park where the Carousel was the current focus of attention. The exterior colour schemes for the Floating Palais, Icy Mountains, Coney Island and Pirate Pete were now completed.

There had been lots of sadness in Martin's family while he was gone. His Grandmother Sharp had died. Uncle Frank also - father to cousins Phillip, Erica, Russell and Rozzie, whose mother, Aunt Edith had died two years before. Martin's mother – Jo – had deteriorating health (scoliosis).

Martin's Australian friends had moved on. 'We all had a lot of irons in the fire,' says Kingo. (21) Living Daylights was about to evolve into Richie Walsh's Nation Review. Richard Neville was courting his interviewer, music journalist Julie Clarke. Tim filmed them. Greg continued his trajectory as a highly sought magazine, art and fashion photographer. George was traveling the south coast of New South Wales surfing and producing a large series of photographs, drawings and paintings. Jonny was preparing his first exhibition for Bonython Galleries in Sydney. Albie was continuing with avant garde films. His understudies were launching their stellar careers – Bruce Beresford, Phillip Noyce and Peter Weir.

Attendance figures at the Nimrod Theatre had soared. Martin's previous poster for Kaspar was well received and knowing how much Martin loved Ginger Meggs, they asked him to design another poster, this one for Ken Horler's play, Ginge's Last Stand, the Nimrod Theatre's opening show for 1975. (22)

Roger Foley was evolving from Ellis D Fogg to 'Roger Foley-Fogg' or 'Mr Fogg'. Only the corporate world could provide the big budgets he required to operate as a light artist. Maggie Tabberer Associates scooped him up. She writes, 'We developed a close working relationship with an exciting new talent, Roger Foley, a lighting and sound whiz who worked under the name LSD Fogg (sic). Roger was wonderful.' (23) Roger and Maggie worked together for the next five years, at least.

And Jeannie was cutting a new album. It featured one of Jeannie's best-loved songs, the Graham Lowndes composition, Till Time Brings Change and a reprise of The Moon is a Harsh Mistress from Tears of Steel & the Clowning Calaveras. Martin offered to do the cover. She says, 'Once we knew each other, Martin was continually a source of inspiration. He and Greg did that cover.' (24) Titled Free Fall Through Featherless Flight it won Australia's 1974 Female Vocal Album of the Year.

In July, six teeth were mysteriously stolen from Martin's face of Luna Park. It was all over the news. No one knew what it was all about. 'That was a raiding party from Kogarah High School,' former student Garry Mallard confessed. He hoarded one of the teeth for eight years before taking it to the tip.

He said, 'It was one of those final year things where you had to nick something. Like, you had to nick like a chair from Central Station, or some famous thing from Hyde Park or a tram wheel from the Tram Museum. We used to make a book on it for charity – you'd take odds, have a party, get pissed and then different people say, "Okay, I'll get the tram wheel" or whatever. If they came back with it, the bet was won and you didn't make any profit. If they didn't come back with it, they lost and you'd make scads. The headmaster knew but he turned a blind eye to it. We were raising money for charity and they were all supposed to go back. It went up for auction at our school. I think they ended up getting $30 for each tooth.

'I didn't take the tooth - I only got the tooth. It didn't look like a tooth. They don't look like teeth close-up. I think it was made of ply. There might have been something about it on the news but I never noticed.' (25)

In August 1974 the Rembrandt of Luna Park, Arthur Barton died. Martin never met him. But Garry had, years before.

Said Garry, 'I'd gone to Luna Park and I came across the artist Arthur Barton. I got talking to him a little bit and I said, This stuff at Luna Park is equivalent to German Expressionist art and I wrote this bullshit article, which was published somewhere, Martin saw it and I think he was quite impressed by that. He got really involved with Arthur Barton's work and carried it on.' (26)

Fresh out of studying art at Caulfield Tech Melbourne, in September 1974, 21-year old Leigh Hobbs was asked to design the exterior colour scheme for the antique Carousel. It was his first commission. The horses were deteriorating and needed attention. All 43 horses were dipped in a bath of caustic soda to strip off the old paint, which the artists would later regret.

15.

PREPARING FOR TINY

There was $thousands to be paid in death duties. So to keep Wirian, Martin entered into an agreement with the Cranbrook School next door.

WILLIAM YANG

When Martin penned 'Anything I can do to help' and handed it to Tiny, Tiny probably didn't quite know what that meant. Neither – I guess - did Martin at that stage. Other than touting around a film script, there was no clear indication that Martin and Tiny would actually work together on any projects. It was little more than a manuscript and hope.

Martin had certainly been around films, recordings and concerts, but always on the sidelines. He didn't know much about direction, location shots, budgets and other complications involved in bringing a film project to fruition. Albie handled all that back at the Yellow House. And while Martin had contributed to Performance and Kaspar, they were really other people's projects.

While continuing his efforts with the Luna Park team, in February, Martin joined the production team of the film, Picnic at Hanging Rock, an Australian mystery drama film directed by Peter Weir, adapted from Joan Lindsay's 1967 novel of the same name. (1)

Said Martin, 'I tried to equip myself for working with Tiny - so I worked in film, I worked in theatre.' (2)

'I took a bit of a change of direction from all the things I enjoyed doing. Picnic At Hanging Rock was a big help. I knew I had to do something, so I tried to prepare myself as best I could by consciously learning. You open yourself up to seeing how it's done and that makes it easier when you have to do it yourself.' (3)

Martin's film credit was Artistic Adviser to the Director. He explained. 'It was to bring what I could to the film - ranging from a script suggestion to a set dressing. I offered what I could to Peter Weir and he took it or left it. He took a good deal of it and left a good deal of it. It was a wonderful experience. I knew people in the film industry but I never really worked closely with them. I'd known individuals but it was great to meet new people who understood and appreciated me, and I felt the same about them, comrades in Art.' (4)

The cast starred Anne-Louise Lambert, Helen Morse, Jackie Weaver, John Jarratt, Rachel Roberts, Vivean Gray, Dominic Guard and Garry McDonald. Garry McDonald was a former Cranbrook boy who was in the process of refining his Norman Gunston character for television. Another Cranbrookian was David Sanderson. Sanderson was working on the film's nature photography and was interested in assisting Martin with his Tiny Tim film, if and when it got going.

Martin's imprint on Picnic At Hanging Rock is slight but present for those who look closely. For example, Martin's Lost Hokusai print hangs on the wall in the headmistress' office. And around the 75-minute mark 'Sara Waybourne' looks through her scrapbook before going to sleep. The scrapbook is filled with Martin's Victoriana-styled collages. Martin also took it upon himself to unpick the symbolic language behind words - the girls' names for example – Irma, Marian and Miranda. The first four letters of each name are the same. 'Three parts of the one whole,' Martin concluded. (5)

Picnic At Hanging Rock was being played against a backdrop of major drama concerning the Wirian estate to which Martin was heir apparent. As well as the house finances, there were constant upheavals. Tim was planning to travel overseas, Sharon moved in with Richard, Martin's cousin Andrew joined them. Victoria Cobden was Martin's new girlfriend - Richard Cobden's sister – plus there was a string of blow-ins. Every relationship drama was being played out before a household audience. Even so, Martin refused to move into his grandparents' quarters while Grandmother Vega was alive.

Caretaker Albert Peck had no such qualms. He moved in while she was still in hospital.

Martin's grandparents had separate upstairs bedrooms. Stuart had the large adjoining room to Vega's palatial bedroom. They shared a common bathroom even though Vega's room also had a private bathroom. Albert moved into Stuart's room. He had his own kitchenette.

Albert knew the nuts and bolts of running Wirian from years of experience whereas Martin could barely cook a meal. Puzzled by his maintenance man's intentions, Martin questioned, 'How long was Albert intending to stay? I don't know. Whether he was staying the length he was meant to stay or whether he was intending to spend his life here? I don't really know. He lived a very separate existence. We didn't use that part of the house at all, so he was living in that whole half of the house. I really respected his space.' (6)

Former Wirian resident, photographer William Yang, explained the conundrum, 'Albert Peck was a tie-over from the old world. He was a retainer from Martin's grandmother. There was an unspoken agreement between Albert and Martin that he came into the house. Albert in return – I was told – looked after Wirian. Albert was a servant in a way. He did the garden, mowed the lawns, took out the garbage, did the repairs. He did all the odd jobs. He even had the key to the place. Martin did not have the key to the place. Martin had to call.' (7)

Finally, Martin's Grandmother Vega died, leaving Martin, and to a lesser extent Jo, as her beneficiaries. Albert had the run of half the house – curtained off – while Martin still lived out of a bedroom in the servants' quarters. The number of residents and overnighters was building. All bedrooms were full, so Kathy Lette and Gabrielle Carey, known as the Salami Sisters, lived under Martin's dining room table for a while. That's where they slept until they moved back to the suburbs and wrote Puberty Blues. Before heading overseas Tim said, 'A lot of people have lived at Wirian at some stage. It was a very exciting time.' (8)

But Martin needed more space to accomplish his projects. The pictures were getting bigger. He was working on a canvas titled Miss Australia and planning another huge Tiny Tim canvas. About dossing down in the servant's quarters, Martin said, 'There was six of us. I couldn't sleep up there anymore. It took a big emotional step to go through to that part of Wirian. Albert wasn't encouraging it at all. He liked the seclusion I'm sure, whereas I wanted him to move a bit further away.'

Martin was referring to the northwest corner of the house where beyond his grandparents' bedrooms was Jo's former bedroom (with its beautiful bay window) and Martin's former nursery. Either would have made an ideal bedroom, but Albert was staying put.

Martin continued, 'I thought, Albert could have the nursery room and the bathroom. A unit - put a door on it. I tried a few times but he thought that room was too hot. As soon as anything is sharp you have to get your way back into it one way or another, and I certainly had to get my way back into this. I hadn't really run a house before, so there was a sort of pressure.' (9)

Albert appeared to have no friends outside Wirian though he had a sister somewhere. For occasional breaks, he went on fishing trips on the Shoalhaven River. As well being 10-15 years older than Martin and friends, Albert was unlike everyone else around the place. He wore short-sleeved polyester shirts, fawn-coloured trousers and pullovers in winter. William

Yang described his appearance as 'totally ordinary', except that Albert loved leather coats. He also admired Adolf Hitler for his Final Solution to the Jewish question and said so openly, which freaked everybody out.

Not only did Martin have to struggle with the internal politics of Wirian, he was also worrying about the Tiny Tim film, Luna Park and the biggest drama of all – death duties – which was like a slow train coming.

William explained, 'There was debate then whether Martin would in fact keep Wirian because there was $thousands to be paid in death duties. So to keep Wirian, Martin entered into an agreement with the Cranbrook School next door. He sold the garage, the tennis court and his circular drive to the school. That was one of the crises.' (10)

Another was the news of David Litvinoff's suicide death in England in April. 'He was a fantastic man. I miss him,' said Martin. Others were not so generous, blaming him for Brett's growing heroin addiction.

Martin reminisced, 'It was great that David came out to Australia. When he went back to London the scene had gone. He liked boys I suppose. He was staying out in the country with a youngish interior decorator who asked him to move on. It was a delicate situation. He rang up a few people, gave a few hints, gave away some nice shirts and everything he had, went to a chemist asked for some pills, took them and that was it. David had no recognisable place in society – something he could earn a living from - he was a sort of court jester, I suppose.' (11)

His friendship with Rock stars had provided Litva with an outstanding collection of tapes. He sold his extraordinary library of reel-to-reel tapes. They finished up in Martin's care, including Bob Dylan's legendary 'Judas' May 1966 concert - a sought after bootleg recording in its day, (12) Brian Jones' Joujouka Music years before its release. Cocksucker Blues by the Rolling Stones – at one stage considered for the soundtrack of Performance. Nobody else had those, not then. Fortunately Martin had a big house. Over the years, residents, drop-ins and passers-through would simply 'leave' stuff at Wirian. Maybe clothes, paintings, books, personal effects, chairs and sometimes - as gifts - figurines.

Martin's Dream Museum grew out of his novelty collection. Sensing the delights of a toy museum, Martin and Richard Liney were discussing the concept perhaps for Luna Park. They occasionally bought figurines that caught their eye. These were added to Martin's childhood toys and accumulation of Mickey Mice, which quickly grew into a small collection.

Said Martin, 'Richard and I had similar taste about Tiny Tim, Luna Park, novelties and popular Art. He's someone I could share these ideas with. We founded the Dream Museum together. We thought that Luna Park should have been snap-frozen. We were entranced by its crumbling plaster dreams. We tried to see an economical way of using the "junk" that had survived there for the past years and adding to it a world of novelties, comic characters and childhood memories. We funded the Dream Museum initially then Luna Park started to put a bit in.

'There's a state of existence which can be described as noveltihood. Certain people from the comic world achieve great success as a comic character and certain human beings become honoured with noveltihood like Prince Charles and Lady Diana, Muhammad Ali, Ginger Meggs, Pinocchio, Jesus, Alice in Wonderland, Popeye, Jiminy Cricket, Sad Sack…you get that interesting world. Where else - in a strange way - would Jesus and Alice in Wonderland meet? And Mickey Mouse and Ginger Meggs…?' (13)

Peeking into bric-a-brac shops and auction rooms, one day Martin spotted a half-peeled tangerine that he took to be somebody's leftover lunch. Martin was surprised it was a legitimate carved object. When it came up for auction Martin bid on it and bought it.

Returning to Wirian, Martin played the song Hello Hello from a bootleg Tiny Tim cassette. The words were, '…would you like some of my tangerine?' which Martin heard as an invocation from Tiny. Visitors may recall seeing that little tangerine object on his desk, table or sideboard all his life, seldom more than a couple of metres away from wherever he was working.

Back at the Park, the main projects were the Carousel and the Games Pavilion. Tim had gone and Peter Kingston (Kingo) had joined. Martin, Richard and Kingo worked together on the Pirate Pete murals. Leigh Hobbs stripped the statues of the Big Boys back to chicken wire and rebuilt them as American tourists, Larry and Lizzie Luna. Jonny Lewis set up a darkroom underneath Wirian where he restored a caché of historical Luna Park photographs. At the start of the year, Jonny's father, Tom Lewis, was sworn in as Liberal Premier for NSW, a position he held for approximately 12 months. In this period, Luna Park was effectively under his jurisdiction. Things might have been okay if it had stayed that way.

The Luna Park lease, held by Leon Fink and Nathan Spatt, was due to expire in October 1975. In the interim the tenancy shifted to a week-to-week basis while new lease documents were being drawn up. All major renovations were temporarily suspended and all development ideas postponed.

Nathan Spatt's son Maurice was appointed general manager and he had ideas of his own, like a restaurant in the shape of an ice cream cone designed by architect Harry Seidler. There were plenty of ideas around, including the one they all dreaded - turning Luna Park into a casino, but none could proceed because everything hung on the all-important lease. Plenty of investment dollars had already been spent. The total cost of the Carousel renovation had been $100,000. The Zipper, the Hurricane and Astrospin had been $90,000 each. (14) Martin's Face cost $28,000 and was fantastic! (15)

The combined artists' efforts were welcomed by the public and by the old timers who had worked at the Park. One day, admiring the work, former manager Ted Hopkins gave the artists his approval, adding, 'If I had a chance there is only one thing I'd like to re-do – the Ghost Train'. (16) The artists were thinking the same way.

A Ghost Train theme is what Jeannie asked of Martin for the set design of Tears of Steel & the Clowning Calaveras, her multi media, double-LP production featuring song, theatre and dance. It was the first show at the new Seymour Centre, a multi-purpose performing venue within the University of Sydney precinct. (17)

Jeannie had been deeply impressed by Kaspar because it centred on a boy who had lost the power of speech. Twelve months before, Jeannie's father had a stroke and suffered the same disability. He never spoke 'language' again. Jeannie dedicated Tears of Steel & the Clowning Calaveras to him.

At the start of the year Jeannie saw the film The Battle of Chile in which she heard the singer Àngel Parra whom she had met in Cuba in 1967. When Jeannie heard him singing she started to weep. In her personal notes Jeannie penned, 'This personal connection to 11 September 1973 added to my commitment-to/compassion-with the people in Chile and those who arrived here courtesy of the Whitlam govt. In the cinema tears surged up and then I got SO angry.' (18)

Soon after, friend/singer Margret Roadknight gave Jeannie a book of Palbo Neruda poems in which Jeannie found the poem that inspired Tears of Steel.

I learned life from your death,
My eyes had begun to mourn
When I discovered within me
Not tears, but undying arms.
Wait for them! Wait for me!

'It's on the album,' said Jeannie. 'Mexico has been a big influence in my life since I was three.' (19)

She described the show, 'There were eight performers, three were singers (who had to do other things), and two dancers and two actors – Lex Marinos and Nicholas Lathouris. Death is very visible in Mexican culture. We hide it and they don't. The calaveras are the skulls. The skeletons represent politicians or different characters in Mexican life and they are "calaveras". It was in two parts. The first part was about people who I saw as martyrs-performers. The costumes for the first half were clown costumes except mine. I wore red because I was the human presence.

'The second half was Tears of Steel which lyrically consisted of the Neruda poem, two poems of mine, a poem of Denis Kevans - all set to music by Michael Carlos. In that half there's an indigenous mask which is half life/half death. The other actors had half their face painted as a skull and I was the normal!

'The piece that Martin did as the backdrop is his interpretation of that life/death mask and that came together across the back of the stage at the end of the second half. Martin was in there painting it at the last minute, technicians going hysterical.

'Martin had done a small painting of that image to go on the back cover of the Tears of Steel LP. I went over to Wirian to pick up the artwork to take to EMI. Martin had torn it into pieces because he said, "Jeannie the death side is too strong". (Years later he framed the pieces in a yellow heart shape frame and gave it to me.) ' (20)

The clown costumes for the show were borrowed by Martin from Luna Park and faithfully returned after the show. Plus, Martin added, 'there was a real piece of the Ghost Train on the stage!' (21) 'I have no idea where,' Jeannie replied. (22)

Said Martin, 'Jeannie is very in touch with things that are happening in the unconscious of the community. She has the power to bring these things through. Not a seer - more of a medium.' (23)

In his notes Martin wrote, 'Because of the Luna Park/Ghost Train connection - humorous horror - Jeannie wanted me to design the show to illustrate her ideas. I provided some clown costumes and masks from Luna Park for the Bravo Pour le Clown song.

'The most ambitious song was The Crucifixion by Phil Ochs, the soon-to-commit-suicide singer songwriter. To illustrate this song, Jeannie wanted the huge sliding panels to come together each side bearing half the skull and half a smiling face. She was still learning to sing the long and difficult song at dress rehearsal and I had left the painting of the Death/Life face to the last minute, hoping she wouldn't insist. I challenged her over the song and its gruesome imagery, but true to herself at all cost, she persisted. The face was done in a heart-shape and became one of the most powerful moments in the show. It was a song I never really understood until the night of the Ghost Train Fire. (24)

'Doing that was so hard - two of those images - Jeannie's record cover. When I did it for the show it was just like a heart-shape, half as a smiling red face, and the other half was a skull and they came together in two big panels behind Jeannie at a certain point of the song. They came together (bang!) like that. Abraxas. So the images are coming through – me, as one who is sensitive to it, and Jeannie - through something unconscious or whatever workings of inspiration.'

One of the cast, Lex Marinos summed up Martin's contribution, 'What was extraordinary was Martin's ability to take stuff and make us see it differently. I was very impressed. Perfect design.' (26)

For a break, Martin and Jonny went on a road trip to Surfer's Paradise and looked up Peter Royles – the Yellow House answer to Bob Dylan - who was working at the Captain's Table restaurant. 'They came and swam with the dolphins', wrote Peter. (27)

At Luna Park the main projects were the Games Pavillion, Pirate Pete, Coney Island and the Orchestral Mural. Richard Liney started restoration of the Floating Palais in January 1976. (28)

Author of Luna Park, Just for Fun, Sam Marshall wrote, 'One third of the Carousel framework was remade, and a new floor and surrounding picket fence were built. Artist Garry Shead painted the wide fascia around the Carousel with postcard scenes.' (29)

Married with a three-year old daughter Gria, Garry and his wife Meryl lived at Lavender Bay where Brett, Kingo and artist John Firth-Smith lived as well. Garry was painting his own canvasses by night and working in a charcuterie (that he would soon own) by day. Martin invited Garry to join the team. His first job was the restoration of Pirate Pete alongside Kingo, Richard and himself. Shortly afterwards Garry was asked to paint the Carousel. Arthur Barton never saw these efforts, reflects Garry, 'that was past his time.

'Martin got me the job - and I really needed a job. He got me to do Pirate Pete with Kingo. I was living at Lavender Bay. I rowed over in the morning, parked the boat and went to work. Martin was working on Pirate Pete as well and I learned so much from him. He was so good with the graphic way he painted. I picked up lots of techniques.'

Everyone involved at the artistic level was handpicked by Martin. 'Martin got the team together,' explained Garry, 'because Fink & Spatt didn't know who to ask for'. (30)

Kingo reflected on the sequence of events, 'Leon Fink bought the rights to demolish the park and then found he couldn't demolish it. He got Martin in and Martin got me in. They certainly weren't interested in paying us much. We were just glad to be there, glad to get some sort of wage. So we're grateful to Leon for that.

'We had full reign of the place over the art side. We tried to save all the Arthur Barton artworks and stabilize the place. I worked on Pirate Pete's Sea Battle, Coney Island, we were trying to tidy up the River Caves and eventually the Ghost Train - we hoped - but the whole thing overtook us.' (31)

In May 1976 Neville Wran was elected Premier of New South Wales. He surprised everyone by not automatically granting another five-year lease. Why the hesitation? Not only was management on a week-by-week tenancy, but staff, tradespeople and artists. 'We were all on it. It could have ended at any time,' said Kingo. (32)

Week-by-week. Every time the document crossed Wran's desk, he put it aside. Week-by-week. The place was starting to run down.

In his notes Martin wrote, 'In 1976 while working at Luna Park, I walked into the deserted Ghost Train building, exploring its twisted black corridors. It took nerves of steel to step into the nightmare tunnels of Hell's Railway armed only with a torch, its pale beam picking out the leering faces of the demons and grotesque laughing skeletons. It was very spooky in there, just me and them.

'I came across a small black cupboard door. It prised open. The torchlight revealed, not a forgotten skeleton, but a glittering track of water, and in a distant grotto, with saxophone raised stood Mickey Mouse, the plaster Pablo of this Magic Theatre. By chance I had discovered the door that links the Ghost Train to the River Caves.' (33)

Meanwhile, death duties were being negotiated on the Wirian estate and Martin had to ensure Jo was okay. Said Martin, 'My mother had laughter, she'd keep going, she couldn't stop herself. It was almost like having a humour fit. So she didn't lose her happiness. All my friends became her friends. They'll all go to see her – the younger generation. She was someone they could talk to.'

As soon as a strategy for death duties was in place, Martin figured he could raise money by mortgaging Wirian. This placed Martin in a position where he realized he might actually have the money to fund the Tiny Tim film himself. He said, 'As soon as I found out I met Mr Morris who was my grandfather's solicitor who didn't understand art. It was a difficult difference but - through Boofhead and things - it's all connected.' (34)

'I found out I could get a mortgage, so I did.' (35)

Wirian with a mortgage over it! Never! Albert was horrified!

Martin was ready for Tiny when he arrived mid-year 1976 for his third Australian tour. In June/July 1976 Tiny played small clubs to a mixed reception. He was booed at an Essendon Hotel in Melbourne but welcomed at Wirian. Martin even had a film script ready. (36)

Tiny had been through quite a bit since their last meeting. He had been evicted from the apartment in Brooklyn where he had lived with Miss Vicki and their daughter little Miss Tulip. Tiny's father had now passed and he rather shamefully moved back in with his mother, back to his childhood home in Washington Heights – avoiding neighbours - before fleeing to Florida.

Then Tiny Tim got his first biographer. Despite years in the public spotlight, no one really knew Tiny's full background until writer Harry Stein tracked him down. Stein's book filled in the early days, where Tiny was born, school, family, first crush, Hubert's Flea Circus, Steve Paul's Scene. Playboy Press published Tiny's first biography. (37) It was generally well received even though stories about the Honey Method and the like seemed unnecessary.

The source? Tiny himself.

Tiny explained, 'Why do I tell them about my showers and everything? Show business is not a private life. If I wanted a private life then I should have been anything but in show business. If I'm a stockbroker or if I'm working in a business, I have a good right to say, What I do in my private life with Miss Vicki, or whoever I'm with, I'm sorry I can't tell you. It's a public business. I also tell them these things because fans want to know what you're doing and who you're doing it with. This is the precise gossip business.

'When I took on myself these things, I said All right, it is a public relations business. Fans want to know. The public wants to know about the star. The public wants to know intimate lives - and the paper is not there to praise the star. The paper is there to get circulated readers. So Tiny Tim, Nice Guy Does Good Show – that's not what they want to hear. They want to hear the other side - Ahh, he can't be like that! That's what they want to hear.' (38)

Unimpressed by Stein's bio, Martin wrote, 'Harry Stein is typical of those who have been drawn by the strange power of entertainers and yet been unable to come to terms with Tiny's real genius, which exists not in the realm of his personal behaviour, fascinating as this may be, but in the area of his greatest magic, his vocal virtuosity. He was fascinated by the man but he never listened to the singer.' (39)

And so Tiny came to Wirian and Martin got to host the Leonardo da Vinci of Popular Song, the Eternal Troubadour, the Chameleon, in the Wirian kitchen. Martin said, 'People talk of great artists – Vincent van Gogh comes immediately to mind. Another one is Tiny – equal magnitudes, different mediums'. (40)

Strumming his ukulele, Tiny harangued against fornication and birth control, while confessing his love for actress Miss Cybill Shepherd and Wirianette Miss Sue Cameron. Tiny proclaimed, 'The early times just in Australia alone were Miss Cameron - Sue Cameron in 1976 in Mr Martin Sharp's house - one wonderful moment's time! (41)

Martin's fascination with Tiny was non-negotiable and Martin taped everything to cassette. Tiny responded in full voice, preached and shared many of his love-fantasies on tape. They also discussed an idea of recording a multi-volume History Of Popular Song (Musical History Tour) starting with Volume One – Henry Burr, through Russ Columbo, Irving Kaufman, Rudy Vallee, Bing Crosby and into the modern period.

However, the main achievement of this Australian tour was that the first footage was shot. Said Martin, 'We shot our first film in 1976. The film started with Tiny arriving at the airport and then in the kitchen here. I don't think we got the sound for it. The Marathon idea was mooted then. He felt the idea of a medley would be best because it was his most popular. He was 100% sure because at all the clubs the people loved this kind of music, which was his ad lib marathon. He said, "Take my word for it." So I said, "Okay."

'And then I was watching Mohammad Ali fight against that Japanese wrestler, Inoki, who looked like a Marvel superhero. It was a big showbiz fight: Ali vs the toughest wrestler in the world.' (42)

The fight between American boxer Muhammad Ali and Japanese professional wrestler Antonio Inoki was held in Tokyo on 26 June 1976. At the time, Ali was the reigning WBC/WBA Heavyweight Champion. Inoki was staging exhibition fights against champions of various martial arts, in an attempt to show that pro wrestling was the dominant fighting discipline.

'Incredible fight,' said Martin. 'A real Barnum-Bailey feel to it, a top showbiz concoction: the two great strongmen, in their own styles, fighting one another. Ali came out with gloves, the wrestler without them, and for 20 rounds he lay down and fought Ali with his feet. I don't think Ali even scored a punch. Everyone thought it was a fake fight, but I thought it was the most exciting fight I've ever seen in my life!

'I watched that fight and thought, that's the idea to make that medley. A Marathon - challenge the world. This is the showcase. So I sent a telegram to Tiny, we talked about it and he mentioned the idea to his manager Joe Cappy, who loved it, and so it was developed from that.' (43)

They talked about the film straight away. Martin mentioned Al Jolson's The Jazz Singer, an idea Tiny liked. From there, they moved to Orpheus and Eurydice and a non-stop singing marathon. Said Martin. 'I added that we have to make it like that fight between Mohammad Ali and Inoki. The idea of the World Non-Stop Singing Record came up. Tiny thought it was a good idea.'

These early discussions were taped at Wirian and at the Southern Cross Hotel Edgecliff where Tiny was staying. Said Martin, 'One was trying to develop the shape of the marathon in the pure historical context so that it went from the first song to the last. He wasn't committed to doing something as formal as that.' (44)

Verbal agreement had been reached. Tiny went off to his next gig in Jamaica, talked it through with his manager and fired back a telegram that read, 'Dear Mr Sharp Mr Joe Cappy is very enthused and very interested in doing your idea of the one hour song marathon all that's required is the following three round trip first class airplane tickets to Australia three paid for rooms in a first class hotel and weekly allowances for me and the financial settlement feel free to call him if you can come up with this sincerely and thanks again for everything Tiny Tim.' (45)

While Luna Park was going wrong, Tiny Tim was going right. Martin applied to the Film Commission for grant, writing an impassioned letter that did not remotely conform to their bureaucratic conventions.

Calling the film project The Lyre Bird – Tiny Tim, Martin wrote, 'I agree that any project involving Tiny Tim may seem quite eccentric, and often I have been considered quite eccentric myself for thinking him more than a "put on" that most people take him for. Nonetheless, nothing can ever persuade me that he is less than a genius.' (46)

To celebrate or announce his success with Tiny, Martin painted what might be called the 'first draft' of a painting called Song of Songs in 1976 and retitled Film Script in 2004 after 28 years of overpainting. (47)

Martin exhibited the earliest version of this picture in his 1976 Hogarth exhibition. That's how he met Willy de la Vega from Argentina whose brother had married Martin's mother's friend.

They met because Willy got roped into carrying Martin's 136 x 319 cm picture into the gallery, after which Willy became terribly enthusiastic about Tiny. He said, 'Martin had an exhibition at the Hogarth Galleries and we came to Wirian to pick him up and that's when I met him. We had to carry the painting to the exhibition while Martin was still painting it.' (48)

Years later, Willy was with Martin on the night of the murder at Wirian.

16.

KOLD KOMFORT

I would keep Martin company while he was working. He was always working on a lot of things at once so there would be preparations for shows, paintings he was working on, various collections, stuff to do with the house, etc, etc, plus endless visitors, interviewers and collaborators.

SUSAN JENSEN

Martin painted less but he wrote more. He started a daily journal/sketch book and he began writing letters, lots of letters, to people in authority – the Premier, for example, mostly about the deteriorating state of Luna Park. He also wrote two magazine articles for Quadrant and two love poems to the Park, penned with the ardour of a teenage romancer.

I care so much about you that my feelings are beyond intellect.

You – Park – are in my blood.

I have explored every inch of your dusty corridors… (1)

Martin also leant towards the Christian faith, there are quiet references throughout his pictures. Did this start with Vincent's Letters? Carl Jung? Arthur Stace? Tiny Tim? Victoria Cobden? Or was this religious fascination ignited when researching the symbolic meaning of the Face of Glory with Tim?

The early-mid 70s has been touted by the media as a hedonistic time, famous for things like LSD, public nudity and free love. There was another side as well. Although conventional churches would never admit it, it was a religious period. Young people rejected organised religions in droves and sparkled with a new type of fervour. Artists and musicians generally weren't atheists. They celebrated gods, gurus and Gaia. Atheists were people with Science degrees.

George Harrison and Donovan favoured Maharishi Mahesh Yogi. We've Been Told Jesus Is Coming Soon was a track on Eric's new album. Tully became a Meher Baba band. Pete Townshend was a Meher Baba devotee. New Zealand band Home displayed Guru Maharaji banners on their stage.

One day, Yellow House itinerant Jesus Adam called on Wirian. Martin describes what occurred, 'We were in the kitchen - he came to stay out of the blue with his wife and baby. And he said, Sometimes I can "do" things - bring through another world - I can do it with a light bulb sometimes and he gestured to the light bulb. I wasn't stoned or anything, this was 11.00am – and his face changed into the Man of Constant Sorrows, like the description in Psalms. He was very moving – directing it at me. Then his eyes brimmed with tears. He was very kind - in agony but still loving. And he said: You're to be a messenger, what I have to say to you can't be said in words – something like that - and then he dragged me back to normality.

'He only stayed a few days. I chased him out in the end'. (2)

What the media called 'cults' were in their heyday. You couldn't avoid the Hara Krishna Temple chanting its mantra all over town. The Children of God marshaled the streets. Muktananda, Bubba Free John, Bhagwan Shree Rajneesh, Krishnamurti, AC Bhaktivedanta Swami Prabhupada and Sun Myung Moon sprang into public consciousness.

Jenny Kee embraced Buddhism. Adrian Rawlins got into Meher Baba. Richard Neville started meditating. And Martin had his own guru – Tiny Tim.

Martin combined Tiny's face with the word Eternity for the cover of the January 1977 issue of the socio-political Quadrant magazine. The issue also featured a full page b/w of Tiny, taken from one of Martin's pictures in London OZ. It was a collage of a collage. (3)

Said Martin, 'I cover a lot of my feelings about Tiny at that time in that article. Eventually it was the feeling that I couldn't convince anyone to do anything with Tiny. Margaret Fink was thinking of making a film with him.' (4)

Margaret Fink's concept was nothing like Martin's. Hers was a comedy to be called The Projectionist, 'but it didn't come through', said Martin. (5) So he ran the idea past Peter Weir who was working on The Last Wave. He seemed more interested in making a film about 'Martin's obsession with Tiny Tim' than about Tiny Tim. Martin also approached Jim Sharman though he didn't expect any real interest. And Philippe was in the country producing his memorable Mad Dog Morgan feature film, starring Dennis Hopper, who was as uncontrollable in real life as the character he was playing. (6)

Martin continued over-painting Song of Songs. It was an evolving picture. Words and images changed continually over the next 35 years. At this early stage the two core images featured Tiny and the Opera House. (7)

For their second show of the year, Nimrod Theatre commissioned a third poster from Martin, this one for Garry McDonald's Young Mo, about the comedian Roy Rene/Mo Mccackie. Martin's poster could not have been more stripped back - no time, no date, not the name of the show, no '…written by Steve Spears', none of that. Just Mo's face and one word – 'Nimrod'. It became the theatre's official logo, on letterheads and mastheads. You could even buy it on a keyring.

Susan Jensen shared an apartment with Jeannie whom she helped with the show Tears of Steel & the Clowning Calaveras. Susan - who never lived in Wirian – was introduced and became one of Martin's main assistants. She writes, 'I would keep him company while he was working on various things and be an extra pair of hands for him, doing whatever needed doing at the time'. (8)

As usual there were lots of ongoing posters, pictures and projects. One of which was the Haymarket poster, with Vincent's Starry Starry Night sky emblazoned with the word Eternity. Susan noted this as a significant spiritual statement, 'The Haymarket poster is an important bringing together of two special spiritual and artistic threads.

'I don't recall seeing the combination of the starry night and Eternity before this. I can almost hear the click in Martin's mind. Martin often noted the parallels between Tiny and Vincent, different gifts but the same link between creativity and spirituality expressed in a uniquely different way. Victoria (Cobden) was one of the first people we all knew who became a truly believing Christian so it was a significant event.' (9)

Sensing that Luna Park was a disaster waiting to happen, Martin and Tim painted the Luna Park towers sinking beneath Hokusai's Wave. Sourced from a collage by Richard Liney, Martin gave it the Biblical title Babylon the Great is Fallen (Revelation 18 v 2). He worked on it for years. (10)

Against a puce-yellow sky a dark form lurks. Redolent of Hokusai's 'great wave' back cover of the back cover of Mick Jagger OZ 15, is it a beast? A shadow? A premonition? Says Tim, 'The brown shape was painted in by Martin several years after I stopped painting the picture.' (11)

Much later in life, Martin's carer and friend Angelica Tremblay, wrote about this picture, 'Martin had many artists, friends and different people working over the years using brown and different coloured pencil drawings in different parts of the work and I was one of them. He never finished the work.' (12)

The formal real estate transaction between Cranbrook School and Wirian began in 1977. When the school finalized its land purchase, they took the garage, tennis court and the circular drive. As for the Cadillac? Martin simply drove it around instead of the Moke. One other task yet remained: cataloging Grandmother's goods. (13)

In the next Quadrant, Martin followed his previous Tiny Tim article with his thoughts on Luna Park. Photos of Martin was the 8-page centerpiece of the February issue. An article by Elwyn Lynn summed up Martin's career thus far and a b/w photographic study by Bernard Cumming shows Martin painting Mo. (14)

Another photograph has Martin sitting at a table in the room that would later become his studio. Visitors and friends know the room well. Martin referred to it as his Studio. They called it his Inner Sanctum. It brimmed with whatever Martin was working on at the time. In this picture, the room is surprisingly sparse.

For Quadrant Martin wrote, 'I love Luna Park, and sometimes I feel Luna Park loves me, but it has been an arduous romance'. Sometimes pure Pop, Martin name-checked, 'Ginger Meggs, Mickey Mouse, Little Nemo, Krazy Kat, The Sentimental Bloke, Tiger Tim, The Phantom, Dr Strange, Captain Marvel, Grock, Santa Claus, Dame Edna, Norman Gunston, Snugglepot and Cuddlepie, Charlie Chaplin, Houdini, Mandrake, Mr Jiggs, Mo, Popeye, Punch and Judy, Boofhead…and all the others'.

He also expressed concerns, 'Luna Park is in a state of flux. Great treasures of popular art are vanishing, it needs an eager army to answer their calls for help'. The article pushed for Luna Park as a Dream Museum, an art gallery to Pop. (15)

Still that lease remained unsigned.

The artists became unsettled. They saw the rides deteriorating before their eyes. They had actually been asked to stop working on some of them and were switched to working on the Mid-Way instead – where a Souvenir Shop (Magic Shop) was introduced. Martin wrote a stream of letters. He said, 'I have a book full with Dear Leon just trying to express how important it was, and how I really felt that - with all my heart - about the place'. Martin wrote to Leon, 'It's no use at this point describing in detail the vast amount of decay that needs rebuilding at Luna Park…'. (16)

Peter Kingston and Garry Shead felt the same and attended meetings with the leaseholders to this effect. Kingo's personal notes reflect the management's indifference to the artists' concerns. He writes of a meeting with Leon Fink (with Nathan Morris and Garry Shead also present). Kingo states that the previous Saturday night some friends had noticed a couple of loose planks on the Coney Island end of the Big Dipper. He quotes Leon's response, 'If we listened everything we heard - followed every rumour - we'd have a fulltime maintenance staff!'

Kingo's meeting with Maurice Spatt fared no better. He wrote, 'Maurice goes – rather proudly, even smugly, no responsible authority approaches us. On our present lease we are a law to ourselves. Amazement expressed by us. Kingo: We must make it safe anyway.' (17)

Was this simply bravado on the manager's part? Underpinning their confident front, the lease document remained unsigned and the week-by-week tenancy must surely have sapped all business confidence.

While all this was going on at the Park, Tiny agreed to tour Australia the following year and Martin scrambled for money to film him. Martin had been haranguing Leon about the condition of the Big Dipper, now he needed a loan. Leon obliged, taking as collateral Martin's Lost Hokusai.

Said Martin, 'I gave it to him as collateral against $3000. I was whinging to him about the Big Dipper and I accepted a cheque from him knowing that I didn't really believe him when he said: I'll do everything possible on the Big Dipper because I didn't want to lose the chance of making the film. That's a confession I've told no one before but I'm telling you now. I felt that was a moment where I should have stuck to my guns, but I was fairly broke and I suppose he almost paid me to keep quiet - when I think about the mechanics of it in that way. So one makes terrible mistakes.

'Leon didn't quite rise to the occasion. He didn't think Luna Park was the most important thing that he owned - but it was you see. He ran a whole lot of other things at the same time and maybe he was too immersed in his other businesses to say, I'll give Luna Park the attention that it needs. I believe at the certain times during the course of events, we personally - by our actions - allowed that fire to occur.

'I thought someone would be killed on the Big Dipper - that was my intuition and that's why I stressed it. I was onto the Big Dipper but I never picked the Ghost Train.' (18)

Still the lease remained unsigned.

So much to do, Martin needed an assistant. Susan Jensen recommended Melody Cooper. Susan writes, 'Martin needed someone to be his right hand person assisting him with all sorts of work relating to both his art and the house. Melody trained in production/set design/costuming at NIDA and was working part time with Linda Jackson at Flamingo Park. I thought she would be the perfect person to help Martin because she has such a variety of really amazing skills.' (19)

Flamingo Park! Another success. Located in Sydney's Victorian-style Strand Arcade, Jenny Kee partnered with designer Linda Jackson and built a creative, attractive and flamboyant business. Martin bought a Flamingo Park dress and presented it to Little Nell's youngest sister, Cressida Campbell, who joined the other artists at Luna Park.

Melody Cooper's arrival at Wirian sparked another room-reshuffle. She moved into the accommodation under the garage until the Cranbrook School asserted its property rights. Melody then settled into Martin's former bedroom in the servant's quarters when he took over his Grandmother's upstairs rooms. Melody also had a downstairs room for her studio, which Martin shared.

Affirming his right to the property was difficult for Martin, not encouraged by Albert. About moving into his Grandmother's grand bedroom Martin says, 'There was a bit of inhibition I suppose - about the house and things like that'. (20)

Richard Neville moved into the nursery room in the northwest corner of the house. 'Richard did his courting at Wirian,' said Martin. (21) Richard was commissioned to write a book about serial killer, charismatic and dangerous Charles Sobhraj, who preyed on western backpackers. This was an unexpected turn coming from someone who had romanticized the Hippie Trail in OZ magazines – he now monstered it. (22)

Richard's co-author was Julie Clarke. She had known Martin since Yellow House days. Julie's name (spelt 'Juli') appears on The Yellow House poster, which is the closest 'official' listing anyone has of the artists who were involved. (23) Tim explained, 'Martin knew Julie before Richard and it was through Martin that Richard met her'. (24) Julie moved in with Richard.

All this coming and going didn't suit Albert who made his likes and dislikes no secret. Richard's friendship with Martin was too entrenched for Albert to call it into question but with Julie it was different. Albert let it be known that he disliked Julie Clarke. Her ABC job didn't help.

Albert liked people who dedicated themselves to the house, people who fixed and cleaned things. Plus he didn't like people wasting electricity. Like, Sharon Liney putting only one pair of knickers through the tumble dryer! To make his point, Albert stretched Sharon's knickers over a giant tin and placed it in the kitchen for all to see. (25)

Describing the caretaker-general, William Yang said, 'You were answerable to Albert. He sort-of ran the place. If you didn't keep the kitchen tidy, Albert would be down on you. If you knocked chips off the wall, Albert would be around. If you scratched the floor, Albert would be onto you. There were a whole lot of little rules that Albert made. He was like the groundsman.' (26)

But Albert did get along with Melody. 'Albert was the glue that held Wirian together', she wrote, 'he made sure the utilities were paid and the rent was collected from the various bodies'. One of her first jobs was to assist Albert in getting Martin's grandmother's things ready for sale, 'so he could pay the death duties and keep Wirian'. (27)

The garage, the driveway, grandmother's effects, all sold – why stop there? Why not sell the lot. When Cleo magazine interviewed Martin for their August issue, they wrote, 'For Sale signs at Wirian, people tug the iron tolling bell and ask to be shown around the house. Martin has an undated ticket to Orlando Florida. He hopes that once in the States he will be able to make a film with Tiny.' (28)

In those days, Wirian did not totally centre on Martin's projects (as it did later). Everyone was busy. Some – like Julie – came-and-went and had their own careers. Richard and Julie also had a book to write about Charles Sobhraj. Susan Jensen worked for Cameron Management, a Double Bay-based agency for models, actors and photographers. Back from overseas, technology-minded Tim was working with video and computers. He interviewed Richard with Julie as his producer. And Jonny created a downstairs darkroom where he was occupied reprinting the Ted Hopkins photographic negatives found at Luna Park. In fact, the whole crew was still loosely engaged at Luna Park.

Martin's fourth poster for the Nimrod Theatre was designed for the cabaret-style show Kold Komfort Kaffee. It must have been quite an opening night as - despite a capacity audience - 'no profit had been made, as all the money was used on food and champagne'. (29)

Knowing that the Premier was expected to attend, Martin went to the Nimrod specifically to engage Neville Wran on the subject of the Luna Park lease and its onerous week-by-week tenancy. Being on friendly terms with Wran's wife Jill Hickson, Martin felt this connection might grant him a sympathetic ear from the Premier.

Said Martin, 'It was the last night of Kold Komfort Kaffee. I went especially to see him. I said, "I'm really worried about Luna Park".

'And Wran said, "I've got nothing against Leon Fink, but while he's got that partner I'll never give him the lease - because he can't say things like that about me. I'm human. I bleed!" This is what he said. I thought it must have been something about his wife or something...?' (30)

And then the problem was revealed. The disagreement stemmed from a gathering at the up-market Pruniers In The Park restaurant in Woollahra some 12 months previously. Someone overheard Nathan Spatt talking about Neville Wran in a derogatory manner but there is some question as to whether Spatt said something insulting about the Premier's new wife, Jill Hickson, or whether he was ridiculing Wran's Socialist roots, citing the Premier's 'hypocritical' attitude to the pilot's strike at the time and restlessness of the union movement in general.

'I'm human, I bleed...' what could that mean? Martin asked Spatt about the meaning of his conversation with the Premier.

'What did you say that could have offended him?" said Martin. 'And he said, "I was only saying what was said in the papers - about him being a scab for flying to Norfolk Island with Abeles (ie. Sir Peter Abeles) and breaking the plane strike.'

A scab.

Martin continued, 'I went to Leon and said, "He's not going to do anything until you get rid of Spatt".

'And Leon said, "I can't get rid of him, so that's that!"

'So the terms were stated. Wran said, "Unless you get rid of Spatt - no lease". And Leon said, "No go".' (31)

Cold comfort indeed.

17.
STREET OF DREAMS PRODUCTIONS

We worked pretty full on for Mart on Street of Dreams and the World Non-Stop Singing Record. Printing posters and t-shirts, making props, painting sets, doing make up and hair for Tiny…
MELODY COOPER

In November 1978 Regency Entertainment brought Tiny to Australia for a tour of Leagues Clubs, shopping centres and other inconsequential venues.

Martin extended the visa and booked Tiny for two concerts plus recording sessions from the close of 1978 to 13 January 1979. Most crucial was the legal agreement with Tiny's management. Without this, prearranged concert plans, studio bookings and the film could fold overnight. Fortunately, there were green lights everywhere.

The 125 x 330 cm Song of Songs picture was to be Martin's 'statement' for the year, yet he still found time to create posters for friends. Actors John Gaden and Kate Fitzpatrick go way back to Sydney University days with Martin. Towards the close of 1978 they played the lead roles in the Paris Theatre Company play Visions. Martin's black and red poster wrapped their faces in a fiery heart with the words Paris and Visions ablaze, like Fitzpatrick's lips.

Martin also did a poster for another play starring John Gaden, Patrick White's play Signal Driver. He sketched a bit too as he always did, in his address book, on scraps of paper or whatever was around.

As well as the marathon, Martin also had ideas for a more intimate Tiny Tim show, which – of course – required an accompanying poster. His Song of Songs Tiny Tim face seemed perfect to replicate, so he re-sketched that. And the Kirk Gallery in Cleveland Street Sydney seemed an ideal venue, providing an opportunity to work with old friends.

Just like the old days – an Ellis D Fogg (Roger Foley) light show!

With the Kirk Concert pencilled in, Martin sketched a new poster, and drafted the words: Martin Sharp and Roger Foley's Magic Theatre proudly present Ellis D Fogg's 10th Anniversary Laser Show starring The Eternal Troubadour Tiny Tim and Dream Theatre of Song at the Kirk 422 Cleveland. (1) Alas, the Australian tour management had another booking for Tiny that night. The Kirk was cancelled.

Roger shrugs it off, 'Tiny couldn't be in Sydney for it. Can't remember why. We were all very disappointed'. (2)

Ellis D Fogg was used to putting on shows. That's what Albie, Seb and he did in the Yellow House. Martin took charge of the walls while they directed the stage. Martin never directed anything. Now, with everything under his baton, Martin was painfully aware that he was moving into areas in which he had little or no experience. Of this Tiny Tim tour Martin confessed, 'He (Tiny) was working with very primitive tools - someone like me who knows nothing about recording!' (3)

How do you organise a recording session?

What does musical copyright mean?

Where do you hire a PA system?

What is the role of a musical director?

Simply finding a venue was tricky enough.

Martin needed all the help he could get and he got it. Melody was his faithful assistant and cousin Russell Sharp set Martin's Street of Dreams

Productions onto a business footing. Russell also assisted Martin with the logistics of producing the LP record that became titled Chameleon.

Said Russell, 'I incorporated Street of Dreams and we also created the Chameleon record covers'. (4)

Plans were constantly changing. The Festival of Sydney became involved: A Century of Song in One Smash Hit - 50-minutes of non-stop singing was to be staged at Sydney Opera House. But the Festival of Sydney didn't pick up the option, so that was on-then-off too.

The Song of Songs picture changed with every new twist, and there were many. Words changed, the image of the venue changed. 'I was changing it from the Opera House to one of the theatres,' said Martin. 'Eventually we settled on Luna Park.' (5) (Later, Luna Park would become the Moon.)

The Regent? The State? Paddo Town Hall? These venues were all considered and others too. Luna Park surfaced as the best idea. It made sense. Tim, Garry, Kingo, Jonny, Cressida, Michael Ramsden, Lee Hobbs, all worked there. The artists knew the administration and they were friends with Leon and Margaret Fink.

Richard Liney had spent his past two years restoring the Floating Palais, a 1935 concrete barge surmounted with an elegant timber pavilion. Martin saw its potential, 'We were trying to get all sorts of different venues. I'd been working at Luna Park and Richard Liney had just restored the Palais beautifully, so the venue was probably at its tiptop best and we hired it.' (6)

'I always had the desire to bring Tiny and Luna Park together. I thought my role in it was to give him a bigger setting and to give the opportunity for him to do what he most wanted to do. I was trusting him absolutely, artistically.' (7)

Martin's assistant Melody was extremely versatile. She needed to be! One day she might be sewing costumes - the next, placing business calls. Lots of others helped too – some were paid, others simply willing hands – like, Richard Wherrett from the Nimrod, Ted Robinson from Clowning

Calaveras plus a production crew, film crew, musicians, hired hands and many more. Especially Nathan Waks.

Jeannie had known Nathan since 1970, when (aged 19) he was Principal Cellist in the Sydney Symphony Orchestra. It was she who introduced Martin to Nathan after one of her shows. (8) In 1978, Nathan was Founding Director and Artistic Adviser to the Australian Chamber Orchestra and best known for his performances with the popular Sydney String Quartet. So we can safely assume that Martin wasn't just being modest when he gave all credit to Nathan for Martin's Tiny Tim shows and recordings.

Meanwhile, Street of Dreams Productions, operating from Wirian, had to cater for everything right down to mundane stuff like the ticketing and booking recording sessions… none of which could go ahead unless the contractual agreements with Tiny's management went smoothly.

They did.

On 4 December 1978, Tiny and his management signed an agreement with Martin's Street of Dreams Productions for Tiny to act (playing himself) in a movie produced by Martin. The film was to be 'a portrait of Tiny' set around a marathon-medley.

Tiny was still keen on a Musical History Tour. Describing his concept of how the marathon should be, Tiny told Martin, 'I would like to put on a non-stop continuous dance singalong medley. Firstly you would have old numbers like Babyface and Four Leaf Clover and then complete Rock songs from the late-40s - of course the Blacks always had it with the Rhythm and Blues - and then up to the White 50s, up to Soul and the 60s, and up to the current time.' Martin taped the discussion.

'This way several things happen: firstly you take what the public liked on stage and put it on record. In fact, the medley has already been proven successful on stage. I find my key thing in the medley are the styles of Harry Richmond, Henry Burr, Bill Murray and the other great artists shown to their best advantage. Secondly, it's never been done before in such a way. Thirdly, it goes on forever, they can dance to it without stopping and they can sing to it. And if this works, then the doors are open because it's no more the Tiptoe image alone!' (9)

Martin was enthused, 'A Marathon - challenge the world! This is the showcase, the backbone of the film. On one level the film is an athletic event - it's also the showcase for talent, singing ability, memory and composition. Tiny had to do the thing off the top of his head and endure! It's a musical tour de force!' (10)

Sydney was just the start. Certain that Tiny would be a sensation, Martin had even bigger plans. He told the Sydney press that the Century of Song marathon concert could pave the way for a lavish production at New York's Madison Square Garden! (11)

Comes a time for everyone to relax. From the handily located Cosmopolitan Double Bay hotel where he was staying, Tiny made frequent visits to Wirian where he sat around the kitchen table, strummed his uke, sang, talked, preached, didn't eat in public, fixated on 'Miss Ingrid' and engaged Richard, Albert and anyone who came through the door in fervent discussions.

Melody's friend - William Yang (who had arrived from Queensland) - photographed Tiny. Les Bean was there. Les – formerly known as Angel Lust - had shifted her devotion from the band Devo to Tiny Tim. Michael Barker was there too. He was a photography student doing an assignment about Martin. And Adrian Rawlins assumed the role of compère. 'Tiny's favourite announcer internationally,' explained Martin, who kept the tape recorder running throughout all this and had a film crew in the room while this was all going on, 'which didn't really come out', he said. (12).

With the show definitely on the road, Martin reworked his Ellis D Fogg/Kirk Gallery image into a new poster, more like a handbill - the b/w World Non-Stop Singing Record - Tiny Tim and the Time Machine, Song of Songs – Eternity. Staged to celebrate the centenary of Thomas Alva Edison's invention of the phonograph, the venue was not named on the handbill because it was printed before that was confirmed. (13)

Then they all got even busier. Les Bean sourced some interesting fabric, which Melody sewed into costumes. Melody said, 'I made costumes for him. The Blue Bird of Happiness Suit, the Mickey Mouse costume and ears, the white satin Pierrot. We worked pretty full-on for Mart on Street of Dreams and the World Non-Stop Singing Record. Printing posters and t-shirts, making props, painting sets. Doing make-up and hair for Tiny (an ordeal I will never forget, getting all Tiny's hair under a Mickey Mouse cap...!) (14)

Nathan called in. He was formally introduced as Tiny's musical director. Tiny established rapport with Nathan and got on particularly well with pianist Marvin Lewis, whose repertoire favoured old time tunes. Stand up and sing for your father an old time tune...! Tiny and Marvin became a type of duo within the seven-piece band comprising Dave Ellis (bass), Dave Donovan (guitar), Tony Ansell (keyboards), Geoff Oakes (sax), John Harding (violin), Doug Gallagher (drums) Marvin and Nathan.

A rehearsal was held at the Floating Palais. Martin described, 'We went down to the Palais to have a rehearsal. Tiny did songs like Lonely Troubadour, San Francisco and a few other songs that weren't in the marathon. He said, "You can do all the rehearsing in the world but if it's not right on the night if there's a spirit of negativity there!" So he was not one to rehearse.' (15)

In mid-December Tiny played the Nimrod Theatre to a packed house. (16) He performed against Martin's set for the previous show, Kold Komfort Kaffee, which had not yet been changed over to a pre-World War 1 set for a play about comedian Stan Laurel's relationship with an Australian singer and dancer.

Martin described Kold Komfort Kaffee as perfect for Tiny. Regrettably, he was not permitted to film the show. 'It was a terrific concert,' Martin said, 'My father was there with Dorothy, his wife'. (17)

Nathan booked EMI Studio 301, the best studio in Sydney, for the second week in January 1979. He also added Peter Haslem (trombone), Eric 'Boof' Thompson (trumpet), Mike Kenny (electric piano) and esteemed actor, David Gulpilil (didgeridoo and click sticks) to the forenamed musicians. Martin was credited as the producer.

Alistair (Al) Jones from the Slim Dusty Band was also present in the studio 'nimbly advising' – as Martin penned on the record credits. Of his own role, Martin explained, 'Nothing made me feel qualified to produce. Tiny said, "You can be my record producer". I said, "I can't produce records!" but he said – I've got it on tape somewhere – "You know enough about my music and I reckon you can". So he just appointed me.' (18)

'The Chameleon sessions was Tiny and Nathan Waks, and me being an absolute fan and saying, "Go for it!" and I probably suggested a few of the songs. He was very happy to do them. I just tried to serve, assisting the artists to do their best.' (19)

Martin described the session as starting with 'about 15 takes' to 'break the musicians in'. He said, 'there's probably some struggle that goes on between performer and musician - they've got to feel each other out.' The first song, Brother Can You Spare A Dime? was recorded in two takes. 'I think it's great', said Martin, 'although Tiny said he liked the Crosby version better'.

The Great Pretender was shaping up as the name of the album until William Yang's louche cover photograph of Tiny begged the title Chameleon.

The inclusion of the Great Pretender track was actually one of Martin's suggestions. Meekly he said, 'I think I actually suggested Tiny sing The Great Pretender. Sometimes if you suggest them, he'll do one. But he really knows what he wants. I just catch it and get it down as well as I can - for the world, I guess.'

Other songs recorded for the album were: Street of Dreams, Tipperary, Deep Night, The Song Without a Name, The Hukilau, My Song, My Way, Staying Alive, St Louis Blues, Dancing in the Street and the Mickey Mouse Club March - which should have been released as a single. 'Tiny said that too,' said Martin, 'It should have been!' (20) (St Louis Blues and Dancing in the Street remained unreleased until 2006.)

The song Country Queen also appeared on Chameleon, a track that was previously recorded and Martin acquired the rights. Martin explained, 'Country Queen was recorded in Nashville on the day that Elvis Presley died. I think it got out as a 45 and hadn't done anything on True Records. Tiny gave us the tapes to use on the album. That song is the only one we didn't record, so it's not us.

'They were spontaneous recordings. There were no arrangements written. Nathan really produced that record. I was the financial producer and getting the people together. So it was a pretty ad lib situation and not the sort of circumstances I would really like to put Tiny in. I think Tiny should have the best equipment at his command and any musician he wants. He speaks through his songs. That's his highest form of communication'. (21)

The following week Tiny returned to the studio with Marvin Lewis on piano and they recorded the 11 tracks that make up the piano-based Wonderful World of Romance album. They recorded an 'unplugged' style album 'direct to disc' with Marvin and Tiny having a jolly good time together, running through old time favourites - She's a New Kind of Old-Fashioned Girl, songs like that. This record was pressed, inserted in a plain white cover and mostly given away to friends. (22)

Chameleon had a more commercial motive. Martin pressed 800 and called it 'an audition record'. But it was much better than that. It certainly ranks among Tiny's best.

One stage show, two LP records and shooting film made for a huge fortnight. As if that was not demanding enough, the marathon was booked for the Floating Palais, 12 January 1979.

But first, Training Camp.

Martin announced the Non-Stop Singing Marathon as an athletic event on par with Japanese wrestler Inoki and boxer Muhammad Ali. Wirian became Training Camp Central. The walls of the room (later known as the Film Editing Room) were tricked up with the yellow curls of Vincent van Gogh's Starry Starry Night sky and Tiny made himself available to the press. Transsexual, Miss Natasha turned up too, all of which was successfully filmed.

Said Martin, 'We had a training camp for him right here on the balcony. Tiny was singing songs, playing ping-pong with his ukulele and it was billed as the World Professional Non-Stop Singing Record Training Camp. We got some good film of that. And then we had a press conference here in the house. Various people asked questions about him and his ideas. He called the marathon an athletic justification.'

'Have you been training this morning?' asked one journalist.

'No,' Tiny replied, 'I've been training for the last eight years!' (23)

Evening came, Tiny returned to his hotel, Martin cleaned the house and prepared for the marathon the following day where he and Tiny crossed the harbour by boat - all filmed. Said Martin, 'The Nimrod provided a boat for us, so there was a good esprit de corps I think.'

Martin described what happened next, 'Dressing room, tune up, the band's there. The crowd starts drifting in – not a lot of people at first but it starts to build up. We had a special costume for Tiny.

'Before the show he ordered a big box of mangoes. He'd always give me anything that was left over so I thought, "I'll get a few mangoes from this" - but he'd eaten them. That was his secret ingredient I think, to give him strength to do the show, he'd eaten this whole box of mangoes!' (24)

The band had arrived, the same line-up as for the Chameleon sessions. Tim Lewis and Richard Liney helped with stage sets. (25) Film crews set up in three vantage points, so nothing was lost if one should stall. Hayden Keenan and George Gittoes were geared for action. Sydney Morning Herald photographer Robert Macfarlane was camera-ready for tomorrow's papers. Roger assisted with lights. Leon Fink was discreetly overseeing. Garry and Ted Markstein watched all this from John Firth-Smith's boat in the harbour. (Ted was about to start a couple of months helping Garry, painting at the Park.) (26)

Tiny splashed a puff of face powder on his cheeks and John McDonald, the ringmaster from Ringling Brothers Circus walked to the mike and announced the opening act - Jeannie Lewis!

After two years out of the country, Jeannie was surprised to come home to a request from Martin. She said, 'I'd only just got back and they had the Non-Stop Singing Record. Martin asked me to come and sing at Luna Park dressed as Pierrette! (Melody may have made that.)' (27)

Martin proudly announced, 'Jeannie Lewis opened the show. She sang some beautiful songs, The Artist's Life, King Kong and one other song. She was dressed as a Pierrette.' (28)

Jeannie was followed by Adrian Rawlins, 'Ladies and gentlemen, guys and gals, welcome to the setting of the world non-stop professional singing record. Would you welcome to the stage America's Ambassador of Song, the Eternal Troubadour, the Human Lyrebird, the Superman of Song, MR TINY TIM!' (29)

Dressed in his comic strip suit, Tiny emerged stage-left, blowing kisses, carrying his shopping bag and trying not to trip over the leads on the way to the microphone.

Said Martin, 'He started off with the first song ever written for the phonograph - My name is Mr Phonograph, I'm not so very old, my father's name is Edison and I'm worth my weight in gold. A great start then he just launched off into this non-stop marathon. Often I had the feeling he was trying to lose the hounds that were after him. The musicians were the hounds trying to catch the fox. He was trying to shake them off. He'd try to find songs they didn't know.

'He knew his material of course and Marvin Lewis knew his material very well. Tiny would sing in blocks of songs. He'd construct this marathon out of these various blocks.' (30)

Jeannie, who joined the audience after performing her set, was astounded. She described what she saw, 'I looked up and there was this band of amazing musicians, some I'd worked with. Amazing musicians! I thought – only they would be able to follow Tiny! I mean, for Nathan who had to produce it! I don't know how he did it because Tiny would just drop bars, go into the next bit and do something else…! I just don't know how they followed him – but anyway, they did! He'd drop bars everywhere - he'd be going into the next song - but they were with him.' (31)

Red shirt, red lights, red hair, red stage. Red was the dominant colour of the comic strip suit, the colour of much of the Palais' sets and décor, and as if that wasn't all red enough, there was a filter on the lights, making Tiny's mop of normally burgundy-dyed hair positively glow.

Without a pause Tiny launched into the up-tempo Goody Goody. Some began to dance but before they could settle into the song it switched to It's A Good Day then Don't Sit Under The Apple Tree (With Anyone Else But Me). The pace slowed, Shine On Harvest Moon. Pennies From Heaven. Faster - Coming In On A Wing And A Prayer, Don't Fence Me In followed by the first song of the night where Tiny used his famous falsetto - Cool Water.

Swanee, For Me And My Gal, I Want A Girl Like The Girl That Married Dear Old Dad then a few songs which seem to relate to his estranged wife Miss Vicki – I Wonder Who's Kissing Her Now, After The Ball and Just One More Chance. Strong audience response, many waltzed, leading to Just A Gigolo, which Tiny sang in firm – not fey - voice. The pace quickened, Accentuate The Positives, followed by The Chattanooga Choo Choo a real tongue twister, which Tiny sang real fast. Everyone got on the dance floor for It's Gonna Be A Great Day.

Through all of this, Tiny never missed a lyric, never played his uke and rarely used the high voice. One minute the audience was swaying, next dancing. They came to a standstill for Mame, an Al Jolson song they might have heard their Grandma sing.

Praise The Lord And Pass The Ammunition, Give Me That Ole Time Religion, Bad Moon Rising, Blue Suede Shoes, I Don't Want To Set The World On Fire. Tiny was peaking.

He slowed the mood for the swaying rhythm of He's Got The Whole World In His Hands during which a bell was heard at the two hour mark.

The audience went wild, Tiny blew kisses and squeezed 'thank you, thank you' between phrases of the song.

'I rang the bell,' said Martin. 'The line was, "Every time I look at the holy book I want to tremble, when I read about where the carpenter clears the temple, but the buyers and the sellers..." - and that's where the bell went - are no different fellas to what you and I profess to be'. A fantastic moment, his artistic endeavour and his religious faith coinciding.' (32)

Michael Row The Boat Ashore came next. Tiny was clear of the two-hour mark. He had achieved what he set out to do and the record was set. Huge applause.

Singing from an interminably long lyric sheet Tiny chose as his encore a power rendition of Staying Alive – an endurance test in itself – 'stayin' alive! stayin' alive…!' The audience of 300 were partying hard, cheering, clapping.

After two hours, 15 minutes and seven seconds Tiny stepped back from the mic, which passed to Adrian Rawlins who proclaimed, 'I think we've witnessed a historic event – the new World Heavyweight Singing Champion, the one and only – Tiny Tim!'

'Thank you, thank you,' responded Tiny, leaving the stage. 'And God bless you all.' (33)

'We filmed it of course,' said Martin. 'Hayden Keenan helped with sound. Martha was helping with the camera. George Gittoes shooting through a prism up the front. Russell Boyd was shooting one of the cameras. Mike Edols was doing another and Tom Cowan too. Wonderful cinematographers – masters. To get the whole show down on three cameras is very different to video. The cueing system was designed by Bill Hicks. So the whole show was captured. Elizabeth Knight was working on the film. She was a great help. She'd been in the Paris Theatre Company. She was the producer really for that concert.' (34)

After the marathon, Tiny chatted to Victoria Cobden backstage then came out to do some more filming dressed in the Pierrot made by Melody.

Martin said 'The crowd had left. It was really just the film crew there and a few other people who were hanging around. We were all very happy with the concert and the filming. The night was a great success. Tiny came back dressed as Pierrot and sang Lonely Troubadour. It was a very touching song. He was very inspired by Miss Ingrid at the time. She was right up the back of the Floating Ballroom and he was singing Lonely Troubadour to her.' (35)

After Tiny, the band and everyone else had packed up and gone, Roger and his assistant needed to double-back to pick up the lights.

With an eerie resemblance to the Sentimental Bloke character that Martin appropriated for his Land of Sweeping Plains cartoon, Roger watched Martin sweeping the dance floor all by himself – he was the last to leave.

Martin was so happy that he didn't want the night to ever end. (36)

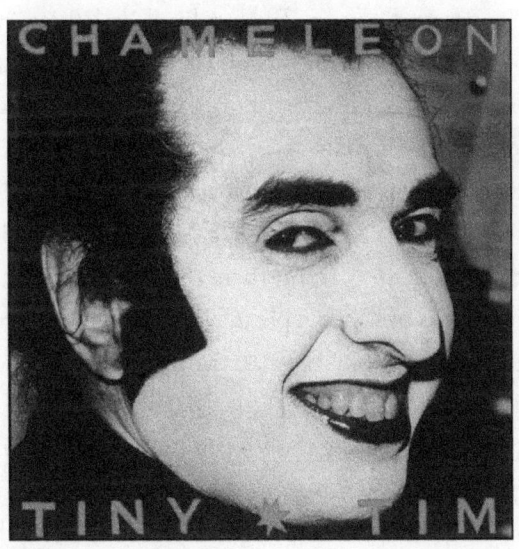

18.

REVENGE OF THE CLOWNING CALAVERAS

The piece Martin did as the Clowning Calaveras backdrop is his interpretation of that life/death mask. He had done a small painting of that to go on the back cover of the Tears of Steel LP. Martin tore it into pieces because he said, 'Jeannie, the death side is too strong'.

JEANNIE LEWIS

Melody Cooper and Steven Teather lived at Wirian now. William Yang had moved in and Martin was on the edge of selling the place. He was hiring out Wirian as a film set. For example, some indoor scenes for Fatty Finn were shot in Wirian.

Film companies negotiated with Albert, not Martin. He only chimed in to enquire about how to proceed with his own film, which was being worked on only a room away from where they were filming. (1)

Martin invited lots of film people to check out his footage of the Non-Stop Singing Marathon, but they all had different opinions - Haydn Keenan, Chris Cordeaux, David Lowrie, Marilyn Karet, Michael Norton.

Since glory days of painting the Face of Luna Park, Premier Wran still refused to sign that bloody lease and the artists' morale was at a trickle. The week-by-week tenancy meant the artists didn't know whether they'd even be back next week and management certainly didn't have the confidence to make an investment in – safety, for example.

Kingo had already forcefully expressed himself, Garry too. Martin was constantly writing to Leon Fink, Nathan Spatt and Nathan's son Maurice (now manager). The Big Dipper was their main concern.

And then came a blast from the past. Martin said, 'I was on the edge of selling Wirian when Dr Pepper, a mad disc jockey and singer from Melbourne came up and gave me a trip and took me to Luna Park. I hadn't had a trip for 10 years and suddenly we decided to take the ferry to Luna Park.'

Dr Pepper goes back to Yellow House days. David Pepperall started Australia's first import Rock record shop and had been a musician, bookseller, record retailer and writer for Daily Planet, Go-Set, Nation Review, Rolling Stone, Digger and Juke. That night, he took back Martin to Luna Park.

At the Circular Quay turnstile Martin and the Doctor were greeted by two enormous people, a man and a woman, 'weighing 25 stone each!' Astonished, Martin said, 'You're going to Luna Park and Lizzie and Larry Luna sell you the ticket. You're in the Magic Theatre. These weren't hallucinations, they were genuine.'

In his pocket Martin was carrying a cassette recorder with a Tiny Tim tape inside. He continued, 'I've got Tiny Tim on a cassette and I'm trying to take it over to Luna Park. This is to meld Tiny and the place together so that I can make the film there. And they said, "You'd better leave Tiny with us (or your recorder) because you don't know what's it's like over there tonight". It was a matter of trust, they were the Guardians at the Gate. I said, "Ok I'll leave it with you, I'll pick it up on the way back - you listen to it!". They said, "Ok" so that felt right because I could tell that they knew somehow that we were on a voyage of seeking reality there. We rode across on the ferry.

'Walking down the mid-way in the Park I saw monsters, werewolves, Draculas and vampires. They were people who'd bought masks that go right over their heads. Thirteen dollars they were selling for. Thirteen. These people were walking through the Park that never had this heavy degree of image. I thought, "The place is being taken over by monsters!" It always had a more fun imagery.

'Where are they all coming from - these monsters? All sorts of terrible things like skeleton horses, grotesques, plastic shit and the terrible end of Psychedelic Art. I tracked this bad vibe to this Magic Shop, painted black. I knew one of the nicest girls who used to work at that shop. I was surprised - I expected to see some witch selling this stuff!

'Anyway the night went on. We went for three rides around the River Caves, just kept rowing. It was amazing, just like a Buddhist shrine. I don't know if we went on the Ghost Train, I can't remember.' (2)

UNESCO had proclaimed 1979 as the International Year of the Child. It was said to be the brainchild of Canon Joseph Moermann, Secretary-General of the International Catholic Child Bureau in Geneva - but Martin disputed that. He reckoned it was the concept of a Sydney woman. That's what Canon James Whild told him when they discussed the matter. Martin said, 'I think it was a warning - the Year of the Child. I could have been making more of a fuss. I was not being as critical as I should have, because I wanted to make the film.' (3)

Martin was also clipping cartoons that he felt related to Luna Park. One, signed Tenat TTO had a pregnant Neville Wran with the Harbour Bridge, the Opera House, Luna Casino in the background and a harbour full of sharks. Also a Jenny Coopes cartoon, 'Mr and Mrs Sin go to Luna Park'. Another, located in hell, which wasn't consciously meant to be Luna Park but it is, if you choose to see it that way - the words above the portal read: Abandon Hope All Ye Who Enter Here. (4)

Eerily, what Martin, Kingo and the others feared most - and virtually predicted - happened. 'On 16 April 1979, 13 people were injured on the Big Dipper when a steel runner came loose and halted a Dipper carriage,' reported Sam Marshall, author of Luna Park Just for Fun, 'The following carriage rammed into the rear, injuring its occupants. A warning had been served.' (5)

'It was the first time the Big Dipper had a smash,' said Martin, 'A lot of the old people then tried to shut down the place because they knew this was it. They knew it was a real warning. They were in touch with the place, the Carneys. Only when they feel safe enough will Carnies settle in a spot and build there instead of moving on. The funfair is a carnival that's settled down. But no, the Park stayed open.

'Tiny was like the Angel Gabriel marking the turf. Coming up to the two hours he starts going into, "Every time I look into the Holy Book it makes me tremble…!" The big statement that he made is "…the money-changers in the Temple." And Luna Park was the Temple in this instance, a holy place but a funfair at the same time. The Big Dipper happened, they didn't do anything. Once the Big Dipper smashed and they didn't close it down, you'd then say that they became culpable.

'As an artist I can occasionally remember the images leading up. There was an intention towards doing up the Ghost Train. There was meant to be a new Ghost Train done by Bruce Petty. Then the struggle for the real estate became so intense.

'Everything was done on the cheap. They had the oldest fire extinguisher, the oldest fire sprinklers. It was meant to look like a funfair, but not meant to succeed like a funfair. That was the whole business principle behind it. So they could say, We can't run a funfair. We've tried hard for five years. We've put everything into it. Were running at a loss. We're honourable. We want to put up our casino on the spot! The Big Dipper smash was a warning. I'm not particularly blaming anyone for it. They kept refusing to give Leon the lease.' (6)

Thursday 7 June, Martin received the first cut of the film. After looking at it Martin said, 'the whole film had a pretty weird feel to it'. (7)

Next day Australian Playboy published a Gahan Wilson cartoon with a face just like Luna Park and two kids asking, 'How come there's no exit?'

This cartoon was drawn from America. (8)

On Saturday 9 June Garry was working on the Carousel until nightfall. He said, 'I happened to walk through the Ghost Train (it was about

5.00 before I went home) and I was amazed how much rubbish there was – stuff thrown out, paper, crap, and I thought, Jeez this is dangerous!' (9)

The evening was calm and warm. The moon was touching full. Around 8.00 Martin walked into the editing room and switched on the Moviola. The screen was frozen on an image of Tiny pointing straight at the viewer and looking severe. Martin wondered what it meant?

'It means I've got to edit the film myself,' he concluded. 'The Moviola can be on every day and you don't take notice of the picture. I interpreted it as, You've got to edit the film yourself which was all I could think of - because I was worried about other people cutting it wrong.' (10)

Then it happened.

Sam Marshall writes, 'On Cracker Night, 9 June 1979, no trains were running due to a rail strike. The Big Dipper was still being repaired. The Ghost Train was the only train operating in Sydney that night. A minimum of three attendants were usually needed to operate the Ghost Train – an operator, a ticket collector and a third person who patrolled the interior for any mischief. On this night, there were only two staff, leaving the interior unpatrolled and vulnerable. What was not supposed to happen happened. A fire broke out and quickly spread in the timber building with its bitumen-covered roof. There were no sprinklers and water pressure was low.' (11)

Martin was in the editing room, cutting Tiny in his Pierrot costume into the film. 'Tiny drew my attention to the fact that something amazing was going on,' said Martin. (12)

'I was anxious when I picked up the film splicer for the first time. I struggled to splice the two pieces of film together. I made one join then the next seemed to spring out of my hands, uncoiling into a perplexity tangle. I made the first cut about the time Luna Park was going up in flames. The phone rang. I left the Moviola with the half completed edit and ran to the next room.' (13)

It was Arkie Whiteley, she said, 'Luna Park's on fire!' Arkie was looking out the window from their place at Lavender Bay with Luna Park directly in front of her. Martin wasn't quick to understand because Arkie's voiceprint sounded like a friend - Mandy Wright.

Mandy Wright.

Said Martin, 'The doorbell rang - it was Mandy and Peter Wright. "We've just come from the Whiteley's and we thought we'd call in". (That's how Arkie picked up her voiceprint.)'

Martin replied, 'Arkie just rang. Luna Park's on fire.'

Peter said, 'We've just left Lavender Bay, it looked like fire. I said to Mandy I've never seen the Park look so bright. The lights were blazing like a huge surge of power going through the place!'

Martin freaked, 'I've got to go over!'

He sped there, thinking through the problems they'd had with management and letters he'd never sent. Martin had mixed feelings at first, 'Initially I thought the fire might be a good thing'.

He felt the fire might be enough to get the park back onto a safer and more artistic footing.

Martin said, 'As I arrived out of the tunnel onto the Cahill Expressway the impact was immediate. The whole centre of the Park seemed to be an inferno with flames gushing into the still sky. I thought, The whole place is going up! (14)

'The whole sky was orange, like a huge bush fire surging out of the middle of Luna Park. You could see it as soon as you got anywhere near the Bridge.' (15)

'By the time I'd reached the Park, through the crowds and blocked traffic, the fire had subsided considerably and the damage was not as vast as the flames had indicated. The superstructure of the Big Dipper was still burning and then the fire was just smouldering. I worked my way round to the entrance.' (16)

Walking into the Park, Martin ran into the leader of the Muktananda crowd, 'Quite a powerful figure, he reminds me of a Crowleyish sort of figure. I'd met him a few times before. He was the first person I knew when I got there. And a beautiful girl called Willow - Tiptoe by the willow tree. When I first met her, I gave her a possum. She was on the merry-go-round at Luna Park. Then I went over to her place and he arrived. It was kinda like a competition. He talked about his film and I talked about mine. He won her and became her boyfriend. The next time I see him it's at the fire at Luna Park! (17)

'It appeared no one was hurt,' Martin continued, 'I sighed with relief, at least this will get some action and prise the dead hand of the management off the place, I thought. Some of the Park may have been lost, but the ludicrous conflict between management and the Premier would be brought into the open and the Park would be saved.

'It was a fire in the Ghost Train. They got everyone out. I saw a gap in the crowd around the gate and pushed through - the security guard's back was turned - I got past him, stepping over fire hoses, drawn onwards. "Hey you! Where are you going?" I hesitated and turned back, "I work here" (Why didn't I have my badge!) "No one's allowed in mate – outside!" I felt if anyone was allowed in, it should be me. I joined the crowd outside the gate, found my way to the car and went home.' (18)

Back at Wirian, Martin rang Kingo who was at Palm Beach. Kingo didn't believe what Martin was telling him. So Martin rang Richard. Martin and he returned to the Park. As they drove, the announcement came over the radio - four dead in the Luna Park Ghost Train blaze... more bodies expected.

'It's over,' Martin said to Richard, 'That's the end. All our dreams for Luna Park had gone up in the Ghost Train blaze!'

Said Martin, 'Richard and I stood outside the entrance and talked with some reporters who had come late to the scene. We saw Maurice Spatt, the new manager being interviewed. We should have gone over and spoken with him but we both hung back. We went home. It was impossible to sleep. We listened to the grim reports on the news and I played Jeannie Lewis' record Clowning Calaveras.' (19)

Said Martin, 'This is all prophecy about Luna Park!' (20)

'It was Jeannie as an artist singing - but it was also Luna Park. No one else could have made that connection. I was involved in both Luna Park and Jeannie Lewis. This concert was three years before the fire. Clowning Calaveras is based on the Festival of the Dead in Mexico where they make death sweets, skulls made of sugar and they dress up in masks. It's like a Ghost Train Festival, if you like. And Jeannie wanted it to be like the Ghost Train, with that sort of imagery. That was the sort of imagery I related to anyway, it was Pop Art.

'There was a real piece of the Ghost Train on the stage – paper skulls, luminous skeletons all around the walls. The image she wanted me to create which I did for the show (but I couldn't do it for her record cover) was that double-faced life/death heart-shaped Abraxas - skull on one side and a loving face on the other. The two came together with two huge sliding walls.'

Horrified by news broadcasts and shocked by what he had witnessed, Martin played the first track,

Glitter and be gay, that's the part I play, forced to bend my soul, to a sordid role...

He explained, 'Luna Park has been a pawn in a political game.

Rising Of The Tide is the second track:

Where does it lead to this madness

the waste of time - pace of time ahead...

Full moon keeps rising on the city,

The sun it keeps moving on the other side,

Am I to rule for quite a while longer,

Before we see the rising of the tide...

(Martin: 'The icecaps are melting the tide is rushing in...!')

The law that rules the land is getting harder.

No one seems to know just how it started...

'...like the fire.'

Once again a child had to be the victim...

'...the kids in the fire.'

These songs followed by The Crucifixion, written by Phil Ochs - the late great American singer-songwriter who hanged himself in 1976. Martin said, 'Before Jeannie recorded the song there was just his version of it. I knew it related but I didn't know how.

'When I played it on the night of the Ghost Train fire, after having been to Luna Park, suddenly I understood the song. I knew the lyrics had meaning because of exactly what we'd just seen. It's got very specific lines about fire, sacrifice of children, it's also about Christ. It all came through so strongly. I think I was weeping in horror and amazement.

'The next day I found out that the man who'd been killed in the fire was named John Godson – God Son - so the song called The Crucifixion was about the death of the Son of God. Suddenly it went bang!' (21)

The TV news was terrible. The charred rumble revealed the bodies of six children and one adult: John Godson and his sons Damian and Craig and Waverley College students Jonathon Billings, Richard Carroll, Michael Johnson and Seamus Rahilly.

'That's another image that bears thinking on, the image of John Godson with his two children, one on each side. The other boys were like the four Apostles - four boys from Waverley College - who'd come from Mass. And then you found out that the Public Relations guy who worked at Luna Park at the time had been the Priest. He actually said, "I knew those boys, I baptised them". He left the Priesthood. So they're strangely following him.' (22)

Martin played The Moon's A Harsh Mistress. There was a big moon on the night of the fire. Kingo had already picked the essence of the song. Before the fire, Martin received a note from Kingo saying, 'Play The Moon's A Harsh Mistress to Leon Fink!'

'The moon's a harsh mistress, the moon can be so cold' said Martin. 'Our dreams about the park and the vision we could see for it. There was such goodwill there - a treasure of the past. So that song we related to'. (23)

'For anyone who's young death is particularly mysterious - in a way that's the point of it. It is sacrifice - showing that we walk on thin rails and outside is the hurricane of destruction. It's the place of Golgotha, the place of the skull - the Ghost Train - you get a Pop-Art parallel. And then you get these whole events that are caused by plotting, not caring for kids, carelessness, living a human life, the way of the world. It was the Year of the Child.

'When Tim and I were researching the history of the face, I read this legend. The earliest ones we could pick up were at Borobudur, the temple in Bali, a Buddhist temple that has Hindu images guarding it. You enter through this mouth-like doorway. We found out it was the Face of Glory.

'An earthly King wanted Krishna's wife – God's wife or whatever - and he sent the heaviest guy that he had - called the Seizer to seize things. The Seizer goes along to Krishna and announces that the other fellow wanted his wife and Krishna creates this creature to opposes the Seizer. (I get characters like Neville Wran - because Neville Wran is an atheist) - and the Seizer threatens Krishna. So Krishna creates a beast, which is Hunger Incarnate. The Seizer sees that he is about to be devoured by this creature and he pleads for mercy and - being the way of gods - Krishna grants mercy.

'But he's created Hunger Incarnate which wants to devour. It pleads for mercy to satisfy its hunger. Krishna - with a stroke of genius - says, "Eat yourself". And it starts from the tail and eats everything up to the face and Krishna says, "For this act of sacrifice you shall forever be known as the Face of Glory and shall guard my Temple".

'In Borobudur the image is the Face of Glory, which is like the Luna Park face even in expression, guarding the Buddha. You see, inside Luna Park there was a real Buddha, a real effigy of the Buddha in marble and gold leaf, surrounded by this court, which is like the Endless River. I see it as a conquest of Buddha by dark forces. The Face has always had an unconscious manifestation - being the Face of Sydney - the largest face visible in the city. Also it's a Horned God. Through the two towers, it has a Satanic element in its look. Like Abraxas – comedy/tragedy.

'One line that freaked my mother out – "Abraxas is - the mother's love for the son is the son's horror of the mother". Unreal reality. Illusion becoming reality, the beauty of a lion the instant it strikes down its victim, the saint and betrayer, the curse of God - of good and evil. Beyond the comprehension of man. If you do try to understand it, it drives you mad. Fear of it is wisdom.

'Luna Park was in the city of Sydney, in fact an unconscious presence that sat on the Endless River. The River Caves went round and round and you flowed down the river eventually past the Buddha. He hadn't been picked consciously for that reason. It was unconscious or naïve art, a folk art gesture of truth. But in the actual image-reality, there was Buddha, and in a strange way, worshipped by unknowing people.

'So unconsciously, it was most probably the most important Buddhist shrine in Australia as far as its set-up was concerned. That was replaced with an act of horror and chaos, dark forces manifested. Does that apply to the world? I think it does. He came in fire you see, "I come in fire".

'It happened where man poked fun at death, the Ghost Train, (you went in and came out alive). So where the fire started, the imitation fire turns into a real fire - with the help of someone pouring petrol and a match on it or it happens in its own right. So it was certainly ready to catch fire. But I do feel that it was helped by characters who were caught up in the whole suction of the event. Sydney was on tenderhooks, as Sydney gets when there's a train strike. People are meeting a whole lot of new people at bus stops, hitching and a whole different thing happens.

'The only train running that day in Sydney was the Ghost Train. It's terrible because it's true. It is hard to get onto, something of another world, but it's crucial to our world to understand it. The whole concept of the Ghost Train is to confuse you. Unpredictable, tricks, illusion. The people going through the Ghost Train saw what had been an imitation fire. So people accepted the beginnings of the fire as an illusion - part of the ride.

'They get burned where man mocks death, in the year dedicated to children. It was a message to Sydney and I think it's made me stronger as a Christian but I'm still pretty bad. I still wouldn't even classify myself as being one - even having so much information. Tiny has always steered me in that direction but also the events at Luna Park.

'I could understand them a bit and then suddenly to just become clear - that there was a poetic language working to say "this is a crucifixion, Golgotha, death by fire". I think all these things are the archetype manifesting itself that was realised in Christ. It doesn't cut out the Egyptian gods that preceded it, it's just the wave that broke eventually on the beach.

'The archetypes are all present in this, the sacrifice of the seven, also Pentecost, the pouring out of the Spirit. It had the dark side but what was revealed by the deaths was the light side. Abraxas if you like. The dark face and the light face. What appeared to be horrendous and chaotic had its beauty, which would sustain the parents at least - especially the Christians.

'Abraxas - God and the Devil in their counterpoint. Darkness/Light. The tide going in and out at the same time. Terrible Abraxas. To look upon Abraxas is blindness. To know it is sickness. To worship it is death. To fear it is wisdom. To assist it not is redemption. I don't know what it means. I've never been able to work that out. It's not for man to know Abraxas. When you're locked up in it, I suppose it destroys you. Abraxas is the Sun, but at the same time the terrible sucking gorge or the void.' (24)

Kingo summed it up, 'Martin never stopped feeling guilty about the Ghost Train fire'. (25)

'I couldn't cope with it,' said Martin, 'the passions of romance and things that make it a hand-to-hand situation. Desire and spirituality.' (26)

That night Martin created a belief system that would be reflected in all his future works and everything that happened next.

Said Susan Jensen, 'The fire was definitely the crisis point for Martin. All those threads that were coming together over time suddenly merged into a complete picture of spiritual reality.' (27)

Martin pulled out some photographs that Michael Barker had recorded of the Ghost Train ride. Examining one of the pictures he said, 'This would appear to be seven clocks which are related to the seven deaths in the Ghost Train. And then on closer inspection, I realized there was another clock that was hidden by a man who was doing some carpentry. I remember feeling uneasy because I thought, "Oh God, I thought it was seven, now it's someone else".

'There was a further one when the North Sydney Swimming Pool had been emptied. When I looked through to the end of the pool I saw there were eight crosses and behind them was Luna Park. I hoped there'd just be seven'.

Martin now expected an eighth death.

Martin fully expected it to be Kingo or himself. He said, 'Kingo and I were very tense – who's going to go?' (28)

NOTES

NOTES

CHAPTER 1

(1) Martin Sharp, interview 11 April 1993.

(2) See Wikipedia, 'Spitfire Squadron 453'.

(3) Martin Sharp, interview 3 March 2011.

(4) See Wikipedia, 'Japanese submarines attack on Sydney Harbour'.

(5) Martin Sharp, interview 11 April 1993.

(6) Martin Sharp, interview 19 March 2005.

(7) Martin Sharp, interview 12 February 2011.

(8) Martin Sharp, interview 12 February 2011.

(9) Margaret Olley, Margaret Olley, Far From a Still Life, Meg Stewart, pp. 113-115, 139-140, 151-154, Random House, 2005. Also, Wikipedia, 'Merioola and the Sydney Charm School'.

(10) Martin Sharp, interview 12 February 2011.

(11) Martin Sharp, interview 11 April 1993.

(12) Martin Sharp, interview 23 April 1987.

(13) A Nightingale Sang in Berkeley Square was a hit song for Vera Lynn in 1939. It would become Henry and Jo's 'song' when they were apart. They may have read into the lyrics references to their own courtship – Berkeley Square, Mayfair and a London moon. See also interview with Martin Sharp, 5 April 2011.

(14) Martin Sharp, interview 12 February 2011.

(15) Martin Sharp, interview 11 April 1993.

(16) Martin Sharp, interview 11 April 1993.

(17) Boofhead is a comic strip by Robert Bruce Clarke which first appeared in the Sydney Daily Mirror in May 1941, continuing until 1970. Also Martin Sharp, interview 5 July 1984.

(18) Martin Sharp, interview 16 October 2003.

(19) Martin Sharp, interview 23 April 1987.

(20) Martin Sharp, interview 5 July 1984.
(21) Martin Sharp, interview 16 October 2003.
(22) AC Child, Cranbrook – The First Fifty Years (1918-1968), Waite & Bull, 1968.
(23) Martin Sharp, interview 11 April 1993.
(24) See Wikipedia, 'Blake Prize for Religious Art'.
(25) Martin Sharp, interview 12 February 2011.
(26) Martin Sharp, interview 5 April 2011.
(27) Martin Sharp, interview 12 February 2011.
(28) Martin Sharp, Memories of Telford, a special interest publication, 2002.
(29) Martin Sharp, interview 6 May 2002.
(30) Martin Sharp, interview 1 February 1983.

CHAPTER 2

(1) Martin Sharp, interview 11 April 1993. Also, AC Child, Cranbrook – The First Fifty Years (1918-1968), Waite & Bull, 1968.

(2) Martin Sharp, interview 12 February 2011. See also former student Tim Lewis, interview 2 June 2014. Because of the brutality Tim's parents removed him from Cranbrook School and enrolled him elsewhere. He says, 'I got caned and all that sort of thing. My parents took me away from Cranbrook because they didn't like those marks on my leg, hit by rulers and bruises and things like that'.

(3) Martin Sharp, interview 12 February 2011.
(4) Martin Sharp, interview Martin 5 April 2011.
(5) Times Educational Supplement, London, 10 January 1986.
(6) Martin Sharp, interview 18 January 1994.
(7) Martin Sharp, interview 11 April 1993.
(8) Richard Neville, Hippie Hippie Shake, p. 49, Wm Heinemann Australia 1995. Also, Martin Sharp interview 17 April 2002.
(9) Martin Sharp, interview 18 January 1994. Martin did not name the perpetrator but added angrily, 'He's got a family, he's got kids in the school now – or he has had – I'd have a word with him if I saw him again!'
(10) Martin Sharp, Catalog, p. 4, 5, 36. Reid Books, 1971.
(11) Martin Sharp, interview 6 September 1982.
(12) Martin Sharp, interview 11 April 1993.
(13) Peter Kingston, interview 28 October 2014.
(14) Martin Sharp, interview 11 April 1993.
(15) Martin Sharp, interview 18 January 1994.
(16) Martin Sharp, interview 5 April 2011.
(17) Martin Sharp, interview 12 February 2011.
(18) Martin Sharp, interview 12 February 2011.
(19) Martin Sharp, interview 11 April 1993.
(20) Martin Sharp, interview 11 April 1993. And, Catalog, p. 4, 5. Reid Books, 1971.

(21) Sydney Morning Herald, Arts and Entertainment, 15 August 2005.

(22) Martin Sharp, interview 16 October 2003.

(23) Martin Sharp, interview 11 April 1993.

(24) Martin Sharp, interview 16 October 2003.

(25) Martin Sharp, interview 31 July 2003.

(26) Martin Sharp, interview 16 October 2003.

(27) AC Child, Cranbrook – The First Fifty Years (1918-1968), Waite & Bull, 1968.

(28) Martin Sharp, interview 29 December 1990.

(29) Martin Sharp, interview 6 September 1982.

(30) Martin Sharp, interview, 6 September 1982. The picture is titled After 'Still Life' by Van Gogh (1957), synthetic polymer paint, water colour on paper.

(31) Martin Sharp, interview 29 December 1990.

(32) Martin Sharp, interview 11 April 1993.

(33) Richard Neville, Hippie Hippie Shake, pp. 19, 49. Wm Heinemann Australia 1995.

(34) Martin Sharp, interview 18 January 1994.

CHAPTER 3

(1) Martin Sharp, Cartoons, p. 8. Scripts Pty Ltd, 1966.

(2) Afferbeck Lauder, Let Stalk Strine, p. 20, Ure Smith, 1965.

(3) Barry Humphries, Wild Life in Suburbia, an EP (extended play) recording on the Score label, 1958.

(4) Nino Culotta (John O'Grady), They're A Weird Mob, Ure Smith, 1957.

(5) Jenny Kee, A Big Life, p. 30, Penguin 2006.

(6) Richard Neville, Hippie Hippie Shake, p. 8. William Heinemann, 1995.

(7) Martin Sharp, interview 16 October 2003.

(8) Garry Shead, interview 13 February 2015.

(9) Martin Sharp, interview 29 December 1990.

(10) Martin Sharp, interview 6 September 1982. A photo of Richard Neville poised to hit Bandstand's dance floor - see Hippie Hippie Shake, p. 121. William Heinemann, 1995.

(11) Martin Sharp, interview 16 October 2003.

(12) Martin Sharp, interview 16 October 2003.

(13) Brian Kennedy, A Passion to Oppose, John Anderson, Philosopher, Melbourne University Press 1995.

(14) Anne Coombs, Sex and Anarchy, The Life and Death of the Sydney Push, Penguin Books 1996.

(15) Martin Sharp, interview 12 February 2011.

(16) Garry Shead, interview 13 February 2015.

(17) Lionel Lindsay, Addled Art, p. 15, 37. Hollis & Carter London, 1946.

(18) Margot Hilton and Graeme Blundell, Whiteley, An Unauthorised Life, p. 46 Pan MacMillan, 1996.

(19) Geoffrey Dutton, The Innovators, p. 190 MacMillan 1986.

(20) Martin Sharp, interview 16 October 2003.

(21) Martin Sharp, interview 6 September 1982.

(22) Garry Shead, interview 13 February 2015. Also, Richard Walsh, The Australian 3 December 2013

(23) Martin Sharp, interview 29 December 1990.

(24) Martin Sharp, interview 6 September 1982.

(25) Martin Sharp, interview 29 December 1990.

(26) Colin Lanceley, Colin Lanceley, p. 19, Craftsman House 1987.

(27) Martin Sharp, interview 6 September 1982.

(28) Martin Sharp, interview 29 December 1990.

(29) Garry Shead, interview 13 February 2015.

(30) Martin Sharp, interview 29 December 1990.

(31) See Arty Wild Oat, University of Wollongong Research Online. ro.uow.edu.au (digital collection)

(32) Albie Thoms, My Generation, p. 100.

(33) Martin Sharp, interview 23 April 1987.

(34) Richard Neville, Hippie Hippie Shake, p. 19. William Heinemann, 1995.

(34) Garry Shead, interview 13 February 2015.

(35) Martin Sharp, interview 6 September 1982.

(36) Garry Shead, interview 13 February 2015.

(37) Martin Sharp, interview

(38) Garry Shead, The Bulletin, 30 June 1962.

(39) Garry Shead, interview 13 February 2015.

(40) Garry Shead, interview 13 February 2015.

(41) Martin Sharp, interview 5 January 1991.

CHAPTER 4

(1) The People of California (plaintiff) V Lawrence Ferlinghetti. The defendant is charged with a violation of Section 311.3 of the Penal Code of the State of California.

(2) DH Lawrence, Lady Chatterley's Lover. The Penguin second edition, published in 1961, contains a publisher's dedication, which reads: 'For having published this book, Penguin Books were prosecuted under the Obscene Publications Act, 1959 at the Old Bailey in London from 20 October to 2 November 1960. This edition is therefore dedicated to the twelve jurors, three women and nine men, who returned a verdict of "not guilty" and thus made D. H. Lawrence's last novel available for the first time to the public in the United Kingdom'.

(3) Richard Neville, Hippie Hippie Shake, p. 23-27, William Heinemann 1995.

(4) Martin Sharp, interview 6 September 1982.

(5) Richard Neville, Hippie Hippie Shake, p. 27, William Heinemann 1995. Oz Magazine, p. 13, August 1963.

(6) OZ Magazine, p. 11, September 1963.

(7) Craig McGregor, People, Politics and Pop, p. 83-84, Ure Smith, 1968.

(8) Ted Markstein, interview, 1 January 2015.

(9) Martin Sharp, interview 29 December 1990.

(10) Darlene Bungey, John Olsen, An Artist's Life, p 179, ABC Books, 2014.

(11) Albie Thoms, My Generation,

(12) Richard Neville, Hippie Hippie Shake, p. 29-30, William Heinemann 1995.

(13) Albie Thoms, My Generation, p. 153.

(14) OZ magazine, 'Obscene or Absurd?' p 12, Xmas and New Year Issue, 1963/64.

(15) Albie Thoms, My Generation, p. 155 and thereabouts

(16) Martin Sharp, interview 29 December 1990.

(17) Martin Sharp, Cartoons, p. 30, Scripts Pty Ltd 1966.

(18) Martin Sharp, interview 6 September 1982.

(19) Martin Sharp, interview 12 February 2011.

(20) Jenny Kee, A Big Life, p. 27, Penguin Lantern, 2006.

(21) Martin Sharp, interview 16 October 2003.

(22) Duncan McNab, The Usual Suspect, the Life of Abe Saffron, p. 84, McMillan 2005.

(23) Richard Neville, Hippie Hippie Shake, p. 36-37, William Heinemann 1995.

(24) Martin Sharp, interview 22 October 2003.

(25) Barry Humphries, Neglected Poems and Other Creatures, p. 49. Angus & Robertson, 1991.

(26) Albie Thoms, My Generation, p.146.

(27) Martin Sharp, interview 29 December 1990.

(28) Richard Neville, Hippie Hippie Shake, p. 35, William Heinemann 1995.

CHAPTER 5

(1) Glenn A Baker The Beatles Down Under...Wild & Woolley 1982.

(2) Martin Sharp, interview 16 October 2003.

(3) Jenny Kee, A Big Life, p. 34-38, Penguin Lantern, 2006.

(4) Martin Sharp, interview 31 July 2003.

(5) Richard Neville, Hippie Hippie Shake, p. 39, William Heinemann 1995.

(6) Bob Whitaker, The Unseen Beatles, Conran Octopus 1991.

(7) Martin Sharp, interview 31 July 2003.

(8) Colin Lanceley, Colin Lanceley, p. 10, Craftsman House 1987.

(9) Cover OZ magazine, No 12 August 1964. Mirka Mora acknowledges this in Wicked But Virtuous, My Life, p. 140-141, Viking, 2000.

(10) Mirka Mora, Wicked But Virtuous, My Life, p. 58, Viking, 2000.

(11) Martin Sharp, interview 31 July 2003.

(12) Bob Whitaker, The Unseen Beatles, p. 7-9, Conran Octopus 1991.

(13) Martin Sharp, interview 5 July 1984.

(14) Martin Sharp, interview 12 February 2011.

(15) Martin Sharp, interview 12 February 2011.

(16) OZ magazine, 'Social Top Twenty' p. 14, Xmas and New Year Issue, 1963/64.

(17) Martin Sharp, interview 5 April 2011.

(18) Martin Sharp, interview 12 February 2011 and 11 April 2011.
(19) Martin Sharp, interview 17 April 2002.
(20) Richard Walsh, The Australian, article 'Wizards of satire put OZ on the map'. 25 March 2013.
(21) Martin Sharp, interview 8 November 2006.
(22) Geoffrey Dutton, The Innovators, p. 225-227, Macmillan 1986.
(23) Craig McGregor, People, Politics and Pop, p. 85-86, Ure Smith, 1968.
(24) Martin Sharp, Cartoons, p. 2, Scripts Pty Ltd 1966.
(25) Martin Sharp, interview 11 April 1993.
(26) Martin Sharp, interview 17 April 2002
(27) Geoffrey Dutton, The Innovators, p. 225-227, Macmillan 1986.
(28) Martin Sharp, interview 17 April 2002
(29) Martin Sharp, interview 6 September 1982.
(30) Mirka Mora, Wicked But Virtuous, My Life, p. 58, Viking, 2000.
(31) Richard Neville, Hippie Hippie Shake, p. 54, William Heinemann 1995.
(32) Garry Shead, interview 13 February 2015.
(33) Richard Neville, Hippie Hippie Shake, p. 54, William Heinemann 1995.
(34) Roger Foley email 16 November 2014, Garry Shead interview 13 February 2015 and my diary notes.
(35) Greg Weight, interview 24 November 2014.
(36) The Everlasting World of Martin Sharp, p. 11, Ivan Dougherty Gallery, 2006.
(37) Martin Sharp, interview 5 January 1991.
(38) Richard Neville, Hippie Hippie Shake, p. 51, William Heinemann 1995.
(39) Jenny Kee, A Big Life, p. 43, Penguin Lantern, 2006.
(40) Martin Sharp, Cartoons, p. 30, Scripts Pty Ltd 1966.
(41) Gary Shearston, 'Sydney Town', An Anthology of Gary Shearston, 2007.
(42) Wikipedia, see OZ magazine.
(43) Martin Sharp, Cartoons, p. 22, Scripts Pty Ltd 1966.
(44) Martin Sharp, interview 11 April 1993.
(45) Martin Sharp, interview 12 February 2011.
(46) Albie Thoms, My Generation, p. 249.
(47) Roger Foley, radio interview with Sally Baillieu (undated, probably 2013).
(48) Albie Thoms, My Generation, p. 249.
(49) Greg Weight, interview 24 November 2014.
(50) Martin Sharp, interview 12 February 2011.
(51) Martin Sharp, interview, 16 October 2003.
(52) Martin Sharp, interview 5 July 1984.
(53) Martin Sharp, interview 12 February 2011.
(54) Martin Sharp, interview 12 February 2011.

CHAPTER 6

(1) Martin Sharp, Cartoons, Scripts Pty Ltd, 1966.

(2) Peter Draffin, Pop, 116 pages, Scripts Pty Ltd, 1967.
(3) Peter Draffin, interview 20 March 2015.
(4) Martin Sharp, interview 22 October 2003.
(5) Peter Draffin, interview 20 March 2015.
(6) OZ Magazine, No 26 (cover) and p. 3, 4, 7, 12, 15, 16, OZ 27 p. 6, OZ 28 p.19.
(7) Craig McGregor, People, Politics and Pop, Ure Smith, 1968.
(8) Martin Sharp, interview 22 October 2003.
(9) Craig McGregor, People, Politics and Pop, Ure Smith, 1968.
See 'Private School' p. 187, 'Three Gaoled Filthy Paper' p. 87, Suburban love goddesses, p. 19, 47, 'Excuse I', p. 35. Beatles collage p. 72 and 'Bobby Dylan' p. 161.
(10) OZ Magazine, No 26 April issue.
(11) Martin Sharp, interview 11 April 1993.
(12) Richard Neville, Hippie Hippie Shake, p. 58-64, William Heinemann 1995.
(13) Martin Sharp, interview 16 October 2003.
(14) Richard Neville, Hippie Hippie Shake, p. 62, William Heinemann 1995.
(15) Martin Sharp, interview 11 April 1993.
(16) Jill Neville, Obituary, The Independent, 12 June 1997.
(17) Martin Sharp, interview 19 March 2005.
(18) Richard Neville, Hippie Hippie Shake, p. 65, William Heinemann 1995.
(19) Jenny Kee, A Big Life, p. 64, Penguin Lantern, 2006.
(20) Martin Sharp, interview 19 March 2005.
(21) Richard Neville, Hippie Hippie Shake, p. 68-69, William Heinemann 1995.
(22) Martin Sharp, interview 11 April 1993.
(23) Martin Sharp, interview 16 October 2003.
(24) Martin Sharp, interview 22 October 2003.
(25) Bob Whitaker, The Unseen Beatles, Conran Octopus 1991.
(26) Martin Sharp, interview 5 July 1984.
(27) Martin Sharp, interview 22 October 2003.
(28) Martin Sharp, interview 16 October 2003.
(29) Martin Sharp, interview 6 September 1982.
(30) Richard Neville, Hippie Hippie Shake, p. 82, William Heinemann 1995.
(31) Richard Neville, Hippie Hippie Shake, p. 77, William Heinemann 1995.
(32) Martin Sharp, interview 6 September 1982.
(33) Martin Sharp, interview 16 October 2003.
(34) Martin Sharp, interview 6 September 1982.
(35) Martin Sharp, Twice Upon a Time, photocopy signed by Martin and held in the author's collection. He wrote, 'Drawn on the Baleric Isle of Formenterra Spain in the late 60s whilst stayed with Peter Draffin.' Martin – 12.6.1985.
(36) Martin Sharp, interview 31 July 2003.
(37) Jenny Kee, A Big Life, p. 67, Penguin Lantern, 2006.
(38) Martin Sharp, interview 6 September 1982.
(39) Greg Weight, interview 24 November 2014.

(40) Eric Clapton, The Autobiography, p. 90, Century London, 2007.
(41) Martin Sharp, interview 5 July 1984.
(42) Martin Sharp, interview 16 January 1991.
(43) Jack Bruce, Composing Himself, p. 97, Jawbone Press.
(44) Dave Thompson, Cream, The World's First Supergroup, pp. 150-154, Virgin 2005.
(45) Wah Wah Pedal, see Wikipedia.
(46) Pete Townshend, Who I Am, p. 108, Harper Collins 2012.
(47) Emanuel Litvinoff, Journey Through a Small Planet, 138 pages, Penguin, 1972.
(48) Martin Sharp, interview 16 October 2003.
(49) Martin Sharp, interview 19 March 2005.
(50) Martin Sharp, interview 6 September 1982.
(51) Martin Sharp, interview 19 March 2005.
(52) Peter Draffin, interview 20 March 2015.
(53) Martin Sharp, interview 16 October 2003.
(54) Richard Neville, Hippie Hippie Shake, p. 72, William Heinemann 1995.

CHAPTER 7

(1) Martin Sharp, interview 16 October 2003.
(2) Eric Clapton, The Autobiography, p. 92, Century London, 2007.
(3) Martin Sharp, interview 5 July 1984.
(4) Martin Sharp, interview 16 October 2003.
(5) Martin Sharp, interview 5 July 1984.
(6) Christine Wallace, Greer – Untamed Shrew, p. 134, Macmillan 1997.
(7) Martin Sharp, interview 23 April 1987.
(8) Martin Sharp, interview 19 March 2005.
(9) Martin Sharp, interview 16 October 2003.
(10) Marsha Rowe, 'Felix Dennis Obituary', The Guardian, 23 June 2014.
(11) Martin Sharp, interview 5 July 1984.
(12) Jack Bruce, Composing Himself, p. 101-102, Jawbone Press.
(13) Bob Whitaker, The Unseen Beatles, p. 151, Conran Octopus 1991.
(14) Martin Sharp, interview 11 April 1993.
(15) Martin Sharp, interview 19 March 2005.
(16) Dave Thompson, Cream, The World's First Supergroup, pp. 187, Virgin 2005.
(17) Angie Errico, author of Rock Album Covers, p. 33, Octopus 1979.
(18) Ginger Baker, Hellraiser, p. 272, John Blake Publishing 2010.
(19) Ginger Baker, Hellraiser, p. 110, John Blake Publishing 2010.
(20) Martin Sharp, interview 11 April 1993.
(21) Martin Sharp, interview 1 February 1983.
(22) Martin Sharp, interview 5 July 1984.
(23) Ginger Baker, Hellraiser, p. 110, John Blake Publishing 2010.
(24) Eric Clapton, The Autobiography, p. 97, Century London, 2007.

(25) Tiny Tim, interview 4 October 1991.

(26) Bill Graham, My Life Inside Rock and Out, p. 226-227, online.

(27) Martin Sharp, interview 22 October 2003.

(28) Martin Sharp, interview 6 September 1982.

(29) Martin Sharp, interview 5 January 1991.

(30) Martin Sharp, interview 5 July 1984. Note: up until early-1967 Cream's road manager was Eric's friend Ben Palmer. See Jack Bruce p. 102.

(31) Martin Sharp, interview 6 September 1982.

(32) Martin Sharp, interview 19 March 2005.

(33) Mirka Mora, Wicked But Virtuous, My Life, p. 99, Viking, 2000.

(34) Richard Neville, Hippie Hippie Shake, p. 105, William Heinemann 1995.

(35) Richard Neville, Hippie Hippie Shake, p. 106, William Heinemann 1995.

(36) Richard Neville, Hippie Hippie Shake, p. 108, William Heinemann 1995.

(37) Richard Neville, Hippie Hippie Shake, p. 114-115, William Heinemann 1995.

(38) Garry Shead, interview 13 February 2015.

(39) Martin Sharp, interview 5 April 2011.

(40) Martin Sharp, interview 12 February 2011.

CHAPTER 8

(1) Lowell Tarling, diary notes.

(2) Eadweard Muybridge, The Human Figure in Motion, Bonanza Books NY, 1989. Also, Martin Sharp interviews, 5 January 1991 and 22 October 2003.

(3) Ginger Baker's Airforce, record album, released 1970.

(4) Michael Organ, Sixties Sharp - the pop & psychedelic art of Martin Sharp, online.

(5) Martin Sharp, interview 6 September 1982.

(6) Martin Sharp, interview 5 July 1984.

(7) Irving Stone, Lust for Life, Grosset & Dunlap, 1934.

(8) The Complete Letters of Vincent van Gogh, in 3 volumes, Thames & Hudson, 1958, 1978, 1988, 1999.

(9) A Letter from a Idle Fellow, OZ 43 July/August 1973.

(10) Martin Sharp, interview 6 September 1982.

(11) Martin Sharp, Cleo August 1977.

(12) Richard Neville, Playpower, 360 p, Jonathon Cape, 1970.

(13) Robert Hughes, Heaven and Hell in Western Art, Weidenfeld & Nicolson, 1968.

(14) Eric Clapton, The Autobiography, p. 103, Century London, 2007.

(15) Martin Sharp, interview 16 October 2003.

(16) Martin Sharp, interview 6 September 1982.

(17) Philippe Mora, Art Monthly, p. 9-10, Dec 2002-Feb 2003.

(18) Darling Do You Love Me? A film by Martin & Bob Whitaker, assisted by Harry Youlden and Alisdair Burke. Starring Germaine Greer.

(19) Martin Sharp, interview 16 October 2003.

(20) Martin Sharp, interview 11 April 1993.

(21) Eric Clapton, The Autobiography, p. 104, Century London, 2007.

(22) Martin Sharp, interview 5 January 1991.

(23) Martin Sharp, interview 5 July 1984.

(24) Martin Sharp, interview 16 January 1991. Also OZ 15 September 1968, back cover.

(25) Mark Lewisohn, The Complete Beatles Recording Sessions, p. 153-154, Hamlyn 1988.

(26) Eric Clapton, The Autobiography, p. 105, Century London, 2007.

(27) Judy Stone, The New York Times, 19 May 1968, see article ' Luna, Who Dreamed of Being Snow White'.

(28) Martin Sharp, interview 5 July 1984.

(29) John Lennon, I Am the Walrus (Lennon-McCartney) 1967.

(30) Eric Clapton, The Autobiography, p. 107, Century London, 2007.

(31) Martin Sharp, interview 5 July 1984.

(32) Richard Neville, Hippie Hippie Shake, p. 125, William Heinemann 1995.

(33) Martin Sharp, interview 5 July 1984.

(34) Richard Neville, Hippie Hippie Shake, p. 125, William Heinemann 1995.

(35) Martin Sharp, interview 5 July 1984.

(36) Eric Clapton, The Autobiography, p. 107, Century London, 2007.

(37) Eric Clapton, The Autobiography, p. 108, Century London, 2007.

(38) Martin Sharp, interview 5 July 1984.

(39) Richard Neville, Hippie Hippie Shake, p. 126, William Heinemann 1995.

(40) Martin Sharp, interview 16 October 2003.

(41) Martin Sharp, interview 6 September 1982.

(42) Lowell Tarling, diary notes.

(43) Tiny Tim, Live at the Royal Albert Hall, released by Rhino, 2000.

(44) Martin Sharp, interview 31 July 2003.

(45) Martin Sharp, interview 16 October 2003.

(46) Martin Sharp, interview 31 July 2003. Martin later changed 'unapproachable' to 'beyond approach' (27 May 2005).

(47) Martin Sharp, 30 October 1968 Diary, diary notes.

(48) Richard Neville, Hippie Hippie Shake, p. 126, William Heinemann 1995.

(49) OZ Magic Theatre, No 16, November 1968.

(50) Jenny Kee, A Big Life, p. 93, Penguin Lantern, 2006. Robert Hughes, University of Wollongong: ro.uow.edu.au/cgi/viewcontent.cgi?article=1015&context=ozlondon

(51) Martin Sharp, interview 16 October 2003.

(52) OZ magazine No 17.

(53) Richard Neville, Play Power, p. 361, Jonathon Cape, 1970.

(54) Timothy Leary, The Politics of Ecstasy, p. 301, Paladin 1970. The original painting was exhibited at the Yellow House in the early 1970s. With Martin's approval, a restored print was made in 2012 by Roger Foley.

(55) Martin Sharp, OZ No 4 June 1967. For the complete Tarot, see Michael Organ, sharp-tarot.blogspot.com.au. Also Martin Sharp, interview 22 October 2003.

(56) The Rolling Stones, Rock And Roll Circus released 1996.

(57) Eric Clapton, The Autobiography, p. 109, Century London, 2007.

CHAPTER 9

(1) Martin Sharp, interview 19 March 2005.

(2) Martin Sharp, interview 16 October 2003.

(3) Philippe Mora, film Trouble in Molopolis written by Philippe and Peter Smalley premiered at the Paris Pullman Chelsea in 1970 in aid of the OZ legal fund.

(4) Ginger Baker, Blind Faith CD Deluxe Edition, liner notes, p. 5.

(5) Martin Sharp, interview 5 July 1984.

(6) Eric Clapton, interview 20 June 2013 with Tom Kovats (youtube).

(7) Martin Sharp, interview 19 March 2005.

(8) Jim Anderson, interview 12 May 2015.

(9) Jim Anderson, Lampoon, p. 8-12, 2011.

(10) Martin Sharp, interview 6 September 1982.

(11) OZ – The Last Issue, Australian OZ p. 2.

(12) OZ – The Last Issue, Australian OZ cover and pp. 8-9.

(13) Albie Thoms, My Generation, p. 343.

(14) Roger Foley, interview 11 February 2014.

(15) Martin Sharp, interview 12 February 2011.

(16) Carl Williams, 'Alternative OZ', Apollo Magazine, 20 September 2013.

(17) Tiny Tim, Beautiful Thoughts, 1969 JP Torcher.

(18) Martin Sharp, print.

(19) Martin Sharp interview 5 July 1984.

(20) Steve Winwood, Atlanta Journal, 'Steve Winwood talks Clapton, Traffic and EDM', 1 May 2015.

(21) Blind Faith CD.

(22) Martin Sharp, interview 16 October 2003.

(23) Richard Neville, Hippie Hippie Shake, p. 171, William Heinemann 1995.

(24) Philippe Mora, email 22 May 2015.

(25) Martin Sharp, interview 5 July 1984.

(26) Martin Sharp, interview 5 July 1984.

(27) Martin Sharp interview, 16 October 2003.

(28) Michael Organ, Sixties Sharp - the pop & psychedelic art of Martin Sharp, online.

(29) Martin Sharp, interview 6 September 1982.

(30) Martin Sharp, interview 16 October 2003.

(31) Martin Sharp, Art Book, p. 31, Mathews Miller Dunbar, London 1972.

(32) Martin Sharp, interview 5 July 1984.

(33) Martin Sharp, interview 11 April 1993.

(34) Martin Sharp, interview 16 October 2003. See also Paul Buck, Performance, A biography of the classic sixties film, Omnibus Press 2012.

(35) Jim Anderson, interview 12 May 2015.
(36) Lowell Tarling, diary notes. Also, Martin Sharp, interview 16 October 2003.
(37) Richard Neville, Hippie Hippie Shake, p. 162, William Heinemann 1995.
(38) Martin Sharp, interview 16 May 1995.
(39) OZ magazine 25, Hippies Atrocities, p. 19-20.
(40) Jim Anderson, email to Lowell Tarling 18 May 2015.
(41) Martin Sharp, interview 31 July 2003.
(42) Martin Sharp, interview 11 April 1993.
(43) Martin Sharp, interview 11 April 1993.
(44) Anthony Bourke and John Rendell, A Lion Called Christian, 180 pp, Bantam Press London, 1971, expanded and updated 2009.

CHAPTER 10

(1) Roger Foley, email dated 4 February 2015.
(2) Philippe Mora, email to Lowell Tarling, 15 October 2014.
(3) John Hewison, Too Much, Art and Society in the Sixties, p.164-181.
(4) Martin Sharp, interview 29 December 1990. Martin says it was he who thought of the Yellow House name, 'I was obviously reading Vincent's letters of the time'.
(5) Martin Sharp, interview 11 April 1993.
(6) Albie Thoms, My Generation, p. 435.
(7) Ian Reid, interview 13 February 2016.
(8) Antoine de Saint-Exupéry, The Little Prince p. 82, Harcourt Inc, 1941. Martin Sharp poster, 1969, authorized by the Arts Vietnam Committee.
(9) Martin Sharp, interview 7 November 1983.
(10) Philippe Mora, emails 22-23 May 2015.
(11) Poster, Crucifixion Exhibition, an exhibition of Degenerate Art, Sigi Krauss Gallery, 23 April-21 May 1970.
(12) Ted Markstein, interview 1 January 2015. Ted lived opposite the Yellow House, at Selsden apartments. He often visited the Yellow House between 1970-1973. Ted ran the fabulous In-Shoppe, Sydney's answer London's Carnaby Street. See The In-Shoppe Drop-Out, POL magazine, 1974. Guest editor: Richard Neville. Interviewer: Louise Ferrier.
(13) Greg Weight, interview 24 November 2014.
(14) Roger Foley, interview 11 February 2014.
(15) Martin Sharp, interview 'just before the opening of the Yellow House', 1971. See also Hazel de Berg interview, 9 June 1970.
(16) Peter Kingston, interview 28 October 2014.
(17) George Gittoes, email 5 July 2014.
(18) Greg Weight, interview 24 November 2014
(19) Martin Sharp, interview 28 October 1984.
(20) Martin Sharp, interview 29 December 1990.
(21) Martin Sharp, interview 16 October 2003.

(22) Ian Reid, interview 13 February 2016.
(23) Martin Sharp, interview 29 December 1990.
(24) Albie Thoms, My Generation, p. 441-451, Media Publishing Ltd, 2012.
(25) Margot Hilton & Graeme Blundell, Whiteley – An Unauthorised Life, p. 92-93.
(26) Johnny Lewis, see Lowell Tarling's diary notes, 21 May 2015.
(27) Brett Whiteley, Another Way of Looking at Vincent Van Gogh, Richard Griffin Publisher, 1983.
(28) Margot Hilton & Graeme Blundell, Whiteley – An Unauthorised Life, p. 92.
(29) Martin Sharp, Catalog, Reid Books, 1971.
(30) Albie Thoms, My Generation, p. 441-451.
(31) Justin Martell with Alanna Wray McDonald, Eternal Troubadour, the Improbable Life of Tiny Tim, p. 210, Jawbone Press 2016.
(32) Jon Lewis and Roger Foley, interview 26 July 2014.
(33) Mal Ramage, interview 8 February 2016.
(34) Jon Lewis and Roger Foley, interview 26 July 2014.
(35) Peter Kingston, interview 28 October 2014.
(36) Albie Thoms, My Generation, p. 441-451, Media Publishing Ltd, 2012.
(37) Richard Neville, Hippy Hippy Shake, William Heinemann Australia, p. 270. For a blow-by-blow description of the London Oz trial, see The Trials of Oz by Tony Palmer, Blond & Briggs, 1971.
(38) Martin Sharp, interview 6 September 1982.
(39) Roger Foley, interview 11 February 2014.
(40) Greg Weight, interview 24 November 2014.
(41) Tim Lewis, interview 2 June 2014.
(42) Jon Lewis and Roger Foley, interview 26 July 2014.
(43) Mal Ramage, interview 8 February 2016.
(44) Ted Markstein, interview, 1 January 2015.
(45) Martin Sharp, interview 14 November 1984.

CHAPTER 11

(1) Martin Sharp, interview 28 October 1984.
(2) Anthony Scaduto, Bob Dylan, Abacus, 1972, p.236, 239. Also, Clinton Heylin, Dylan: Behind the Shades, Viking Penguin, 1991, p. 161.
(3) Greg Weight, interview 24 November 2014.
(4) Roger Foley, interview 26 July 2014.
(5) Germaine Greer, The Female Eunuch, Granada Publishing, 1970.
(6) Adrian Rawlins, interview on film by Roger Foley, at the Yellow House Retrospective, 1990.
(7) Ian Reid, interview 13 February 2016.
(8) Martin Sharp, interview 7 November 1983.
(9) John A Walker, Art Into Pop, see Illustrations 54, Thames and Hudson, 1975.
(10) Jeannie Lewis, interview 7 May 2015.

(11) Greg Weight, interview 24 November 2014.

(12) Ian Reid, interview 13 February 2016.

(13) Ted Markstein, interview 1 January 2015.

(14) Jon Lewis, interview 26 July 2014.

(15) The Yellow House 1970-1972, published by Art Gallery of New South Wales, 1990.

(16) Albie Thoms, My Generation, p. 441-451.

(17) Martin Sharp, interview 14 November 1984. Peter Kingston disputes that the Stone Room was Martin's idea. He says, 'I was sort-of stuck in the Stone Room, which is really my idea…' interview, 28 October 2014.

(18) Greg Weight, interview 24 November 2014.

(19) Jon Lewis, interview 26 July 2014.

(20) Roger Foley, interview 26 July 2014.

(21) Albie Thoms, My Generation, p. 441-451.

(22) Peter Royles, email to Lowell Tarling, 5 January 2015.

(23) Betty Roland, The Eye of the Beholder, Hale & Ironmonger 1984. 'An insider's portrait of the establishment of Monsalvat, Eltham Victoria, under the magnetic influence of painter Justus Jorgensen' – cover lines.

(24) Marcus Skipper, email 21 June 2014.

(25) Martin Sharp, interview 16 January 1991, referencing Le Petit Prince by Antoine de Saint-Exupéry.

(26) Martin Sharp, interview 5 January 1991

(27) Greg Weight, interview 24 November 2014.

(28) Jo Sharp, interview with Martin Sharp, 5 April 2011.

(29) Jon Lewis, interview 26 July 2014.

(30) Ted Markstein, interview 1 January 2015. Ian Reid is amongst several to say they never saw David Litvinoff have anything to do with smack. However, most people (Ian and Mal Ramage amongst them) reckon that when it came to Litvinoff stories, you never knew what was fictionalized and what was true. The Bali story? The Kray Brothers hanging him from a window ledge? The 'big smile'? Maybe he made it all up.

(31) Nic Lyon, interview 16 August 2015.

(32) Albie Thoms, My Generation, p. 441-451.

(33) Jon Lewis, interview 26 July 2014.

(34) Clayton Simms, interview 23 October 2014.

(35) Ian Reid, interview 13 February 2016.

(36) Martin Sharp, taped interview 1971.

(37) Albie Thoms, My Generation, p. 441-451.

(38) Ian Reid, interview 123 February 2016.

(39) Martin Sharp, interview 16 October 2003.

(40) Mic Conway, interview 24 January 2015.

(41) Roger Foley, email 6 February 2015 and interview 11 February 2014.

(42) Roger Foley, Notes on the Yellow House, 2015.

(43) The Yellow House, a mimeographed A3 newsletter-style publication re-printed by Roger Foley with the encouragement of Albie Thoms 2013.

(44) Tim Lewis, interview 2 June 2014.

(45) Ted Markstein, interview 1 January 2015.

(46) Ian Reid, interview 13 February 2016. Also, 27 February 2116.

CHAPTER 12

(1) Germaine Greer, The Female Eunuch, 354pp, MacGibbon & Kee, 1970.

(2) Juno Gemes, Facebook 2014.

(3) Jim Anderson interview, 12 May 2015.

(4) Jim Anderson interview, 12 May 2015.

(5) Jim Anderson interview, 12 May 2015.

(6) John Lennon, Wonsaponatime CD, track 8. Jim Anderson, Michael Ramsden and a chorus of others were on the original recording, all eliminated by Phil Specter who only used John Lennon's guide vocal in the final recording.

(7) Geoffrey Robertson wrote both the stage show and the film script. The most comprehensive book on OZ is Tony Palmer, The Trials of OZ, 275 pp, Blond & Briggs 1971. See also, Nigel Fountain, Underground – the London Alternative Press 1966-1974, pp. 231, Routledge, 1988. And Jonathon Green, Days in the Life – Voices from the English Underground 1961-1971, pp. 468, Heinemann, 1988.

(8) Martin Sharp, interview 16 January 1991.

(9) Martin Sharp, interview 5 April 2011.

(10) Lex Marinos, interview 25 May 2015.

(11) Martin Sharp interview, 5 April 2011.

(12) Martin Sharp, interview 11 April 1993.

(13) Martin Sharp, interview 16 October 2003.

(14) Martin Sharp, interview 29 December 1990.

(15) Martin Sharp, Art Book, 40 pp, Mathews Miller & Dunbar, 1972.

(16) George Melly, Double Exposures, I have the cutting, not its reference.

(17) Brian Rice & Tony Evans, The English Sunrise, 80pp, Mathews Miller & Dunbar, 1972. Reprinted in 1987 by Chatto & Windus.

(18) Martin Sharp, interviews 6 September 1982 and 16 January 1991.

(19) Martin Sharp, interview 19 March 2005.

(20) Tiny Tim, Tiny Tim's Second Album released January 1969.

(21) Tiny Tim, Concert in Fairyland released August 1969.

(22) Tiny Tim, For All My Little Friends released 1969.

(23) Martin Sharp, interview 13 April 1983.

(24) Martin Sharp, interview 13 April 1983.

(25) Zandra Rhodes and Anne Knight, The Art of Zandra Rhodes, Jonathon Cape, 1984.

(26) Georgina Howell, In Vogue, Sixty years of celebrities and fashion from British Vogue, p. 327, Penguin Books 1975.

(27) Neil Baldwin, Man Ray – American Artist, p. 351, Da Capo Press 2001.
(28) Martin Sharp, interview 5 July 1984.
(29) Martin Sharp, interview 5 July 1984.
(30) J Hillier, Hokusai, Phaidon Press, 1955.
(31) Martin Sharp, interview 16 January 1991.
(32) Martin Sharp, interview 29 Dec 1990.
(33) OZ magazine 43, July/August, p. 4-6. Also Martin Sharp, Art Book, p. 2, Mathews Miller Dunbar, London 1972.
(34) Martin Sharp, Letter to Monseigneur, 13 June 1986.
(35) Sam Marshall, Luna Park – Just for Fun, p. 105-106, Luna Park Reserve Trust, 1995.
(36) Martin Sharp, Cartoons, p. 22, Scripts Pty Ltd 1966.
(37) Martin Sharp, Letter to Monseigneur, 13 June 1986.

CHAPTER 13

(1) Doug Aiton & Terry Lane, The First Century, p. 103-106, Information Australia 2000.
(2) Roger Foley film, The Aquarius Festival, Nimbin 1973, restored by Fogg Productions 2014.
(3) See David Litvinoff, Wikipedia.
(4) Albie Thoms, My Generation, p. 415-441.
(5) Julian Meyrick, See How It Runs, Nimrod and the New Wave, p. 226-227, Currency Press, 2002.
(6) Julian Meyrick, See How It Runs, Nimrod and the New Wave, p. 277, Currency Press, 2002.
(7) Julian Meyrick, See How It Runs, Nimrod and the New Wave, p. 75, Currency Press, 2002.
(8) Jeannie Lewis, interview 7 May 2015.
(9) Gary Shearston, interview 1 November 2001.
(10) Gary Shearston, Dingo, recorded in London in 1974 on the album of the same name.
(11) Martin Sharp, interview 5 April 2005.
(12) Martin Sharp, Cleo magazine, August 1977.
(13) Tim Lewis, interview 2 June 2014.
(14) Tim Lewis, interview 2 June 2014. Martin also told me this, in my diary notes.
(15) Tim Lewis, interview 2 June 2014.
(16) Tim Lewis, interview 2 June 2014.
(17) Roger Foley film, Martin Sharp Prepares, 21st March 1973, restored by Fogg Productions 2014.
(18) Martin Sharp, interview 12 February 2011
(19) Tim Lewis, interview 2 June 2014.
(20) Martin Sharp, interview 29 December 1990.
(21) Tim Lewis, interview 2 June 2014. Also 19 May 2015 (Facebook message).
(22) Martin Sharp, interview 16 October 2003.
(23) Tim Lewis, notes on telephone conversation 5 June 2015.
(24) See Wikipedia, Sydney Opera House. Utzon was not invited to the ceremony, nor was his name mentioned.

(25) Martin Sharp, interview 3 March 1984.
(26) Martin Sharp, interview 16 October 2003
(27) Martin Sharp, interview 7 November 1983.
(28) Sam Marshall, Luna Park – Just for Fun, p. 106, Luna Park Reserve Trust, 1995.
(29) Tim Lewis, interview 2 June 2014.
(30) Martin Sharp, Cleo magazine, August 1977.
(31) Martin Sharp, 'Notes from the River Caves', Quadrant, February 1977.
(32) OZ – The Last Issue, No 48, Winter 1973.
(33) Jim Anderson, Lampoon, p. 20-21, Dennis Publishing, 2011.
(34) Martin Sharp, interview 5 July 1984.
(35) Martin Sharp, interview 5 July 1984.
(36) Martin Sharp, interview 5 July 1984.
(37) Martin Sharp, Cleo magazine, August 1977.
(38) Lex Marinos, Blood and Circuses, An Irresponsible Memoir, p.92, Allen & Unwin, 2014.
(39) Lex Marinos, interview 25 May 2015.
(40) Keith Dunstan, Ratbags, Golden Press 1979.
(41) Martin Sharp, interview 5 January 1991.
(42) Tim Lewis, interview 2 June 2014.

CHAPTER 14

(1) Martin Sharp, interview 16 October 2003
(2) Martin Sharp, interview 24 January 1997
(3) Martin Sharp, interview 1 February 1983.
(4) Martin Sharp, interview 24 January 1997.
(5) Martin Sharp, interview 6 September 1982.
(6) Martin Sharp, interview 27 May 2005.
(7) Martin Sharp, interview 11 February 1983.
(8) Zandra Rhodes and Anne Knight, The Art of Zandra Rhodes, p. 123, Jonathan Cape 1984.
(9) John A Walker, Art Since Pop, Illustration 54, Thames and Hudson, 1975.
(10) Carl Jung, Synchronicity – An Acausal Connecting Principle. Routledge and Kegan Paul, 1972.
(11) James A Michener, The Hokusai Sketchbooks, Charles E. Tuttle, 1959.
(12) Martin Sharp, interview 27 May 2005.
(13) Martin Sharp, interview 16 October 2003.
(14) Pete Townshend, Who I Am, p. 108, Harper Collins, 2012.
(15) Martin Sharp, interview 13 April 1983.
(16) Martin Sharp, Street of Dreams film script, the first draft.
(17) Martin Sharp, interview 13 April 1983.
(18) Martin Sharp undated letter to Monseigeur.
(19) Tim Lewis, notes on telephone conversation 5 June 2015.
(20) Tim Lewis, interview 2 June 2014.

(21) Peter Kingston, interview 28 October 2014.

(22) Julian Meyrick, See How it Runs, Nimrod and the New Wave, p. 232, Currency Press. 40,550 attendees in 1973, 72,478 in 1974.

(23) Maggie Tabberer, Maggie, Allen & Unwin, 1998.

(24) Jeannie Lewis, interview 7 May 2015. Also see Free Fall Through Featherless Flight CD.

(25) Garry Mallard, interview 9 November 1983.

(26) Garry Shead, interview 13 February 2015.

CHAPTER 15

(1) Picnic at Hanging Rock, a film by Peter Weir premiered in August 1975.

(2) Martin Sharp, interview, 16 October 2003.

(3) Martin Sharp, interview 5 January 1991.

(4) Martin Sharp, interview 13 April 1983.

(5) Martin Sharp, Cleo magazine, August 1977.

(6) Martin Sharp, interview 5 August 1983.

(7) William Yang, interview 5 August 1983.

(8) Tim Lewis, interview 2 June 2014.

(9) Martin Sharp, interview 5 August 1983.

(10) William Yang, interview 5 August 1983.

(11) Martin Sharp, interview 14 November 1984.

(12) Bob Dylan, The Bootleg Series Vol 4, known as the 'Albert Hall' concert, it was recorded in Manchester 17 May 1966. It became commercially available in 1998.

(13) Martin Sharp, interview 5 January 1991.

(14) Sam Marshall, Luna Park, Just for Fun, pp. 106-110, Luna Park Reserve Trust 1995.

(15) Martin Sharp, Luna Park Timeline, a private document.

(16) Ted Hopkins, Report on Luna Park, p. 27, 1980.

(17) Martin Sharp, interview 3 March 1984.

(18) Jeannie Lewis, Tears of Steel & the Clowning Calaveras, see liner notes, 1976.

(19) Jeannie Lewis, email 8 May 2015.

(20) Jeannie Lewis, interview 7 May 2015.

(21) Martin Sharp, interview 7 November 1983.

(22) Jeannie Lewis, interview 7 May 2015.

(23) Martin Sharp, interview 3 March 1984.

(24) Martin Sharp, Luna Park notes on Clowning Calaveras retyped in 1983.

(25) Martin Sharp, interview 3 March 1984.

(26) Lex Marinos, interview 25 May 2015.

(26) Peter Kingston, interview 28 October 2014.

(27) Peter Royles, email 6 February 2015.

(28) Report on Luna Park, p. 27, 37, 39, 42, 43. Published 1980.

(29) Sam Marshall, Luna Park, Just for Fun, p. 110, Luna Park Reserve Trust 1995.

(30) Garry Shead, interview 13 February 2015.

(31) Peter Kingston, interview 28 October 2014.
(32) Peter Kingston, interview 28 October 2014.
(33) Martin Sharp, undated notes (retyped by me in 1983).
(34) Martin Sharp, interview 5 April 2005.
(35) Martin Sharp, interview 16 October 2003.
(36) Martin Sharp, interview 27 May 2005.
(37) Harry Stein, Tiny Tim, Playboy Press, 1976.
(38) Tiny Tim, interview 4 April 1992.
(39) Martin Sharp, 'The Real Tiny Tim', Quadrant, January 1977.
(40) Martin Sharp, interview 6 September 1982.
(41) Tiny Tim, interview 4 October 1991.
(42) Martin Sharp, interview 13 April 1983.
(43) Martin Sharp, interview 13 April 1983.
(44) Martin Sharp, interview 29 November 2004.
(45) Tiny Tim, telegram to Martin Sharp, 16 July 1976.
(46) Martin Sharp, The Lyre Bird – Tiny Tim, application to the Film Commission 1976.
(47) Kym Bonython, Modern Australian Painting 1975-1980, p. 66, Martin Sharp, Song of Songs – Festival of Sydney 1978, Rigby, 1980. And, The Everlasting World of Martin Sharp, p. 24, Ivan Dougherty Gallery 2006.
(48) Willy de la Vega, interview 27 April 1992.

CHAPTER 16

(1) Martin Sharp, two poems – in the author's collection.
(2) Martin Sharp, interview 7 July 1984.
(3) Martin Sharp, cover and article 'The Real Tiny Tim', Quadrant, January 1977. Also Martin Sharp, interview 27 May 2005.
(4) Martin Sharp, interview 16 October 2003.
(5) Martin Sharp, interview 29 November 2004.
(6) Martin Sharp, interview 27 May 2005. Philippe Mora's Mad Dog Morgan, starring Dennis Hopper and Jack Thompson (1976) is available on DVD.
(7) Kym Bonython, Modern Australian Painting 1975-1980, p. 66, Rigby Ltd 1980. This depiction shows Martin's picture as it was in 1978, before the over-painting. Titled Song of Songs – Festival of Sydney, it later became known as Film Script.
(8) Susan Jensen, email 4 July 2015.
(9) Susan Jensen, email 11 July 2015.
(10) The Everlasting World of Martin Sharp, p. 27, Ivan Dougherty Gallery, 2006.
(11) Tim Lewis, Facebook 13 December 2014.

(12) Angelica Tremblay, Facebook 30 December 2014.
(13) Martin Sharp, personal notes, Sharp Papers Vol 3 (held by the author).
(14) Elwyn Lynn, 'Those Silver Scissors', Quadrant, February 1977.
(15) Martin Sharp, 'Notes from the River Caves', Quadrant, February 1977.
(16) Martin Sharp, interview 29 January 1985.
(17) Peter Kingston, notes held in Martin Sharp's papers. Tape: 29 January 1985.
(18) Martin Sharp, interview 29 January 1985.
(19) Susan Jensen, email 4 July 2115.
(20) Martin Sharp, interview 5 August 1983.
(21) Martin Sharp, author's diary notes.
(22) Richard Neville and Julie Clarke, The Life and Crimes of Charles Sobhraj, 352 pp, Jonathon Cape Ltd, 1979.
(23) The Yellow House, a mimeographed A3 newsletter-style publication re-printed by Roger Foley with the encouragement of Albie Thoms 2013.
(24) Tim Lewis, interview 2 June 2014.
(25) Melody Cooper, email 5 July 2015.
(26) William Yang, interview 5 August 1983.
(27) Melody Cooper, email 5 July 2015.
(28) Cleo magazine, August 1977.
(29) Julian Meyrick, See How it Runs, Nimrod and the New Wave, p. 141, Currency Press.
(30) Martin Sharp, interview 3 March 1984.
(31) Martin Sharp, interview 3 March 1984.

CHAPTER 17

(1) Martin Sharp, photocopy of sketch, in the author's collection.
(2) Roger Foley-Fogg, Facebook message, 20 May 2115.
(3) Martin Sharp, interview 2 February 1983.
(4) Russell Sharp, interview 6 June 2015.
(5) Martin Sharp, interview 29 November 2004.
(6) Martin Sharp, interview 13 April 1983.
(7) Martin Sharp, interview 29 November 2004.
(8) Martin Sharp, interview 16 October 2003.
(9) Tiny Tim, talking to Martin Sharp at the Cosmopolitan Motor Inn, Sydney 4 December 1978. Tiny is reading the contract aloud and discussing it.
(10) Martin Sharp, interview 13 April 1983.
(11) Martin Sharp, Sydney Morning Herald, 8 January 1978.
(12) Martin Sharp, interview 29 November 2004.
(13) Martin Sharp, poster Tiny, produced as a postcard by Lamella Sydney, 1981.
(14) Melody Cooper, email 5 July 2015.
(15) Martin Sharp, interview 29 November 2004.
(16) Julian Meyrick, See How it Runs, Nimrod and the New Wave, p. 273, Currency Press.

(17) Martin Sharp, interview 29 November 2004.
(18) Martin Sharp, interview 1 February 1983.
(19) Martin Sharp, interview 24 January 1997.
(20) Martin Sharp, interview 5 July 1984.
(21) Martin Sharp, interview 1 February 1983.
(22) Wonderful World of Romance, Custom Records, a facility of Studio 301.
(23) Tiny Tim, film Street of Dreams.
(24) Martin Sharp, interview 29 November 2004.
(25) Tim Lewis, Facebook message, 1 July 2015.
(26) Ted Markstein, Facebook message, 23 June 2115. 'It was for the 360 degree projection attraction in Luna Park. April-May 1979. I did two 8' x 4' panels.'
(27) Jeannie Lewis, interview 7 May 2115.
(28) Martin Sharp, interview 29 November 2004.
(29) Tiny Tim, film Street of Dreams.
(30) Martin Sharp, interview 29 November 2004.
(31) Jeannie Lewis, interview 7 May 2115.
(32) Martin Sharp, interview 29 November 2004.
(33) Tiny Tim, film Street of Dreams.
(34) Martin Sharp, interview 29 November 2004.
(35) Martin Sharp, interview 29 November 2004.
(36) Roger Foley-Fogg, author's diary notes 2114.

CHAPTER 18

(1) William Yang, interview 5 August 1983.
(2) Martin Sharp, interview 3 March 1984.
(3) Martin Sharp, interview 3 March 1984.
(4) Undated photocopies are in the author's collection, original clippings at Wirian.
(5) Sam Marshall, Luna Park, Just for Fun, pp. 112, Luna Park Reserve Trust 1995.
(6) Martin Sharp, interview 3 March 1984.
(7) Martin Sharp, interview 13 April 1983.
(8) Australian Playboy, June 1979. Undated photocopy in the author's collection.
(9) Garry Shead, interview 13 February 2015.
(10) Martin Sharp, interview 3 March 1984.
(11) Sam Marshall, Luna Park, Just for Fun, pp. 112-113, Luna Park Reserve Trust 1995.
(12) Martin Sharp, interview 3 March 1984.
(13) Martin Sharp, notes on Luna Park that I rekeyed for him 1982/83.
(14) Martin Sharp, notes on Luna Park that I rekeyed for him 1982/83.
(15) Martin Sharp, interview 3 March 1984.
(16) Martin Sharp, notes on Luna Park that I rekeyed for him 1982/83.
(17) Martin Sharp, interview 3 March 1984.
(18) Martin Sharp, notes on Luna Park that I rekeyed for him 1982/83.

(19) Martin Sharp, notes on Luna Park that I rekeyed for him 1982/83.
(20) Martin Sharp, interview 11 December 1983.
(21) Martin Sharp, interview 7 November 1983.
(22) Martin Sharp, interview 3 March 1984.
(23) Martin Sharp, interview 7 November 1983.
(24) Martin Sharp, interview 3 March 1984.
(25) Peter Kingston, interview 28 October 2014.
(26) Martin Sharp, interview 7 November 1983.
(27) Susan Jensen, email 11 July 2015.
(28) Martin Sharp, interview 7 March 1984.

INDEX

A

Abbey Road Studios – 113,
Abeles, Peter – 232,
Aboriginal Tent Embassy – 184, 186,
Abraxas – 101, 119, 157, 166, 216, 253, 256-257,
Abraxas (album) – 177,
Adams, Phillip - 32,
The Adventures of Barry McKenzie – 55, 176,
Ahearn, David – 164,
Ain't Misbehaving – 155,
Ali, Muhammad – 33, 212, 220, 240,
Ali, Tariq – 118,
Alice in Wonderland - 212,
Allen, Johnny – 71, 79,
Amédée Joubert & Son – 81,
Amphlett, Patricia (Little Pattie) – 54,
Anderson, Colin – 72,
Anderson, Jim – 121, 123, 131-132, 146-147, 169-171, 181, 194,
Anderson, John – 34,
Andrews Sisters – 26,
Anglican Press – 50,
Angry Penguins – 36,
Animal Crackers – 175,
Another Way of Looking at Vincent Van Gogh – 142,
Ansell, Tony – 238,
Anyone for Tennis – 101-104,
The Apple Boutique – 98,
Aquarius Festival – 156, 184, 194,
Archdale, Betty – 66,
Are You Experienced – 96,
Argyle, Michael – 147, 171,
Armstrong, Louis – 26, 34,
Arp, Jean – 128,
The Art of Australia – 103,
Art Book – 109, 128-129, 173-174, 177-178, 181, 187-188, 199-200,
Art Exhibition (Sharp Art Exhibition) – 109, 128, 140, 186, 188, 190-191,
Art Gallery of New South Wales – 32, 83,
Art for Mart's Sake – 68, 187,
Arts Lab – 135-136, 146,
Art Since Pop – 200,
Artoons – 128-129,
Atherden, Geoff – 42,
Arty Wild Oat – 41-43, 47,
Atlantic Studios – 89, 99, 103,
Australia (poem) – 25, 76, 196,
Australia Council (formerly Australia Council for the Arts) – 185-186,
The Australian – 61,
Australian Broadcasting Commission (ABC) – 19, 32, 45, 47, 67, 105, 150, 161, 230,
Australian Chamber Orchestra – 236,
Australian Film Commission – 221,
The Australian Londoner/The London Australian - 76,
Avalon, Frankie - 34,

B

Babyface – 236,
Babylon the Great is Fallen (Revelation 18 v 2) – 226,
Bacon, Francis – 112, 142,
Baker, Ginger – 88-89, 94, 96-99, 104, 108, 114, 116, 122, 126, 137,
Baker, Karen – 97-98,
Bardot, Brigitte – 107,
Barker College – 19, 28, 38,
Barker, Michael – 237, 258,
Barrett, Syd – 80, 99, 171,
Barton, Arthur – 24-25, 191-192, 206, 216-217,
The Basic Wage Dream - 69,
Bass, Tom – 63,
Baudelaire, Charles – 73,
Baume, Eric – 50,
Bazaar – 81,
Beardsley, Aubrey – 83,
Beatles - 27, 54, 57-60, 69, 72, 81-83, 94, 107, 113, 131, 150, 171,
Beatles Calendar – 77, 82-83,
Beck, Jeff – 99,
Bee, John – 150, 167,
Begin the Beguine – 203,
Belafonte, Harry – 26, 34, 53,
Bell, Cheery – 25,
Bell, John – 38, 135, 185,
Beresford, Bruce – 42, 55, 120, 138, 205,
Berlin, Irving - 143,
Bhagwan Shree Rajneesh – 224,
Bhaktivedanta Swami Prabhupada – 224,
Bianchi, Vittorio – 134,
Biba's Boutique – 79,
Big Dipper – 228-229, 247-251,
Big O Posters – 84-85, 92, 95-96, 102, 108, 128, 173, 177,
Bill Haley & the Comets – 26-27,
Billings, Jonathon – 254,
Billy Thorpe & the Aztecs – 54,
Bilu, Asher – 60,
Binkie's Burgers – 48-49, 80,
Binns, Vivienne – 154,
Birth of Venus – 190,
Bitches Brew – 177,
Blackman, Barbara – 60,
Blackman, Charles – 60,
Blake, Peter – 40, 84, 93,
Blake Prize – 13, 20,
Blind Faith – 115, 126, 169,

Bliss – 142, 144, 167,
Blonde-Headed Stompie Wompie Real Gone Surfer Guy – 54,
Blonde On Blonde – 79,
Blue Groper – 15, 200,
Blue Skies – 143,
Bond, Grahame – 176,
Bonnard, Pierre – 128,
Bono, Sonny – 117,
Bonython Galleries – 190, 205,
Bonzo Dog Doo-Dah Band – 130, 169,
Boofhead – 10, 76, 195, 200, 218, 227,
Borges, Jorge Luis - 127,
Borobudur – 191-192, 255,
Botticelli, Sandro – 128-129, 190,
Bourke, Anthony (Ace) – 132,
Bowlly, Al – 116-117, 150,
Boyd, Arthur – 36, 39, 60, 122,
Boyd, Jamie - 122,
Boyd, Russell – 244,
Brando, Marlon – 26,
Bravo Pour le Clown – 215,
Brennan, Christopher – 133,
Brennan, Richard – 42,
Bresslau, Erica, née Sharp – 14, 22, 204,
Brett, Chrissie – 159,
Brian Poole & the Tremeloes – 54, 58,
Brissenden, RF – 65,
British Broadcasting Corporation (BBC) – 78, 80,
Bowie, David – 131,
Broken Hearted – 71,
Brother Can You Spare a Dime? – 116-117, 202, 239,
Brown, Bruce – 54,
Brown, Mike – 39, 79,
Brown, Pete – 89, 98, 102,
Brown, Peter (Charlie) – 28, 32, 35, 68, 125, 137, 140, 144,
Brodziak, Ken – 57,
Bruce, Jack – 88-89, 90, 96, 98-99, 102, 111, 122,
Bruce, Janet – 96,
Bubba Free John – 224,
Buddha – 192, 255-256,
Buddhism – 224,
Budinger, Vicki (Miss Vicki) – 126, 174, 199, 218-219, 243,
The Bulletin – 39, 41, 44,
Burns, Tim – 158, 164, 167,
Burns, Tommy - 33,
Burr, Henry – 220, 236,

Burton, Richard – 130,
Butterfield Blues Band – 101,
Byrne, Cynthia – 49,

C

Caesar's Palace – 127,
Café Au Go Go – 99,
Cahill, Tony – 122,
Calwell, Arthur – 30,
Cameron, Sue – 220,
Cammell, Donald – 112-113, 130, 176,
Campbell, Cressida – 229, 235,
Campbell, Laura (Little Nell) – 143, 146, 155, 163, 172, 177, 194, 229,
Canberra Times – 49,
Cannes Film Festival – 200,
Can't Buy Me Love – 57,
Cappy, Joe - 221,
Captain Marvel – 227,
Captain Matchbox Whoopee Band – 163,
Carlos, Michael – 215,
Carroll, Judy – 71,
Carroll, Richard – 254,
Cartoons – 16, 76, 87,
Cash, Johnny – 34,
Catalog – 19, 24, 29, 45, 143, 157-158, 161,
Caton, Michael – 176,
Caulfield Tech (Melbourne),
Cell Block Theatre – 165,
Central Station – 205,
Cezanne, Paul – 128,
Chameleon – 235, 239-241,
Chaplin, Charles – 227,
Charles II – 90,
Checker, Chubby – 34, 53,
Chelsea Arts Club – 81,
Chelsea Hotel – 142,
Chevron Hotel – 69, 138-139, 148,
Children of God – 224,
Christesen, Clem – 65,
Christie, Lou – 131,
A Christmas Carol – 200,
Christo – 155,
City Lights Books – 46,
Clapton, Eric – 87-94, 96-107, 110-117, 120-123, 126-130, 158, 171, 184, 200, 224,
Clark, John – 71,
Clark, Terry – 137, 140,
Clarke, Julie – 167, 204, 230,
Clay's Books – 134,
Cleo - 193, 230,

A Clockwork Orange – 138,
Clune Gallery – 37, 48, 68, 72, 75, 79-80, 125, 128, 135-137,
Clune, Frank – 135,
Clune, Terry – 135,
Clune, Thelma – 135,
Cocksucker Blues – 211,
Cocker, Joe - 130,
Cobden, Richard – 188-189, 196, 209,
Cobden, Victoria – 209, 223, 226, 244,
Cole, Nat King – 26,
Collins, Judy – 86,
Collingwood, Lyn – 38,
Columbo, Russ - 220
Company Caine (Co-Caine) – 155,
The Complete Letters of Vincent Van Gogh – 87, 109-110, 121, 135, 223,
Concert in Fairyland – 175,
Conway, Janie - 163,
Conway, Mic – 163-164,
Cooper, Melody – 229-230, 233-235, 237-238, 242, 244, 246,
Cooper, Robyn – 47,
Cordeaux, Chris – 246,
Cosmopolitan Hotel - 237,
Country Life – 116, 120,
Country Queen – 240,
Country Radio – 155,
Cowan, Tom - 244,
Coward, Noel – 62,
Cranbrook School – 6, 12-13, 17-28, 37, 68, 77, 105, 140, 143, 145, 187, 207-208, 211, 226,
Cream – 87-90, 92-104, 108, 110-113, 116, 122, 173,
Cream (poster) – 108,
Cream - The World's First Supergroup – 97,
Crocker, Barry – 55,
Crosby, Bing – 11, 15, 116, 143, 199-120,
Crossroads – 104,
Crothall, Ross – 39,
Crows Over the Cornfield – 196,
The Crucifixion (song) – 215, 254,
Crumb, Robert - 103, 107, 143, 157, 170,
Cullen, William Portus – 64,
Cumming, Bernard – 227,

D

Daley, Bob – 167,
Dalí, Gala – 178-179,
Dalí, Salvadore – 118, 128, 179-181,

Daltrey, Roger – 179,
Daily Mirror – 12, 78,
Daily Planet – 247,
Daily Telegraph - 42, 80, 145,
Dame Everage, Edna – 31, 76, 227,
Dancing in the Street – 239,
Dantalian's Chariot – 99,
Darling! – 76,
Darling Do You Love Me? – 112,
Davis, Miles – 175, 177,
De Chirico, Giorgio – 128, 174, 189, 190, 199,
De La Vega, Willy – 222,
De Saint-Exupéry, Antoine – 137,
Deep Night – 239,
Demoiselles d'Avignon – 126, 189,
Dean, James – 26,
Degas, Edgar – 128,
Degenerate Art Show (aka Crucifixion Show) – 138,
Dellasandro, Joe – 180,
Dennis, Clarence (CJ) – 191,
Dennis, Felix – 95, 106, 121, 123, 131, 146, 156, 169-171, 194,
Dennis Publishing – 194,
Derek & the Dominos – 171,
Devo – 237,
Diamond, Neil – 202,
Dickens, Charles – 200,
Dickinson, John Nodes – 64,
Digger – 247,
Dignam, Arthur – 38,
Ding A Ding Day – 39, 45, 67, 76, 163,
Dingo – 186,
The Dirty Mac - 120,
Disraeli Gears – 89-90, 93, 96-98, 101, 108, 177,
Do the OZ – 171,
Do You Love Me? – 102,
Dobell, William – 36, 133,
Donegan, Lonnie – 27,
Donovan – 84-85, 95, 114, 175, 224,
Donovan, Dave - 238,
Don't Be Cruel – 26,
Don't Leave Me Here Standing All Alone – 125,
Don't Pass Me By – 113,
Doring, Geoff – 32,
Douglas, Kirk – 28,
Dr Strange – 227,
Draffin, Peter – 76-77, 85-87, 92, 105,
Dream Museum – 195, 212, 227,
Driscoll, Michael – 185,

Drooker, Eric - 202,
Drummond, Pat – 185,
Drysdale, Russell – 36,
Duchamp, Marcel – 128,
Duke of Edinburgh – 118,
Dundas, Douglas – 44,
Dunstan, Keith – 197,
Dutton, Geoff – 37, 57, 63, 65,
Dylan, Bob – 72-73, 77, 79, 83-85, 117, 130-131, 150, 156, 211, 216,

E

Edols, Mike – 244,
Eastman, Linda – 96,
Edison, Thomas Alva – 237, 242,
El Alamein Fountain – 134, 156,
El Greco (Doménikos Theotokópoulos) – 28,
El Rocco – 134-135,
Ellis, Bob – 38, 42, 55,
Ellis, Dave – 238,
The Endless Summer – 55,
The English Sunrise – 174,
Epstein, Brian – 57-61, 150,
Ernst, Max – 94-95, 113, 128,
Errico, Angie – 97,
Ertegun, Ahmet – 89,
Essex, David – 177, 201,
Eternity – 45, 72, 119, 197, 224, 226, 237,
Etting, Ruth – 116,
Evening Standard – 80,
Eviston, Gina – 47-48,
Ewbank, John – 186,
Expatriotism – 124,
Exploding Galaxy – 99,

F

Fabulous Furry Freak Brothers – 131,
Fall Girl – 78,
Family – 126,
Fancy Our Meeting – 128, 195,
Fatty Finn – 246,
The Female Eunuch – 110, 151, 168,
Feldman, Marty – 164,
Ferlinghetti, Lawrence – 46,
Ferrier, Louise – 48, 67, 70, 75, 77, 79-80, 84, 92, 95, 104, 117, 119, 127, 168-169, 184, 198, 200,
Ferrier, Noel – 176,
Festival of Sydney – 235,

*Film Script (*also *Song of Songs)* - 188, 222, 225, 233-234,
Fink, Leon – 181-182, 193, 213, 217, 227-228, 231-232, 235, 247, 249, 254,
Fink, Margaret, née Elliott – 35, 182, 193, 225, 235,
First No Pinky – 72, 75, 154,
Firth-Smith, John – 42-43, 71, 216, 241,
Fisher, Meredith (Meme) née Millear – 22,
Fisher, Peter – 79,
Fitzgerald, Ella - 26,
Fitzgerald, Tom – 65,
Fitzpatrick, Kate – 40, 233,
Flamingo Park – 184, 229,
Fleischmann, Arthur – 7,
Foley, Roger (Ellis D Fogg) – 71-72, 76, 124-125, 134, 139-140, 151, 154-155, 164-167, 184, 189, 205, 234,
Fonda, Jane – 130,
The Fool (Simon Posthuma, Marijke Koger and Barry Finch) – 98,
For All My Little Friends – 199,
For Your Love – 88,
Fox, James – 94, 113,
Francesca, Piero Della – 128,
Free – 130,
Free Fall Through Featherless Flight – 205,
Freedom Ride – 137,
Freudenstein, George – 160,
Fresh Cream – 87-89,
Freud, Lucien - 91
Friend, Donald - 7, 133,
Fromm, Erich – 157,
Fuller, Lyn – 167,

G

Gaden, John – 38, 233-234,
Gallagher, Doug – 238,
Ganpatsingh, Hazel – 117,
Garland, Judy – 34, 81,
Gas Lash – 49, 69, 80, 137,
Gaughin, Paul - 28, 128, 174,
Gemes, Judy (Juno) – 169,
Gernreich, Rudi – 134,
Gerry & the Pacemakers – 54,
Get Folked – 64, 76,
Ghost Train – 202, 213, 215-218, 229, 248-249, 250-258,
Glasheen, Mick – 47-48, 55, 71, 79, 142, 146,
Gilliam, Terry – 68,
Ginger Baker's Airforce – 108, 137,

Ginger Meggs – 10, 205, 212, 227,
Ginger Meggs Memorial School of Arts – 146,
Ginge's Last Stand – 205,
Ginsberg, Allen – 46, 155, 159,
Gittoes, George – 125, 136, 140-141, 151, 153, 160, 163, 167, 184, 195, 204, 241, 244,
Gittoes, Joyce – 153,
Glitter and Be Gay – 253,
Go-Set – 247,
God Bless Tiny Tim – 104, 117,
God Save OZ – 171,
God Save the Queen (Sex Pistols song) – 201,
Godson, Craig – 254,
Godson, Damien – 254,
Godson, John – 254,
Goold, Bruce – 144, 151, 154-156, 159, 167, 184,
Gordon, Lee – 26-27, 34, 53,
Gorton, John – 124,
Gould, Bob – 35,
Goya, Francisco – 128,
Graham, Bill – 83, 100,
Granny Takes A Trip – 81, 94, 121, 171,
Grateful Dead - 107,
Gray, Vivean – 208,
The Great Pretender – 239,
The Great Society Blows Another Mind – 103,
Great White Wonder (bootleg) – 131,
Greenough, George – 153, 160, 164, 176,
Greer, Germaine – 35, 38, 65, 75, 95, 102, 110, 112, 120, 151, 165, 168-169, 182, 186, 200,
Greig, Julian (Jewellion the Mime) – 145, 155, 160,
Gresch, Rick – 126,
Griffin, Rick – 83,
Grock – 227,
Grose, Peter – 41-42, 47-48, 50-51, 61,
GTK-TV (Get to Know) – 150, 161,
Guard, Dominic – 208,
Gulpilil, David – 6, 239,
Gunston, Norman – 208, 227,
Guru Maharaji – 224,
Gwynn, Nell – 90-91,
Gye, Hal – 195,

H

Hair – 134,
Hamilton, Richard – 107, 128, 199,
Handke, Peter – 191, 196,
Hapsash and the Coloured Coat - 121,

Hara Krishna Temple – 134, 224,
Harcourt Brace & Jovanovich – 194,
A Hard Day's Night – 57,
Harding, John – 238,
Haring, Keith – 84,
Harrigan, John – 53,
Harris, Chester – 165,
Harris, Max – 65,
Harrison, George – 57, 61, 82, 98, 113-114, 224,
Harrison, Patti – 82,
Hartley, Ian – 165,
Haslem, Peter – 238,
Hawkins, Gordon – 66,
Hayden-Guest, Anthony – 112,
Haymarket – 226,
Haynes, Jim – 135,
Haywood, Chris - 196,
He's Got the Whole World in His Hands – 27, 243,
Heartbreak Hotel – 26,
Heaven and Hell in Western Art – 103, 110,
Heaven Is My Home – 200,
Heide (Heide Museum of Modern Art) – 36, 59,
Hello Hello – 212,
Helpmann, Robert – 165,
Henderson, Brian – 32, 40, 70,
Henderson, Don – 69, 185,
Henderson, Marion – 185,
Henderson, Jane, née Massy-Greene – 22,
Hendrix (painting) – 96, 108, 166,
Hendrix, Jimi – 90, 96, 104, 156, 175,
Herbst, Peter – 65,
Heseltine, Harry – 66,
Hesse, Herman – 157, 160,
Hester, Joy – 60,
Hicks, Bill – 244,
Hickson, Jill (Wran) – 231,
Hipgnosis – 107,
Hillier, Joseph – 180,
Hippie Hippie Shake (book) – 67, 77,
Hippy Hippy Shake (song) – 34,
Hobbs, Leigh – 206, 213, 235,
Hobby, Karen – 167,
Hockney, David – 84,
Hoffman, Abbie – 104,
Hogarth Galleries – 222,
Hokusai – 128, 151, 173, 179-180,
The Hokusai Sketchbooks – 201,
Hokusai's Wave – 113, 119, 153-154, 197, 200, 226,

Holbein, Hans – 128,
Holdsworth Galleries – 140,
Hollingsworth, Keith – 23, 35, 71,
Holly, Buddy – 126,
Home (band) – 224,
Honi Soit – 39, 41-42, 47, 61, 76,
Hooton, Harry – 35,
Hopkins, Livingstone (Hop) – 10, 157,
Hopkins, Ted – 213, 231,
Hopper Dennis - 225,
Horler, Ken – 135, 185, 205,
Horn, Clayton – 46,
Houdini – 227,
Howl – 46, 64, 155,
Hubert's Flea Circus – 100, 219,
Hughes, Davis – 70-71,
Hughes, Danne (née Emerson) – 103,
Hughes, Robert (Bob) – 35, 42, 47, 55, 65, 75, 80, 103, 110, 119, 122, 135, 171, 200,
The Hukilau - 239,
The Human Figure in Motion - 108,
Humphries, Barry – 31, 49, 52, 55, 57, 75, 120,
Hurtwood Edge – 120, 171,
Hyde Park (London) – 85, 123,
Hyde Park (Sydney) – 205,
Hynde, Chrissie – 173,

I

I Am the Walrus – 114,
IBC Studios – 98,
I Got You Babe – 117, 202,
I Was Rolled by the Stones – 69, 76,
The Icecaps Are Melting – 119, 253,
I'm So Glad – 92,
In Bed with the English – 95,
In the Presence of the Lord – 126,
Inoki, Antonio – 220-221, 240,
In Shoppe – 148,
Incredible OZ Band – 156,
Incredible Shrinking Exhibition – 133, 138-139, 141, 143,
Ingres, Jean-Auguste-Dominique – 128,
Innermost Limits of Pure Fun – 153,
International Year of the Child 1979 – 248, 255,
I've Got a Loverly Bunch of Coconuts – 16,
In His Own Write – 57,
International Times (IT) – 83, 124, 135,
Isle of Wight Festival – 130, 174,

J

Jackson, Linda – 184, 229,
Jagger, Mick – 69, 85, 91, 94, 108, 112-114, 118, 147, 189, 226,
James, Nikki – 188-190,
Jamieson, Laura – 108,
Jarratt, John – 208,
Jarry, Alfred – 51,
James, Clive – 35, 38, 65,
James, Francis – 50, 64-65,
The Jazz Singer – 202, 221,
Jefferson Airplane - 107,
Jensen, Susan – 223, 225, 229, 231,
Jessop, Clytie - 111, 129,
Jesus Adam – 224,
Jesus Christ – 118, 138, 226, 254, 257,
Jewish News – 61,
Jimi Hendrix Experience - 96,
Jiminy Cricket - 212,
John, Elton – 130,
John Mayall's Bluesbreakers – 88, 94,
Johnny Carson Show – 174,
Johnson, Franklin – 151, 167,
Johnson, Jack – 33,
Johnson, Keith – 72,
Johnson, Michael – 254,
Jolson, Al – 15, 116, 197, 202, 221, 243,
Jonathon Cape publishers – 123,
Jones, Alistair (Al) – 239,
Jones, Brian – 85, 114, 211,
Jones, Gillian – 155,
Jorgensen, Justus – 156,
Jorgensen, Sebastian (Seb) – 156, 157, 160, 163-165, 166, 186, 234,
Joubert Studios – 81,
Jovic, Slavka – 167,
Juke – 247,
Julian Ashton Art School – 7,
Juillet, Patric – 159,
Juillet's Restaurant – 155, 159,
Jumping Jack Flash – 91, 129, 147,
Jung, Carl – 119, 201, 223,
Just For Fun – 192, 216,

K

Kaleidoscope – 167,
Kaiser, Ann – 47,
Karet, Marilyn – 246,
Karvan, Arthur – 158, 166-167,
Kaspar – 172, 191, 195-197, 205, 207, 214,
Kaufman, Irving – 220,
Kay Kyser – 15,
Kaye, Danny – 16,
Kee, Jenny – 32, 53, 58-59, 69, 75, 79, 84-85, 87, 119, 122, 169, 184, 224, 229,
Keenan, Haydn – 241, 244, 246,
Kelly, Anne – 189,
Kenny, Mike – 238,
Kerr, John – 66,
Kevans, Denis – 215,
Khaury, Butros – 99-100,
Khaury, Tillie – 100,
Khaury, Tulip – 199, 218,
King, BB – 101,
King, Bill – 112,
King, George – 100,
Kirk Gallery – 234, 237,
Kissler, Anou – 33, 47-48, 50, 58-60, 67, 72, 77, 85-86, 104,
Kings Cross Whisper – 49, 135,
Kingston, Peter (Kingo) – 19, 47-48, 55, 71, 79, 119, 138, 140, 142, 145-146, 153, 167, 176, 204, 213, 216-217, 227-227, 235, 247-248, 252, 254, 257-258,
Klarwein, Matí – 107, 177,
Klarwein, Sophie – 177-178,
Klippel, Robert – 49, 135,
Knight, Elizabeth – 244,
Kogarah High School – 205,
Kold Komfort Kaffee – 231, 238,
Koltai, Christine – 165,
Kouloori, Miss – 4, 13,
Kray Brothers – 90, 129, 147-148,
Krauss, Sigi – 129-130, 138, 174,
Krazy Kat – 227,
Krishna – 255,
Krishnamurti – 224,
Kubrick, Stanley – 138,

L

L'Amour – 180,
Lady Chatterley's Lover – 35, 46, 66, 146,
Lady Diana – 212,
Lagerfeld, Karl – 180,
Laing, RD -112,

Lanceley, Colin – 39-40, 43, 59-60, 75, 189,
Landa, Paul – 66,
Lansell, Ross – 161,
Laine, Frankie – 62,
Lambert, Anne-Louise – 208,
The Last Wave – 225,
Lathouris, Nicholas – 214,
Laugh-In (Rowan and Martin's Laugh-In) – 175,
Laurel, Stan – 238,
Lawson, Peter – 48,
Lear, Amanda – 178,
Leary, Timothy – 104, 119, 170,
Led Zeppelin – 123,
Ledeboer, Peter – 84,
Lee, Brenda – 34,
Legalise Cannabis – 85,
Legalise Pot Rally, Hyde Park - 85, 123,
Lennon, Cynthia - 87,
Lennon, John – 57, 59, 61, 82, 87, 98, 113-114, 118, 120, 130, 171,
Leonard, Roma (Nursy) – 5, 12-13, 72,
Les Bean – 237-238,
Leunig, Michael – 195,
Lewis, Jeannie - 67, 137, 152, 155, 166, 184-186, 201, 205, 213-216, 225, 236, 242, 246, 252-254,
Lewis, Jon (Jonny) – 142, 144-146, 148, 153-154, 157-158, 161, 167, 184, 187, 204, 213, 216, 231, 235,
Lewis, Marvin – 238, 240, 242,
Lewis, Tim – 17, 68, 148, 151, 167, 187-194, 196, 197, 203-204, 209-210, 213, 223, 226, 230-231, 235, 241, 255,
Lewis, Tom – 213,
Lichtenstein, Roy – 56, 84, 128, 157,
Lieberson, Sandy – 176-177, 201,
Lindsay, Joan – 207,
Lindsay, Lionel - 36,
Lindsay, Norman – 43,
Liney, Richard – 188, 191, 193, 197, 199, 203, 209, 211-212, 216, 226, 235, 241,
Liney, Sharon – 191, 209, 230,
Lisztomania – 177,
Little Nemo – 118, 227,
The Little Prince (Le Petit Prince) – 137, 143, 157, 197, 200,
Litvinoff, Barnet – 91,
Litvinoff, David – 90-91, 112, 129, 147-149, 156, 158, 161, 167, 185, 189, 211,
Litvinoff, Emanuel - 91,
Live Give Love – 95,

Living Daylights – 194-196, 204,
Lloyd, Owen (Bird Man of Kings Cross) - 134,
Locke, Gerald – 64-65,
London, Laurie – 27, 58,
Lonely Troubadour – 238, 245,
Lozano, Carlos – 178,
Lorca, Federico – 127,
The Lost Hokusai (Abalone Diver) – 179, 180, 208, 228,
Love Machine – 68,
Love Me Do – 54,
Lovin' Spoonful – 89,
Lowe Chica – 7,
Lowndes, Graham - 205,
Lowrie, David - 246,
Luckock, Elizabeth (Lizzy), née Millear – 22,
Luckock, Sally, née Millear - 22,
Luna, Donyale – 114,
Luna Park – 24, 39-40, 58, 71, 181-182, 189, 191-194, 200, 202-207, 211-213, 215-217, 221, 223, 226-229, 235, 242, 246-258,
Luna Park Holdings P/L – 181,
Lust for Life (film) – 28,
Lust for Life (book) – 28, 109,
Lynn, Elwyn – 66, 227,
Lyon, Nic – 144, 155, 155, 160, 163, 167, 184,
The Lyre Bird – Tiny Tim – 221,

M

Macallum, Mungo – 35, 42, 61, 66,
Macfarlane, Robert – 241,
Macquarie University – 197,
Mad – 31,
Mad Dog Morgan – 225,
Madame Tussaud's – 58,
Madden, Nikki – 163,
Madison Square Garden – 237,
Magic Theatre OZ – 119, 121-123, 143,
Magritte, René – 99, 107, 109-110, 118, 128-129, 135, 141, 146, 151, 153-154, 157, 167, 173, 178, 181, 188, 190,
Maharishi Mahesh Yogi – 224,
Maher, Vickii – 58-59,
Mallard, Garry – 205,
Malley, Ern - 36,
Man Ray – 109, 128, 177-178,
Mandrake the Magician – 227,
Mantegna, Andrea – 128,
Marceau, Marcel – 155,
Marinetti – 146,

Marinos, Lex – 172, 196, 214, 216,
Markstein, Ted – 48, 138, 148, 153, 158, 167, 241,
Marsh, Berys – 196,
Marshall, Sam – 192, 216, 248, 250,
Martin, Charlotte – 87-88, 110, 113, 123,
Massy-Greene, David – 22,
Massy-Greene, Elizabeth, née Sharp (aunt) – 8,
Massy-Greene, Kate – 22,
Massy-Greene, Roger – 22,
Mathews, Miller & Dunbar publishers – 174,
Matthews, Freja – 111, 114,
Matisse, Henri – 128, 179, 188,
May, Phil – 10,
May, Professor - 66,
Mayall, John – 88,
Mavis Bramston Show – 49,
Mayne, Robert – 42,
Max's – 104,
Max – the Birdman – Ernst – 94-95, 113,
McAuley, James – 65,
McCartney, Paul – 57, 59, 61, 82, 113,
McDonald, Garry – 208, 225,
McLaren, Malcolm – 173,
McGregor, Craig – 48, 64, 77, 105,
McGuinness, Paddy – 35,
McKeon, Phillip (aka Phillip Arts) – 165,
McNicoll, Penny – 42,
McPherson, Lennie - 70,
McTell, Ralph – 175,
Meanjin – 65, 77,
Meher Baba – 150, 224,
Melbourne Museum of Modern Art and Design – 40,
Melly, George - 121, 168, 174,
Menzies, Robert – 30, 36, 50, 124,
Mercury, Freddy – 172,
Merioola artists – 7, 13, 189,
Meyrick, Julian – 185,
Michener, James – 201,
Mickey Mouse – 11, 127-128, 137, 160, 169-170, 172, 195-196, 200, 212, 218, 227, 238-239,
Mickey Mouse Club March – 239,
Miles Twins – 178-179,
Millear, Katherine, née Sharp (aunt) – 8,
Millear, Katherine (Margie) – 22,
Minstrel Boy – 130,
Miss Australia – 210,
Miss Natasha – 241,
Missing Links – 58,
Mitchell, Guy – 16,

Mitchell, Joni – 175,
Mitchell, Mitch – 120,
Mo – 225, 227,
Moby Grape – 107,
Moermann, Joseph – 248,
Moody Blues – 130,
Molnar, George – 35,
Mondrian, Piet – 128,
Monet, Claude – 128,
Money, Zoot - 99,
Montsalvat – 156,
The Moon is a Harsh Mistress – 205, 254,
Mora, Georges – 60, 67,
Mora, Mirka – 60, 67, 102,
Mora, Philippe – 60, 102, 107, 112, 114-116, 118-120, 122-123, 127, 129, 135, 138, 151, 159, 171-172, 176, 186, 200, 225,
Morrison, Alastair (Afferbeck Lauder) – 30,
Morrissey, Paul – 180,
Morse, Helen – 208,
Mortimer, John – 147,
Moscoso, Victor – 83, 109,
Moth – 155, 167,
Mouse, Stanley – 83,
Mr Jiggs – 227,
Mr Tambourine Man (poster) – 83-84, 110,
Mr Tambourine Man (song) – 72,
Muggeridge, Malcolm – 103,
Muktananda – 224, 251,
Munch, Edvard – 128, 157, 178,
Munro, H – 65,
Murao, Shigeyoshi (Shig) – 46,
Murawalla, Black Allen – 67-68, 185-186,
Murdoch, Rupert – 61,
Murphy, Lionel – 66,
Murray, Bill – 236,
Murray-Smith, Stephen – 65,
Museum of Sydney – 132,
Muybridge, Eadweard – 107-108, 118, 125, 143, 157,
My Canary Has Circles Under His Eyes – 163,
My Generation (book) – 146,
My Song – 239,
My Way – 239,
Myriad, Carrl – 163,

N

Nancy – 10,
Nation Review – 204, 247,

National Art School (East Sydney Tech) – 32-33, 36, 39-40, 43-44, 49, 58, 167, 187,
National Gallery Canberra – 190,
Nelson, Sandra – 134,
Neruda, Pablo – 214-215,
Neville, Jill – 75, 78-80, 84, 92,
Neville, Judy – 78,
Neville, Richard – 32-33, 37, 41-44, 47-48, 50-52, 54-56, 58-59, 62, 63-67, 69-70, 73, 75-80, 82, 84, 87, 92, 95, 102-104, 110-111, 115-119, 121-123, 127, 131, 146-147, 156, 168-171, 184, 188, 194-195, 198, 200, 204, 224, 229-231, 237, 252,
New York Times – 114,
News of the World – 85,
Newport Arms – 54,
National Institute of Dramatic Art (NIDA) – 231,
Nimrod Theatre – 135, 185-186, 191, 195, 205, 225, 231, 235, 238, 241,
Nixon, Richard – 118,
Noffs, Ted – 134,
Nolan, Sidney – 36, 40, 60,
North Shore – 73,
North Sydney Swimming Pool – 258,
Norton, Michael – 246,
Norton, Rosaleen – 135,
Noyce, Phillip – 140, 205,
Nye, Alan – 73,

O

Oakes, Geoff – 238,
The Observer – 80,
O'Brien, Justin – 7, 12-13, 19-21, 24-25, 28-29, 32, 68, 109, 187,
O'Brien, Richard – 112,
Ochs, Phil – 215, 254,
Octopus's Garden – 113,
Odetta – 105,
O'Dowd, Bernard – 25,
O'Grady, John (Nino Culotta) – 31,
O'Keefe, Johnny – 26, 58,
The Old Pacific Sea – 55,
Old Shep – 26,
Oldham, Andrew Loog – 69,
Olley, Margaret – 7,
Olsen, John – 37, 40, 49, 60, 64, 66, 133, 135,
On Stage OZ – 76,
On The Good Ship Lollipop – 175,
On the Road to Tarascon – 13, 87, 109, 128, 160, 202,

Ono, Yoko – 118, 171,
Organ, Michael - 108, 128,
Ormsby-Gore, Alice – 123,
Orpheus and Eurydice – 202-203, 221,
Oswald, Lee Harvey – 118,
The OZ Guide to Sydney's Underworld – 70,
OZ (Australia) – 41, 43-44, 46-52, 54-58, 60, 61-73, 75-80, 82, 94, 103-104, 115, 119, 122-124, 135, 182, 186,
OZ (London) – 78, 80, 85, 92, 95, 102-105, 107-108, 110-111, 113, 117-118-119, 121-123, 126, 129, 131-132, 135, 143, 146-147, 156-157, 165, 168-171, 177-178, 181, 185, 194, 200, 225-226, 229,
OZ Newsletter – 123,
OZ? (tapestry) – 25,

P

Packer, Frank - 32,
PACT Folk- 163, 186,
Page, Jimmy - 123,
Paint Your Own Gallery – 137, 139, 141,
Paladin Granada publishers - 119,
Pallenburg, Anita – 113,
Palmer, Tony – 171,
Paolozzi, Eduardo – 112, 159,
Pappalardi, Felix – 89, 99.
Paradise Club – 134,
Paris Theatre Company - 233, 244,
Parra, Angel – 214,
Peanuts – 157,
Peck, Albert – 191, 203-204, 209-211, 218, 229-230, 237, 246,
Pengally, Vivienne – 151,
Penguin Books – 46, 66, 91,
Pentecost – 128, 188,
People, Politics and Pop – 77, 105,
Pepperall, David (Dr Pepper) – 247,
Perceval, John – 60,
Perceval, Mary – 60,
Performance - 94, 112-113, 122, 129, 146, 171, 176, 178, 201, 207, 211,
Perry, David – 71,
Perry, Richard – 117,
Peter, Paul and Mary - 34, 100,
Petit, Philippe – 194,
Petty, Bruce – 61, 249,
The Phantom – 157, 227,
The Pheasantry – 90-92, 94-97, 99, 102, 107, 109-112, 114, 116, 119-128, 136-137, 171, 173, 177,

Philadelphia Museum of Modern Art – 178,
Picasso, Pablo – 36, 126, 128, 178, 189-190,
Picasso's – 81,
Piccolo Bar – 132,
Picnic at Hanging Rock – 207-209,
Pilcher, Norman – 84-85, 114-116,
Pink Floyd – 80, 99, 107, 125, 164,
Pink Pussycat – 134,
Pinniger, Gretel (Madam Lash) – 165, 184,
Pinocchio – 10, 212,
Plant A Flower Child – 102, 201,
Playboy – 50, 249,
Playboy Press - 219,
Popeye – 212, 227,
Proud, Philip (Pip) – 135,
Pitney, Gene – 34,
Plant a Flower Child – 102, 201,
Play Power – 110, 119, 123,
Plunkett, Brad - 90,
The Politics of Ecstasy – 119,
Poor Little Rich Girl – 62,
Pop (novel) – 76-77, 85, 105,
Pop Into Popism – 84,
Pope Paul VI - 118,
Popov, Alex – 47,
Portrait of Tiny Tim – 197,
Powditch, Peter – 32, 49, 53, 151, 159, 187,
Presley, Elvis – 26, 34, 117, 131, 240,
Pressed Rat and Warthog – 104,
Pretenders - 173,
Primavera – 129,
Prince Charles – 212,
Princess Margaret – 131,
Private School – 77,
The Procurer – 91,
The Projectionist – 224,
Pruniers in the Park Restaurant– 231,
Punch and Judy – 227,

Q

Quadrant – 65, 77, 223-224, 226-227,
Quant, Mary – 81,
Queen – 172,
Queen Elizabeth II – 50, 58, 112, 118, 191, 201,
Quill, Greg – 155,
Quinn, Anthony - 28,

R

Rainey, Michael – 91,
Rahilly, Seamus – 254,
Ramage, Mal – 144-145, 148, 155, 162, 166-167,
Ramsden, Michael - 129, 138, 159, 235,
Ratbags – 197,
Rawlins, Adrian - 61, 124-125, 150, 152, 155-156, 184, 224, 237, 242, 244,
Ray, Johnny – 16, 26,
Ray Price Jazz Quintet – 137,
Rebel Without a Cause – 26,
Read, Aggy – 48, 71, 124, 140, 142, 167,
Ready Made Bouquet – 129,
Reed, John – 59-60,
Reed, Sunday – 59-60,
Regency Entertainment – 233,
Reid, Barrett – 60,
Reid, Catherine (Katie), née Sharp – 22, 106, 163,
Reid, Ian – 136, 141, 145, 149, 152-153, 156-157, 159, 162-163, 166-167,
Reid, Jamie - 201,
Rendall, John – 132,
Rene, Roy (Mo Mccackie) – 225,
Reprise Records – 100, 199,
Restivo, Johnny – 34,
Reuben Tice Memorial Band – 156,
Revolver – 82,
Revue of the Absurd – 49, 51,
Rhodes, Zandra – 159, 167, 177, 200-201,
Rich, Buddy - 26,
Richard, Cliff - 27,
Richards, Keith – 69, 85, 108, 114, 120, 130,
Richmond, Harry – 236,
Riley, Bridget – 76, 83,
Rip It Up – 26,
Rising of the Tide – 253,
Ritchie Bros – 5, 21, 36,
Ritchie, Harold – 37,
Ritchie, James (great-paternal grandfather) – 5,
Ritchie, Stuart (maternal grandfather) – 6-7, 10, 14, 21, 23, 36, 62, 74, 209,
Ritchie, Vega (Vee) née Kopson (maternal grandmother) – 5, 11, 13, 105, 191, 209-210,
Roadknight, Margret – 185, 214,
Roberts, Rachel – 208,
Robertson, Geoffrey – 147,
Robinson, Ted – 235,
Rock Album Covers – 97,

Rock Around the Clock – 26,
Rock Island Line – 27,
Rock and Roll Circus – 120,
Rocky Horror Show – 112, 172, 176, 194,
Roeg, Nick – 112,
Rolling Stone – 247,
Rolling Stones – 58, 69, 78, 85, 117, 120, 188-189, 211,
Rousseau, Douanier – 117,
The Roving Kind – 16,
Rowe, Alfred (The Great Onzalo) – 194,
Roxon, Lilian – 103-104,
Royal Albert Hall – 16, 33, 116-117, 122, 130, 174, 176,
Royal Easter Show (Sydney) – 24, 192,
Royal George Hotel – 34,
Royles, Peter – 156, 160, 167, 184, 216,
Rubin, Jerry - 104,
Rubin, Victor – 188,
Rudy Komon Gallery – 40,
Rule Brittania - 175,
Rushton, Ernest – 42,
Russell, Ken – 177,
Rydell, Bobby – 34, 53,

S

Sad Sack – 212,
Saffron, Abe – 53,
Sagan, Carl – 87, 118,
Sale, Julia – 151, 153,
Sanderson, David – 208,
Sangster, John – 135,
Santa Claus – 23, 227,
Santana, Carlos – 177,
Scripts P/L – 76,
See How it Runs – 185,
See You Later Alligator – 26,
Seideman, Bob - 107, 115, 126, 169,
Seidler, Harry – 50, 213,
The Seizer – 255,
Self Portrait (album) – 130, 150,
Self Portrait (painting) – 94,
Self Portrait (Tim Lewis exhibition) – 204,
The Sentimental Bloke – 191, 195, 227, 245,
Seurat, Georges – 128,
Seven Sermons to the Dead – 119,
Seventeen Minutes to Four – 68,
Sex! (poster) – 95,
SEX (punk clothes shop) – 173,
Sex Pistols – 173, 201,
Seymour Centre – 214,

Signac, Paul – 127,
Sgt Pepper's Lonely Hearts Club Band – 93, 96,
Shannon, Del - 34,
Sharman, Jimmy – 24,
Sharman, Jim – 76, 112, 140, 166-167, 172, 225,
Sharp Alan (uncle) – 8, 22, 73,
Sharp, Alexander (Sandy) – 22, 106, 176,
Sharp, Andrew – 22, 106, 176, 196, 209,
Sharp, Barbara (née Davies) – 52-53,
Sharp, Dorothy, née Muller (stepmother) – 23, 35, 62, 105, 125, 186, 238,
Sharp, Edith (Dinks), née Lycett – 14, 52-53, 204,
Sharp, Frank (uncle) – 8, 12, 14, 22, 37, 204,
Sharp, Henry Ritchie (father) – 4-14, 17, 22-23, 35, 37-38, 52, 62-63, 71, 73, 105, 115, 125, 128, 186,
Sharp, Joan (Jo) née Ritchie (mother) – 5-16, 20-21, 23, 26-27, 35, 52-53, 58, 62, 65, 71-72, 74, 105, 113, 125, 158, 166, 183, 187, 189-190, 204, 210, 218, 222, 256,
Sharp Martin and his Silver Scissors – 130,
Sharp, Phillip – 14, 22, 204,
Sharp, Roslyn (Rozzie) – 14, 22, 106, 204,
Sharp, Russell – 14, 22, 106, 204, 234-235,
Sharp, Walter Ramsay (paternal grandfather) – 8, 13, 17-18, 22, 37,
Sharp, Elizabeth (Bessie) née Ritchie (paternal grandmother) – 8, 22, 37, 53, 62, 125, 191, 204,
Shaw, Artie – 26,
Shea Stadium – 82,
Shead Garry – 30, 33, 36-45, 47-48, 55, 67, 71, 73, 77, 79, 105, 120, 125, 146, 163, 176, 184, 186, 205-206, 216-217, 227, 235, 241, 247, 249-250,
Shead, Gria – 216,
Shead, Meryl – 216,
Shearston, Gary – 67, 69-70, 183, 186,
Shepherd, Cybill – 220,
Sheraton Hotel – 60,
She's A New Kind of Old Fashioned Girl – 240,
Shrimpton, Jean – 108, 114, 188, 190,
Signal Driver – 234,
Simms, Clayton – 162,
Singleton, John – 32,
Skinner, Ian – 14-15,
Skinner, Ida – 14,
Skinner, Jan – 14-15,

Skipper, Marcus – 156-157,
Slessor, Kenneth – 133,
Slim Dusty Band – 239,
Smartiples – 119, 125,
Smilde, Roelof – 35,
The Small One – 11,
Snugglepot and Cuddlepie – 227,
Sobhraj, Charles – 229, 231,
Social Deviants – 99,
Solomon, David – 61,
The Song of the Disembraining – 51,
Song of Love – 190,
Song Without A Name – 239,
Southern Cross – 197, 200,
Southern Cross Hotel (Melbourne) – 61,
Southern Cross Hotel (Edgecliff) – 221,
Spatt, Maurice - 213, 228, 247, 252,
Spatt, Nathan – 181, 213, 227, 231, 236, 247,
Speakeasy Club – 87-88, 127, 198,
Spears, Steve – 225,
Spectator – 80,
Spencer Davis Group – 126,
Spoonful – 92, 104,
St Barnabas Church – 197,
St John, Colette – 144, 188, 204,
St John, Edward – 66,
St Louis Blues – 239,
St Paul's College – 37,
Stace, Arthur – 197, 223,
Starkiewicz, Antionette – 158,
Starr, Ringo – 57, 61, 113, 130, 177, 201,
Starry Night – 180, 194, 197, 202, 226, 240,
Stayin' Alive - 239, 244,
Steele, Jackie - 70,
Steele, Tommy – 58,
Stein, Harry – 218,
Steve Paul's Scene (The Scene) - 100, 116, 177, 219,
Stevenson, Pamela - 176,
Stigwood, Robert – 99, 114,
Strachan, David – 38,
Street of Dreams – 239,
Street of Dreams Productions – 233-238,
Stone, Judy – 114,
Stone, Sandy – 31, 52,
Strange Brew – 89-90, 104,
Stanshall, Viv – 169,
Street, Philip Whistler – 64,
Subterranean Imitation Realists (also known as the Annandale Imitation Realists) – 39-40, 60,
Sue-Ellen – 158, 167,

Summer in the City – 89,
Sunshine City – 146, 185,
Sunshine of Your Love – 89, 104,
Sunshine Superman (poster) – 84, 95,
Superman – 10, 194,
Surf City – 53-54,
Sun (band) – 155,
Sun Myong Moon – 224,
Sunbury Music Festival – 184,
Sutinen, Asco (Axel) – 164-165,
The Sweet Shop – 108,
Sydney Harbour Bridge – 19, 41, 140, 194,
Sydney Morning Herald – 17, 39, 41, 67, 76-77, 139, 241,
Sydney Opera House – 70-71, 186, 191, 193, 202, 225, 235, 248,
Sydney Push – 34-35, 46, 51, 67-68, 78, 137, 151, 169, 182,
Sydney Showground – 188,
Sydney Stadium – 26-27, 33-34, 58, 73,
Sydney String Quartet – 236,
Sydney Symphony Orchestra – 236,
Sydney Town – 70,
Sydney University Revue (Dramatic Society) – 38, 51, 185,
Synchronicity: An Acausal Connecting Principle – 201,
Swastika – 176, 200,

T

Tabberer, Maggie – 205,
Tales of Brave Ulysses – 86-90, 104, 184,
Tanner, Les – 39,
Tate Gallery – 36-37, 142,
Tatlock Miller, Harry – 7,
Taylor, Derek – 59,
Taylor, Elizabeth – 130,
Tears of Steel & the Clowning Calaveras – 205, 213-214, 225, 235-236, 246, 252-253,
Teather, Steven – 246,
Telford – 5, 14-15, 33, 105,
The Toff – 25,
Thames & Hudson – 200,
Tharunka – 41-43, 47, 51, 76,
That'll Be the Day (film) – 177, 201,
There'll Always be an England – 175,
Thompson, Dave – 97,
Thompson, Eric (Boof) – 238,
Thoms, Albie - 39, 42, 46, 49, 51-52, 55, 71-72, 120, 122, 124, 135-136, 140-150, 154-156,

160, 161-163, 165-167, 176, 185-186, 205, 207, 234,
Thomson, Brian – 167,
Three Gaoled Filthy Paper – 77,
Three Little Fishies – 15,
The Times – 80,
Tiger Tim – 227,
Til Time Brings Change – 205,
Tiny Tim (Herbert Khaury) – 16, 92, 99-102, 104, 107, 116-119, 126-127, 130-131, 138, 143-144, 150, 157, 174-177, 181, 197-203, 207-208, 210-212, 218-226, 228, 230, 233-245, 247, 250, 257,
Tiny Tim's Second Album – 126, 174,
Tipperary – 239,
Tiptoe Through the Tulips – 100, 104, 117, 237, 252,
Toad – 104,
Tommy – 177,
Townshend, Pete – 90, 177, 201, 224,
Tracey, Dick - 70,
Traintime – 104,
Tremblay, Angelica – 226,
Trials of OZ (book) – 171,
Trials of OZ (film) – 171,
Trials of OZ (off-Broadway production) – 171,
Trouble in Molopolis – 122, 171, 176,
True Records – 240,
The Twist – 34,
Tucker, Albert – 36, 40, 60,
Tully – 124-125, 135, 150, 224,
Turner, Joseph – 81,
Twice Upon a Time - 87, 102,
Twiggy – 108, 114,
Two Innocents Abroad, the Adventures of Martin and Richard - 76,
Two Innocents Abroad, Part 2 – 76,

U

Ubu Films – 71, 124, 140,
UFO Club – 80, 99, 103,
Uluru – 200,
University of New South Wales – 37, 41, 43, 137,
University of New South Wales Revue – 72, 74,
University of New South Wales Roundhouse - 42, 152,
University of Sydney – 34, 38-39, 41, 43, 137, 140, 145, 151, 158, 185, 232,
University of Wollongong – 108, 128,

The Unexpected Answer (Whaam) – 157, 190,
The Unseen Beatles – 59, 82, 97,
Untitled Red Painting – 37, 142,
Ure Smith Publisher – 77,
Utamaro – 180,
Utzon, Jorn – 70-71, 191, 193,

V

Vadim, Roger – 130,
Vadim's Restaurant – 33, 35, 40, 47, 58,
Vallee, Rudy – 117, 220,
Van Gogh, Theo – 110, 181,
Van Gogh, Vincent – 13, 28, 87, 107, 109-110, 118, 121, 128, 135-137, 140, 142, 152, 157, 161, 181, 200-201, 219, 223, 226, 240,
Van Gogh-Bonger, Johanna – 110,
Van Rijn, Rembrandt – 151,
Van Wieringen, Ian – 42-43,
Vehka Aho, Eija – 83, 110,
Velvet Underground – 107,
Vermeer, Johannes – 128,
The Very Best of Cream – 104,
Victoria and Albert Museum – 180,
Village Theatre – 99,
Vincent van Gogh (collage) – 152, 201,
Visions – 233,
Visions of Johanna – 79,
Vogue – 177,
Voorman, Klaus – 82,
Voss – 36,

W

Wahroonga Lady and Her Naked Lunch – 73,
Wake In Fright – 183,
Waks, Nathan – 236-239, 240, 242,
Walker, John - 200,
Waller, Fats – 155,
Walsh, Janthia – 69,
Walsh, Richard (Ritchie) – 19, 28, 37-38, 41-42, 44, 47-48, 50-52, 55-56, 63, 65-66, 73, 76, 95, 102-103, 105, 115, 123-125, 194, 204,
Walsh, Sue, (née Phillips) – 103,
Warhol, Andy – 56, 84, 104, 107, 128, 145, 180-181, 195,
Warwick Electronics – 90,
Waters, Darcy – 35,
Watters Gallery – 73, 154,
Watts, Charlie – 130, 189,
Waverley College – 254,
Waymouth, Nigel - 121, 127,

Weaver, Jackie – 208,
Webster, John – 134,
Weight, Greg – 32, 58, 67-68, 72-73, 75, 88, 125, 133, 139-140, 145, 148-154, 158, 164, 167, 184, 186-187, 204-205,
Weight, Richard (Dicky) – 140-141, 144-145, 150-151, 162, 165, 167, 186,
Weight, Suzie (née Cuthbert) – 87-88, 184,
Weir, Peter – 140, 176, 205, 207-208, 225,
Well All Right – 126,
Welles, Orson – 10,
Westwood, Vivienne – 173,
We've Been Told Jesus Is Coming Soon – 224,
Wheels of Fire – 97-99, 101, 103-104, 112, 124,
Wherrett, Richard – 185, 191, 195-196, 235,
Whild, James – 248,
While My Guitar Gently Weeps - 113,
Whistler, James – 128,
Whitaker, Robert (Bob) – 59-61, 75, 77, 80-83, 87, 91-92, 95-97, 103, 110, 112, 120,
Whitborne, Tim – 112,
The White Album (actually titled *The Beatles*) – 107, 113,
White, Patrick, 36, 234,
Whiteley, Arkie – 151, 158, 251,
Whiteley, Brett – 32, 36-37, 142, 149-151, 154, 158-159, 167, 176, 184, 186, 188-189, 211, 216, 251,
Whiteley, Wendy – 142, 158, 167, 251,
White Room – 104,
Whiter Shade of Pale – 86,
Whitlam, Gough – 183, 186,
The Who – 90, 130, 177,
Wighton, Rosemary – 63,
Wild Life in Suburbia – 31,
Wild One (song) – 26,
The Wild One (film) – 26,
Wilde, Oscar – 81,
Williams, Carl – 126,
Williams, Esther – 27,
Williams, Fred – 60,
Wills, David – 131, 170,
Wilson, Gahan – 249,
Winwood, Steve – 126,
Wirian, 3 Victoria Road, Bellevue Hill – 4-8, 18, 26, 35, 105, 133, 166, 187, 191, 203-204, 207, 209-215, 218-226, 229-231, 236-237, 240, 246-247, 252,
Witzig, Paul – 54, 176,
Wonderful World of Romance – 240,
Wood, Sue – 42,
The Word Flashed Around the Arms – 54-55, 64,

Worker's Club Newcastle – 198-199,
World Non-Stop Singing Marathon – 220-221, 234, 236-238, 240-246,
World Trade Centre P/L – 181,
Wran, Neville – 66, 217, 231-232, 246, 248, 255,
Wright, Mandy – 251,
Wright, Peter – 142, 144, 151, 155, 167, 251,

X
Y

Yang, William – 207, 209-211, 230, 237, 239, 246,
Yardbirds – 88,
Yarrow, Peter – 100,
Yellow House Catalogue – 166,
Yellow House – 19, 24, 28, 45, 72, 121, 128, 135-136, 139-177, 184, 186-190, 198, 207, 216, 224, 230, 234, 247,
Yellow House Retrospective (AGNSW) – 45, 153,
Yesterday and Today ('the Butcher Cover') – 82,
Young Mo – 225,

Z

www.ingramcontent.com/pod-product-compliance
Lightning Source LLC
Chambersburg PA
CBHW032036150426
43194CB00006B/296